I0083649

WHEN
DIVORCES FAIL

WHEN DIVORCES FAIL

Disillusionment, Destructivity, and High-Conflict Divorce

Arthur Leonoff

ROWMAN & LITTLEFIELD
Lanham • Boulder • New York • London

Published by Rowman & Littlefield
An imprint of The Rowman & Littlefield Publishing Group, Inc.
4501 Forbes Boulevard, Suite 200, Lanham, Maryland 20706
www.rowman.com

6 Tinworth Street, London SE11 5AL, United Kingdom

Copyright © 2021 by The Rowman & Littlefield Publishing Group, Inc.

All rights reserved. No part of this book may be reproduced in any form or by any electronic or mechanical means, including information storage and retrieval systems, without written permission from the publisher, except by a reviewer who may quote passages in a review.

British Library Cataloguing in Publication Information Available

Library of Congress Cataloging-in-Publication Data
Names: Leonoff, Arthur, 1947– author.
Title: When divorces fail : disillusionment, destructivity, and high-conflict divorce / Arthur Leonoff.
Description: Lanham : Rowman & Littlefield, 2021. | Includes bibliographical references and index.
Identifiers: LCCN 2021014411 (print) | LCCN 2021014412 (ebook) | ISBN 9781538153710 (cloth) | ISBN 9781538153727 (paperback) | ISBN 9781538153734 (epub)
Subjects: LCSH: Divorce—Psychological aspects. | Conflict management—Psychological aspects.
Classification: LCC HQ814 .L46 2021 (print) | LCC HQ814 (ebook) | DDC 155.9/3—dc23
LC record available at https://lccn.loc.gov/2021014411
LC ebook record available at https://lccn.loc.gov/2021014412

This book is dedicated to Ryan, Scott, Tavyn, Isabelle, and Adelyn.

Contents

Acknowledgments

Writing has always been my way of thinking, and this book is no exception. It weaves together concepts that have helped make sense of the most challenging work I have done as a clinical psychologist and psychoanalyst. I am always grateful to my wife, Lynda, whose patience and loving support when it comes to my engrossing preoccupations makes this scholarly work possible. Gratitude as well to Jean Whieldon, friend and astute editor, whose assistance has been invaluable. I also offer a special thanks to Mark Kerr and Courtney Packard of Rowman & Littlefield, who supported this project despite the significant upheaval of the 2020–2021 coronavirus pandemic.

Finally, I wish to acknowledge how much I have learned from the family law lawyers and judges who work in this extremely taxing field. It takes a very special skill to balance legal representation with the overall goal of protecting the welfare of children whose parents are going through such a complex and difficult time. I have been in awe of judges whose legal decisions and guidance from the bench make a huge difference in the lives of the people who come before them. The family law system, as I have experienced it as a consultant, clinician, and expert witness, is a vital societal tool that toils for our mutual benefit and deserves to be recognized.

Author's Note

This book relies on clinical examples to illustrate the important themes that emerge when writing about the complexity of high-conflict divorce. These fictionalized cases are very much informed by a long clinical experience contributing to the divorce domain. Working at the heart of family law has offered a unique opportunity to observe and study an aspect of the human mind not commonly afforded to psychotherapists or analysts. For this experience, I am grateful.

Introduction

When I began practicing as a psychologist in the middle 1970s, I received several poignant referrals, one of which came from the pediatrician of an 11-year-old boy caught in a severe divorce crisis. His mother had temporarily gone into hiding after his father had been detained by the police for skulking in the bushes in front of his ex-wife's house. He had apparently been hoping to catch her in the arms of a lover to prove her bad character in family court. This same man had frozen family bank accounts, lobbied his son for his support, and stole utility bills from his ex-partner's mailbox to create extra hardship.

Needless to say, this child was anxious and confused and found it hard to fall asleep. He knew too much of his parents' struggles, all the sordid details, and this played over repeatedly in his young mind. His mother could not conceal her fury and contempt for her now ex-husband. She made sure her son knew it all. His skulking father, aiming to destroy his mother, became an object of derision between mother and son. It was unclear what feelings belonged to the son and what belonged to his mother. In any case, it was a radical disillusionment for the boy. His father's bizarre violations and his mother's equal failure to protect him were exceedingly damaging.

I was filled with questions that stayed with me and gradually formed the ideas in this book. What would motivate someone to go to that extent to retaliate against a former partner, someone who presumably had been loved and cherished and is the mother of his children? Why would both parents expose their child to such a toxic spectacle? How could the mother counterattack by so devaluing her son's father that the boy effectively lost a father to love? I had to conclude that there is a distinct phenomenon bearing the understated moniker of "high-conflict divorce." It is one saturated with destructive energies and targeting family members while collaterally inflicting severe damage on others.

These questions percolated for decades. My psychoanalytic training helped me to conceptualize these issues and ponder the origin of the destructive in human nature. During this time, I gained substantial experience working with the complications of divorce in the context of family law. This included completing hundreds of family assessments over four decades as a part of my clinical practice. Now, in this late stage of my career, I feel ready to put pen to paper and explore these issues in depth.

There are a set of ideas that link the various concepts elaborated in the text that follows. One concerns the essential destructiveness of high-conflict divorce that sets it apart from other forms of divorce conflict. I suggest that the destructiveness is primary and not an untoward consequence of personality deficiencies or disorder. The attack is on the family crucible in one way or another, and its manifestations are legion, making use of every tool that might be weaponized and aimed at the other, including children.

At its core, all destructiveness represents a violation of trust. It is inherently unethical. Someone turns on another in what amounts to a severe betrayal of human values of care and responsibility. It is a boundary violation. A major premise is that this core destructiveness must be acknowledged in this subgroup of divorcing couples in order to make progress in assisting them.

Secondly, there is the singular importance of disillusionment as a trigger for high-conflict destructiveness. One regularly finds a personal history of disillusionment in the narratives of high-conflict couples, layers of disillusionment that culminate in a union precariously balanced on unstable illusions that crumble when tested by real life. Disillusionment in this subgroup is experienced traumatically with consequent rage and persecutory anxieties. There is a close link between high-conflict divorce and psychic trauma.

Thirdly, I underline the importance of ethics as a framework, not only to understand what goes terribly wrong in high-conflict divorce, but also to anchor a treatment strategy founded in the irreducible responsibility for the other, even someone now in the ex-partner category. Conceptualizing the ethical and its relation to divorce is emphasized.

This severe high-conflict group places a strain on the mental health and family court systems attempting to guide them toward ethics. They represent a minority of divorce cases but are extremely high utilizers of legal and psychological services. These cases preoccupy family courts. What distinguishes them is that conflict takes on an entirely different hue than its usual variant, and conflict resolution must be supplanted by the more feasible goal of case management. These cases do not resolve other than by attrition.

In the chapters that follow, I rely on constructed case histories that recreate prevalent themes to bring these concepts to life for the reader. Whatever its manifestations, there is often an urgency to intervene in severe high conflict due to children suffering from entrenched destructive interparental dynamics. At the same time, there is a sense of futility when the tools available to family law, including mediation, parent coordination, family therapy, judicial case management, and even trials, fail to contain the destructiveness that is so evident. These couples are often impervious to influence.

High-conflict cases test the mettle of the family law system and push it to its limits—sometimes beyond. It would be very gratifying if this book helped extend understanding and gave rise to treatment and judicial approaches that could help these afflicted families and those dedicated professionals trying to make a difference in their lives.

High Conflict
An Ethical Dilemma

Community concern regarding the impact of divorce is no longer focused on its ubiquity but on those cases of severe conflict and dysfunction that represent a serious risk to children and adults alike. It is tragic to witness the devastation to families caught in the maelstrom of severe high-conflict divorce. What is most remarkable about this relatively small percentage of divorces is how recalcitrant they are to clinical, legal, and judicial intervention. Minor or not in frequency, they preoccupy the family courts and the health and social service professionals working to address their specific needs.[1]

One family law judge estimates that the court spends 40%–50% of its time dealing with high-conflict cases, which require ongoing case management and are prone to relitigation.[2] This seems very plausible. Conflict might be legal, but what emerges between the parties is hardly contained in the term *conflict*. There is a serious struggle amounting to a war, with the threat of emotional and socioeconomic depletion a present danger. These painful, protracted divorce struggles place significant strain on the family law legal system and, of course, on children and parents who must cope with the deleterious consequences.[3] How do divorcing and divorced couples reach such a point of relationship turmoil that they risk serious psychological and sometimes physical harm to themselves and their children?

[1] Fidler, B., Bala, N., & Saini, M. (Eds.), (2013), *Children who resist post separation parental contact*, Oxford University Press; Wallerstein, J., & Kelly, J., (1980), *Surviving the breakup: How children and parents cope with divorce*, Basic Books.

[2] Braver, S., Cohen Hita, L., & Wheeler, L., (2016), A randomized comparative effectiveness trial of two court-connected programs for high conflict families, *Family Court Review*, 54(3), 349–363.

[3] Hetherington, E. M., Bridges, M., & Insabella, G. M., (1998), What matters? What does not? Five perspectives on the association between marital transitions and children's adjustment, *American Psychologist*, 53, 167–184; Wallerstein, J., Lewis, J., & Blakeslee, S., (2002), The unexpected legacy of divorce: A 25-year landmark study, *Journal of the American Academy of Child & Adolescent Psychiatry*, 41, 359–360.

The theory that explains severe divorce dysfunction mainly focuses on individual psychopathology and impaired couple dynamics. High-conflict-prone individuals are described as more personality disordered, projecting, blaming, and nonreflective than their divorcing peers. The latter, who are the more normal divorcing group, are generally amenable to treatment and legal intervention. Their conflicts do not reach toxic and destructive proportions that lead to alienated children, ongoing abusive interactions, and postseparation domestic violence.

Bill Eddy, lawyer, social worker, and a major contributor to the high-conflict literature, stresses this connection between high conflict and disordered personality. A recent book, for example, *5 Types of People Who Can Ruin Your Life: Identifying and Dealing With Narcissists, Sociopaths, and Other High Conflict Personalities*, makes this link explicit.[4]

Psychoanalyst and forensic psychologist Michael Donner captures the dire essence of this special population: "I believe that these perpetual struggles serve to hold off hateful and murderous wishes directed against the other parent and against their own children."[5] Donner views high-conflict cases as an attempt to ward off psychic collapse, as if the individual or couple uses hatred and interminable conflict to reverse suffering and despair.

Smyth and Moloney observe correctly, in my view, that the nonspecific term *high conflict* greatly oversimplifies the destructive aspect that engulfs this minority of families but that extracts a high societal price.[6] Focusing on the hatred itself, they describe two forms: one that is reactive to the situation as well as time limited, and the other that is enmeshed and intractable. It is only the enmeshed and chronic form, in my view, that deserves the understated label "high conflict."

Donner's article concerns the most severe cases, although the ones for which a solution is badly needed. Postmarital conflict occurs on a continuum of intensity, but whether it is low or high is not necessarily the most salient variable. Two 30-year-olds who conceive a child before ever establishing a stable relationship and who struggle over their rightful place with their baby (the new mother wanting

---

[4] Eddy, B., (2018), *5 types of people who can ruin your life: identifying and dealing with narcissists, sociopaths, and other high-conflict personalities*, Tarcher Perigee (Penguin).

[5] Donner, M., (2006), Tearing the child apart, *Psychoanalytic Psychology*, 23(3), 542.

[6] Smyth, B. M., & Moloney, L. J., (2017), Entrenched postseparation parenting disputes: The role of interparental hatred? *Family Court Review*, 55(3), 404–416.

boundaries and the father wanting equal inclusion) might be considered high conflict, especially if initial conduct was poor. They would likely need case management and therapy in order to mature and find their footing as a parenting team. This case hardly compares to a couple who fights to mutual exhaustion over a decade, where the marriage ends with violence and where both parents initiate serious physical altercations and emotionally charged episodes, both between them and with their children, who become psychologically battered and even ill during the long period of turmoil. Nonetheless, both might be labeled "high conflict." It is clearly a spectrum.

Additionally, as Johnson notes, most severe high-conflict disorders usually occur in the limited sphere of the divorce itself.[7] Reality testing and adaptation do not necessarily suffer beyond the toxic bubble of the divorce, and the behavior of afflicted individuals often fails to meet the clear criteria of personality disorder in the pervasive sense of mental health diagnostics.

What becomes evident is that there is a need for a clear clinical framework in which to understand this minority of entrenched high-conflict divorces that demand so many therapeutic and legal resources with such limited success. Whether it is personality disorder, situational madness, hatred, or some measure of the degree of conflict itself, there is something qualitatively unique about these cases, often chilling and at times dangerous.[8]

Let us begin with a snapshot of such a scenario to give some sense of the subject matter.

Sylvia and Murray

Sylvia and Murray met in high school. Each took comfort in knowing that they both came from turbulent, dysfunctional family homes where violence was commonplace. They had witnessed explosive, alcohol-fueled episodes growing up, and they vowed never to repeat this experience in their own lives. Their childhood disillusionment was

---

[7] Johnson, J., (2017), Commentary on "Entrenched postseparation parenting disputes: The role of interparental hatred," *Family Court Review*, 55(3), 424–429.

[8] Gottlieb, M., Gould-Saltman, D., & Bow, J., (2015), Risks from clients and opposing parties for family law attorneys, *Family Court Review*, 53(2), 317–325; Pickar, D., (2006), On being a child custody evaluator: Professional and personal challenges, risks, and rewards, *Family Court Review*, 45(1), 103–115.

huge, and they needed to feel hope and the promise of a different, healthier destiny.

Yet by the time the marriage self-destructed, with two children, a daughter, four, and a son, eight, there were a thousand episodes that for each defined the inherent and out-of-control abusiveness of the other. The police and child protection agency were involved a dozen times with ongoing judicial intervention. Even before they officially separated, Sylvia found Murray highly critical, explosive, retaliatory, and selfish. He felt depressed, belittled, rejected, and at times suicidal. He could not bear living with a woman who seemed to hate him, helped herself to money from their line of credit, and regularly disparaged his physique and appearance.

Murray erupted one day, provoked, he believed, by his wife, who recorded his outburst in front of the children: "The fucking nonsense that comes out of you. I hate you. You are a piece of shit. I can't honestly wait until the day I fucking die so that I don't have to deal with you anymore." It had gone too far, even for this embattled couple, and they separated. Nonetheless, the roiling conflict did not abate.

In the aftermath, their four-year-old daughter returned from a visit with her father with redness in her vaginal area. Questioning by her mother led to a disclosure that her father had her touch his penis. There were further giggling accounts of dances with a penis, a penis waterfall, penis licking, and many other variations that soon engulfed the family in police and child protection investigations. All of this led to nothing other than a family in tatters and two confused, emotionally stressed children whose parents could not even discuss parenting issues.

Sylvia continued to assert that Murray was the perverse predator behind the penis touching, and he saw his access reduced from days and overnights to just hours. If she could have had him jailed and excommunicated from their children's lives, she would have. To be sure, it was a near-knockout blow, although he was able to claw his way back through the recommendation of a court-ordered family assessment. Nonetheless it was evident that whatever trauma, abuse, and violence these two parents had experienced in their early lives was revisited on their offspring. They fought to impasse over who would be the therapist for the child to the extent that there was no therapist. The eight-year-old boy seemed relegated to the sidelines of this drama, which focused almost entirely on his sister. He seemed shocked into silence.

The Concept of High Conflict

In her original, multidecade longitudinal study of divorce, the late Judith Wallerstein underlines the unique aspect of this subgroup of severe high conflict.[9] In a 1991 article, she elaborates on her findings and observations:

> [The] tormented families who are locked into protracted high conflict are not accurately considered as representing the far end of the divorcing spectrum. They represent instead a separate subgroup that is relatively new in many respects to the mental health profession, in part because they rarely seek out therapy. Consequently, they challenge the limits of our psychological knowledge and clinical skills. Children in these families remain at very high risk, whether or not the family arrives at a legal resolution of their dispute. In some of these families, the divorce appears to trigger a thought disorder in one or both parents that involve the child and the other parent in a focused or encapsulated delusional system. This is something difficult to diagnose because the adults are often capable of functioning with competence in other domains of their lives.[10]

In another broad study focusing on the children of divorce, Heatherington and Kelly observe that 20%–25% of children of divorce, all four years of age when their parents separated, were troubled as adults based on self-reported psychiatric symptoms, compared to 10% of the average population, confirmed in the control group of intact families.[11] The authors add that this divorce effect is larger than that between smoking and cancer.

These severe high-conflict individuals and couples seem to become "mad" in a way that is reminiscent of thought disorder. There is a radical disconnect akin to a refusal to acknowledge the core humanity of the ex-spouse. Paranoid thinking can run wild—the other becomes a monstrous antagonist in a battle of good versus evil that is litigated endlessly, no matter the price or psychological cost. As Wallerstein observes, litigation is no answer in many of these cases. Indeed, it is but a blip in a long saga that only dissipates when the children finally grow up.

---

[9] Wallerstein, J. S., & Kelly, J. B., (1980), *Surviving the breakup: How parents and children cope with divorce*, Basic Books.

[10] Wallerstein, J. S., (1991), Tailoring the intervention to the child in the separating and divorced family, *Family and Conciliation Courts Review*, 29, 457

[11] Hetherington, E. M., & Kelly, J., (2002), *For better or for worse: Divorce reconsidered*, Norton.

There has been extensive clinical work linking severe high-conflict divorce and a host of mental health conditions as well as substance abuse and family violence.[12] In other words, it is incontrovertible that toxic divorce can leave a transgenerational traumatic footprint. Children who endure their parents' divorce wars have particular trouble believing in relationships, developing social skills, and managing conflict in their own marriages.[13]

In the latter part of her career, Wallerstein grew pessimistic about the impact of divorce based on her extensive interviews over decades with children and their parents. She not only reported on the data she collected but also communicated her abiding clinical impression that divorce in general comes with a significant price for children, even when conflict levels are within a normal range. In 2004, she wrote in conjunction with a colleague,

> How is the inner template of the child of divorce different from that of the young adult in the intact family, especially if the child has access to both parents and the parents refrain from fighting? As every "child of divorce" in our sample told us, no matter how often they see their parents through the years, the image of them together as a couple is forever lost; and a father in one home and a mother in another does not represent a marriage. Joint custody does not teach children how to create adult intimacy and mutual affection, how to resolve marital conflicts, or how to deal, as a couple, with a family crisis. As they grew up, these children lacked this central reassuring image. By strong contrast, the children from intact families told many stories about their home life and how their parents met and married. They had spent their growing-up years observing their parents' interactions and learning about marriage, and they were well aware of the expectable ups and downs. For the children of divorce, the parents' interactions—including the courtship, the marriage, and the divorce—collapsed into a black hole, as if the parents as a unified couple had vanished from the world and from the child's inner life.[14]

---

[12] Johnston, J. R., (2006), A child-centered approach to high-conflict and domestic-violence families: Differential assessment and interventions, *Journal of Family Studies*, 12, 15–36; Johnston, J. R., Roseby, V., & Kuehlne, K., (2009), *In the name of the child: A developmental approach to understanding and helping children of conflicted and violent divorce* (2nd ed.), Free Press.

[13] Amato, P. R., (2000), The consequences of divorce for adults and children, *Journal of Marriage and the Family*, 62, 1269–1287; Amato, P. R., & DeBoer, D. D., (2001), The transmission of marital stability across generations: Relationship skills or commitment to marriage? *Journal of Marriage and Family*, 63, 1038–1051.

[14] Wallerstein, J., & Lewis, J. M., (2004), The unexpected legacy of divorce: Report of a 25-year study, *Psychoanalytic Psychology*, 21, 368.

All of this accords with clinical experience, although my impression is that Wallerstein underestimated childhood resiliency as well as the extent to which many divorced parents go to acknowledge a link with the other parent and to provide a different adaptive model to their children. Divorce itself is less the problem, it seems, than how it occurs.[15] What is ascribed to the clinical and developmental consequences of divorce as a splintering event and life change masks the more crucial contribution of the parties' conduct during and after the breakup. It is the ethical dimension that needs to be accorded an important place in both understanding and working with these individuals, couples, and families.

When I use the word *ethical*, as I do in this book, it is not to finger wag or moralize. This would be futile and condescending. Rather, I use the word in its most elemental sense, as *ethos*, from the Greek word meaning *nature* or *disposition*. It is our human nature that calls us to ethics, and this nature is inextricably linked with the first relationships, those with the parent(s) at the beginning of life. It is the parents' gaze that conveys our particular individuality. We come into being through parental love. There is no self that does not include otherness, and this represents a continuing obligation that touches all relationships. Whether this particular person, the ex-partner, leaves or is left, there is always a residue, a remainder, the obligatory imprint of otherness for which there is no escape from responsibility.

In this interpretation of ethics, I am influenced by the writing of the late philosopher Emmanuel Levinas, whose phenomenology was grounded in the face-to-face encounter with the other.[16] For Levinas, responsibility for the other is not something based on a rational argument or whether the other is deserving. It is more primary. The other is installed in our being at the most elemental level of experience, and the subject both has and feels that they have an ethical responsibility. This arises because of the intense human desire for otherness, something beyond the self that provokes reverence and duty to care. It is a realm of "not-me" that cannot be possessed or mastered.

Fast-forward, then, to adult marital relationships; the offer that the other makes to love, care, and recognize us is itself a summons to ethics. This core responsibility to the other, embedded in the social unit of the family, is irreducible, permanent, and unaltered by later

---

[15] See Leonoff, A., (2021), *The ethical divorce: A psychoanalyst's guide to separation, divorce and childcare*, Friesen Press.
[16] Levinas, E., (1969), *Totality and infinity* (A. Lingis, Trans.), Duquesne University Press.

events, including divorce. When I work with divorced couples at all levels of complications and conflict, this ethical lens structures my thinking. It is indispensable to outcome.

One can think of those who refuse to feel responsible. They turn away from the other, as if this other can be mastered, defeated, replaced, or extinguished. They effectively turn away from ethics. The result is as expected: deeply dysfunctional, often immoral behavior and attitudes that quickly become destructive. We might say to this person, devoid of ethics, that hope is not in the negation and destruction of the other, the former spouse, but in embracing a fundamental respect and responsibility to and for them. This is freedom, whereas the alternative route breeds interminable conflict while trying to kill off what cannot be murdered, which is the legitimate presence of the other on whom one depends.

There is a difference between divorce as a solution to a troubled relationship and a radical break with the other that is negating and destructive in its ferocity. As such, it is neither anger nor conflict necessarily that is central to the problem. Rather, it is a profound denial of responsibility that both facilitates and expresses the destructiveness that becomes high conflict. When the other, and especially any responsibility for the other, is so denied as to render this other person alien or so dissociated that there is no connection, link, or stake, then total war becomes a real possibility.

Thus, it is the destructive element that is determining in high conflict. Spouses can be abandoned without warning, for example, never given the chance of repairing or even understanding what has occurred. Communication, essential to coparenting, can be replaced by constant verbal attack. Acts of sabotage are legion in this subgroup, including attacks on the other parent's relationship with a child. Nothing is off-limits or considered sacred. Children are regularly betrayed during exchanges when one or both parents use it as an opportunity for denigration, cold staring matches, or overt fighting. Physical violence can erupt, and children will learn to fear their parents ever occupying the same physical space. Accusations made to authorities, especially egregiously false and defamatory ones, show how child protective services and police can be weaponized to undermine the other in this all-out destructive struggle. Automobiles often feature large in these toxic high-conflict sagas. They are used for surveillance, recording, intimidating, blocking, and physical threat.

The main narrative in severe high conflict is aimed at the heart of what it means to be a self among others for whom we owe a duty of care. High conflict invariably involves a rejection of this duty, although it is often rationalized as a reaction to how one is treated. The "good" does not survive in high-conflict divorce, or if it does manage to survive, it is leveraged on fragile conditions that prove unattainable. There is no live and let live. Failed expectations, especially major disillusionments, and perceptions of the other as unworthy lead to unending vitriol and vengeance. Once the other is negated and discarded, there are often few limits to the harm the person is willing to inflict, even if this directly or indirectly hurts the shared children. Such sagas of destructiveness are narrated repeatedly in courtrooms around the world.

In this regard, the ultimate destructiveness is to deny this connection with the other and what responsibility it imposes. This profound disidentification then facilitates the no-holds-barred conduct that can be disturbing in its severity. Such couples lose their connection to the ethical when the other is deemed alien and beyond care or responsibility. One would need to refind it for any meaningful reparation to occur.

Hence, I make ethics a focus of this book, a touchstone to point the way to understanding and solutions. A family is a matrix, the place where separate elements come together within an ethical framework. The word *matrix* derives from the Latin word for *womb*. The family is a womb that is gestational because of this infinite responsibility for the other. Divorce does not lessen or eliminate the ethical demand, even though the high-conflict subject or couple rails against this imperative. We are always the one who is ultimately responsible. Of course, divorce does shift how this responsibility is delivered, but it does not end it.

Looking into the face of the other, the high-conflict subject does not respond to the other's validity, need, or vulnerability. Rather, they become mired in grievance or attempts at control, as if the other can be dominated, excluded, or vilified to the point of being totally undeserving. Often, such individuals are phobic about meeting the other and will raise all manner of objections to ever sharing the same physical space. They communicate electronically and avoid the face-to-face encounter that might stir them to admit the other's validity and the obligation to care. They cannot appreciate the vulnerability of the other as an extension of their own. At worst, they communicate through lawyers, which only adds to the aloneness, persecutory anxiety, and alienation. Levinas would say that we cannot choose whether to be responsible. It is in the other's face.[17]

Psychoanalyst Donald Winnicott observed this same irreducible intersubjectivity, which he grounds in the primary encounter between baby and mother. He noted that there is no such thing as a baby apart from the nurturing, providing mother at the beginning of life.[18] It is the mother's reflective gaze that allows the self to emerge within the matrix of this primal relationship. In other words, this original setup anticipates an emergent self but one in which there is always a fundamental debt and indissoluble reliance on the other. Being happens before we know that we are being, but it is always tied to another. Solitude is wonderful as long as there is access to an internal presence of the other. Otherwise, it would be a state of intolerable aloneness and nonbeing. Babies raised in foundling homes in Britain in the early 20th century, where they were fed but not touched or loved, were severely impaired psychologically; some even died.[19]

As noted previously, the high-conflict-prone individual radically rejects this indissoluble link to the other and, in so doing, splits from an ethical imperative. This can be observed in the silo of high conflict that is cut off from normal social interaction and interrelationship. There is a lethality to high conflict that is concealed by its claim to justice and children's well-being. Mental health and legal professionals and family members can be drawn into the turmoil—a maelstrom from which there is no seeming exit.

The illusion of the high-conflict mind-set is that divorce should provide absolute freedom from the other, the right to a parallel universe. This is the philosophy behind parallel parenting: two solitudes that never touch, even though they raise common children. Yet, one is never free of this inherent responsibility, with its links to child raising, which is what makes the high-conflict scenario so persecutory and, at the same time, so unethical.

The court's focus on justice thus often clashes with the high-conflict fixation on retribution and even annihilation of the other. The

[17] Levinas, E., (1978), *Otherwise than being or beyond essence* (A. Lingis, Trans.), Kluwer Academic.

[18] Winnicott, D. W., (1975), *Through paediatrics to psycho-analysis*, Hogarth/Institute of Psycho-Analysis.

[19] Spitz, R. A., (1945), Hospitalism—An inquiry into the genesis of psychiatric conditions in early childhood, *Psychoanalytic Study of the Child*, 1, 53–74.

turning to ethics needs to be the therapeutic and legal goal. The individual caught in the churn of conflict must come to face the other, accept responsibility for this person, gaze into the face of the former partner, and see their own vulnerability and need and that of their shared offspring. Of course, this is not something that can be ordered. It requires a process that must begin with the individuals themselves, who often can only rage about the other or anyone perceived at supporting this other. The destructive current is so intense that hope cannot easily survive. A sense of helplessness takes over, but nothing seems to spur a change of heart.

William and Julie

William had been separated for two and a half years, but there was scant progress in settling the business or parenting matters with his ex-wife, Julie. He described the transition where their two school-aged children passed from one parent to the other in the parking lot of a local coffee chain. It was William's ex-wife who insisted on a public setting because she expressed fear of his temper and his ongoing sense of blame and victimhood. William denied any responsibility for temper or intimidating behaviors. He saw the whole process of divorce as an unnecessary and self-serving plot to gain maximum financial support and bleed him dry. He was very bitter.

> WILLIAM: I can barely control my anger. Look at what she is doing to the kids: forcing them into this humiliating exchange just so that she can make me look like a monster. She's good at playing the "poor me" card, shakes when we are in court to impress the judge. I feel so used by her, and now she wants to take everything.

> ANALYST: What do you feel inside when you look at Julie? Is there something other than anger and bitterness?

> WILLIAM: The problem is that I can't look at her. I look everywhere else—up, down, the kids, other people in the parking lot. For a moment this week, I thought I might look at her, but then I just got bitter. What if she was hurt? Would I even help her? I hope not, but the kids would expect me to. They ask me if I love Mommy. I want to tell them that I hate her. She should just disappear. Julie might be the mother of my kids, but I want her out of my life. You are probably like everyone else. She looks sweet, so she must be. It is very different though.

ANALYST: You seem to feel shamed and controlled by Julie. It's hard to find a way out.

WILLIAM: It's all on my shoulders, like I am this brute who has to be kept in his place. Julie planned this, and I didn't see it coming. It's all crap!

ANALYST: If you could completely discredit Julie, then you would be free of having to look after her in any way.

WILLIAM: The kids will figure it out. They will come to understand who their mother is.

ANALYST: Yes, but it seems that you see the remedy as turning the tables on Julie. I wonder whether in your pain about what has happened that you don't really see Julie anymore—her vulnerability and insecurity, her pain at what has happened between you.

WILLIAM: I don't see her that way.

ANALYST: I agree; the problem is seeing. Perhaps that is why you can't look at her. Seeing her might move you to feel concern and to see something of yourself reflected back.

WILLIAM: I can't bear what she has done to me and to us. How could she?

William's strained and discordant postseparation relationship with Julie had not lessened over more than two years. His attention was focused inward, trying to find justification for his ill temper, constant grievance, sense of victimization, and inability to mourn. He was self-absorbed and caught in a circle of negativity that was much more bondage than freedom. He needed to transcend the situation, which was oppressing him, his ex-wife, and his children. William needed to see Julie as a human being, not as just someone who hurt him on purpose. This could only be found by getting outside himself and perceiving Julie in her vulnerability, with her own pain and distress. It would be an ethical solution, one that acknowledged the other and the duty to care for even someone who was a source of pain and disappointment.

William retained some capacity for reflection and was struggling to find a way through his feelings and what was transpiring legally. He had trouble seeing himself through Julie's eyes and acknowledging his contribution to the problem. He had difficulty seeing Julie.

What would have perhaps made it worse would have been a radical disavowal of Julie, amounting to a negation of her being and any link to her. If this had occurred, then destructiveness could take hold, giving rise to high conflict. William would kill his pain by killing off Julie in his mind. At the same time, he would have to deal with her as a coparent.

Boundary Violation

In parallel with the priest who abuses the parishioner or the doctor who violates the patient, there is an individual or couple who turns on the family itself, whether this be the ex-partner, the children, or both, and exacts a destructive toll. Of course, this is never acknowledged, but the destructive impact is irrefutable. The destructive catalyzes high conflict.

These situations are seemingly impervious to influence. They are impenetrable and function within a closed system that allows no new input or new learning. With no receptivity to new perspectives, high-conflict-prone individuals often seek aligned legal counsel and therapists and force all involved to be with or against them. They demand victory, not justice.

It is the theme of radical disconnect from the other that resonates through severe high-conflict cases. The experience of injury leads to a rageful and often vicious response. The fact that these two people share offspring is an inconvenient truth. The children do not stand a chance. If they try to stay in a neutral zone between their parents, they get pummelled by the interminable conflict. If they align with one, they stand the risk of losing the other.

This underlines the paradox of high conflict. There is a failure to divorce precisely because there is such a radical disconnect and disidentification with the ex-partner. Identification needs to shift in divorce with children to raise but not to be destroyed. It takes connection to divorce well.

An illustrative example might help further introduce this problem.

Marianne and Derek

Marianne, a 44-year-old business professional, was separated from her 45-year-old husband, Derek, a public servant. Lea was their young, adolescent daughter and the eldest of two children. The other was a boy who continued to follow the defined parenting schedule. Derek had not seen his daughter, though, for almost two years. It had been a gradual erosion of Lea's willingness to spend time with her dad. Finally, she refused to see him at all. Since then, she changed her surname to that of her mother's new partner. Lea wanted her father effaced from her life and family history.

When asked to articulate her complaints, Lea was vague. He had not allowed her to watch the movies she wanted. He wanted to talk rather than let her do her own thing. He was nosy.

Marianne's personal history was as troubled as was her marriage to Derek. She saw the family law system as protecting Derek from the consequences he deserved. She felt deeply violated by her husband, the legal system, and potentially anyone who stood in the way of freeing Lea and her from the offensive, traumatic hold of this horrible ex-husband. Curiously, this same mind-set did not generalize to the son.

Derek had an obsessional personality and was perfectionistic and somewhat rigid. He denied most of Marianne's complaints against him. He loved his daughter and wanted to find a way to get back into her life. Yet the more he insisted, the more he was vilified and labeled a threat to their collective welfare. Hence, mother and daughter became unified in their resistance against him.

Even asking mother and daughter to participate in therapy was perceived as violation. Although Lea claimed to have her own very negative experience of her father, it seemed more that she held her father responsible for her mother's emotional condition and, in this regard, shored up her mother. Marianne was very brittle and vulnerable. She felt very violated by Derek in every way, including sexually.

We should distinguish the destructive from the traumatic. Marianne was clearly traumatized, and Derek could well have contributed to her fear and hatred of him, but this was unclear. I suspect that she suffered some form of sexual abuse in childhood, likely from a close male relative, and that whatever she experienced with Derek was less a reminder than a repetition of the severe psychic threat this represented. Marianne said little regarding her origins, but what she offered was negative: Her father was a weekend alcoholic who preferred his garage workshop to the family home and his drinking friends to his family. She felt little connection to him. For the most part, Marianne refused to discuss him.

This traumatic aspect was solely linked to Derek, who she insisted was a vile pervert. He was the abuser who had to be expunged from the daughter's life. I suspect that this allowed Marianne to have a better relationship with her new partner. This second man could be freed from the poison of abuse through splitting good from bad. However, trauma is not inherently destructive other than to the self. It is an experience of suffering.

What Marianne demonstrated was more than the clinical effect of trauma. She was filled with hate and directed her attack on the father-daughter relationship. This was not accidental or collateral. My thought is that Marianne would have envied Lea too much if the daughter could have had the kind of positive, affirming father-daughter bond that Marianne was denied. In this regard, the destructive revealed itself. Marianne's attack was as much or more on her daughter than her ex-husband. Lea would never be allowed to have more than her mother. Additionally, Derek would be required to wear a sign of damning perversity, whether he had earned this label or not.

Such is the nature of the destructive current in high conflict. It is masked as justice but bears no resemblance. There is no thinking or pondering of different points of view. The other is caricatured or stereotyped, frozen in an image of badness by whatever name. It is not whether one party is innocent and the other guilty, for there is usually enough fault and blame to go around. It is rather that the other is treated as alien, a screen for unholy projections. The accumulated rage and destructivity are turned against the family identity, whether this be the ex-partner, the children, or the parent-child relationship. It is a severe attack with few limits and seemingly no awareness of consequences.

In a healthy perspective, divorce represents a loss on many levels that must be mourned. It takes maturity and courage to do so, especially because marital rupture often opens old wounds as well as new. Anxieties can flood the personality, and at least temporary regressions in adaptive functioning are common. When there are children involved, the complexity is magnified. While the adults are coping with disillusionment and disappointment, they must parent together and attend to the legal termination of the union. It is not surprising, then, that divorce is a major risk factor for the destructive. Once this takes hold in the couple, it can be very hard to stop or mitigate it.

What unleashes the destructive in the family context is understandably complex. I emphasize, however, the role of disillusionment, especially of the traumatic kind that seems to threaten hope itself. It is as if one's dreams and sense of the world as a hopeful place is exposed as a lie. This is very different from an experience of disappointment, a lack of fulfillment that makes it necessary to compromise or moderate expectations but does not endanger hopefulness.[20]

High-conflict, toxic divorce is a world without hope. There is an unleashing of fury on the family crucible, which is attacked in some way or another. The results are predictably harmful to all family members. In the psychological history of one or both ex-partners, one observes a layering of severe disillusionments that create a very real vulnerability. When the marriage ends, hope ends with it, and this sends the person or couple over a cliff.

The family courts today have developed effective case-management programs to divert resources to this challenging population. Still, however, there will never be enough resources to deal with the family-law equivalent of total war. It is also frustrating and depleting for the entire system—judges, lawyers, mental health professionals, child protection workers, and police—when they fail to make a dent in the mind-set of these individuals and couples.

Statistically, based on available data, severe high-conflict divorce would be expected to be a major societal issue with reverberating effects. Assuming that there are 500,000 married couples or families living in a hypothetical urban community, approximately one-third of these would divorce (based on a CDC reported divorce rate of almost 333 per 1,000).[21] Of those divorce cases, assuming the lowest sampling estimate of 5% in the high-conflict range, there are 8,350 cases at any point in time. The worst high-conflict situations can endure for a decade if the children are young enough when the breakup occurs. Hence, the numbers and impact accumulate. Clearly, this is no small problem for communities and society as a whole. It spurs us to find solutions.

It is the destructive in high-conflict divorce that blocks help for these individuals and couples. They are far away from ethics and the constructive path that an ethical frame allows. The high-conflict situation, saturated with projection, attack, and struggle, is hard to manage even for professionals. In many ways, it deserves danger pay. In part, this has to do with a type of perverse inversion that gives preference to hatred, destruction, and attack over love, construction,

[20] LaFarge, L., (2015), The fog of disappointment, the cliffs of disillusionment, the abyss of despair, *Journal of the American Psychoanalytic Association*, 63(6), 1225–1239.
[21] National Center for Health Statistics, (2018), *Marriage and divorce*, Centers for Disease Control and Prevention, https://www.cdc.gov/nchs/fastats/marriage-divorce.htm

insight, and resolution. These individuals and couples do not fit the social, psychological, and legal framework to manage divorce. They become "special cases," although misunderstood, in my view, as suffering from a surfeit of conflict rather than the destructiveness that is behind the drama that unfolds.

Certainly, it is not the stuff for which therapists, or lawyers for that matter, normally train. Psychoanalysts, however, have been keenly aware since Freud that there is something beyond the pleasure principle needed to explain the compulsive repetition of painful experience and the immense destructiveness of which human beings are capable.[22]

It is essential, in my view, to see the destructive unmasked and unrationalized as something else, such as narcissistic fragility, fury, or a defense against emotional injury. It might benefit understanding to consider another case example, this time from the clinical literature where the therapist clearly assisted the family through a destructive divorce.[23]

The therapist, a social worker, was contacted by the psychiatrist of two boys, ages 8 and 10. Their father had been arrested for assault and spent a night in jail. Their mother alleged that the children were afraid of their father, unsafe in his care, and that he had lurid, pedophilic fantasies, including watching child pornography and had solicited one of the boys to touch him sexually. She claimed to have suffered emotional and physical abuse in their 10-year union and only chose to report this when it occurred in front of the children.

The therapist found the father to be passive, submissive, and self-suffering, He was unable to set appropriate boundaries for the children but meant well. The boys were comfortable and happy in his care. He had to learn that his sons wanted him and not what they could get from him. He also needed to accept that passive surrender to his ex-wife was never going to solve the problem.

Skillfully, the therapist claimed her own neutral space and responded supportively to each parent. When the mother realized that the therapist was not buying her version of reality and would not serve as her ally, she stopped participating. As is common in these

[22] Freud, S., (1920), Beyond the pleasure principle, in *The standard edition of the complete psychological works of Sigmund Freud: Vol. 18, 1920–1922: Beyond the pleasure principle, group psychology and other works*, 1–64, Hogarth Press.
[23] Scharff, K. E., (2004), Therapeutic supervision with families of high-conflict divorce, *International Journal of Applied Psychoanalytic Studies*, 1, 269–281.

cases, the mother found a sympathetic counselor who allied with her self-identification as a victim of abuse. She changed lawyers as well, finding an attorney who also accepted her stance unequivocally, one who "specialized" in spousal violence and sexual abuse.

As father and sons improved together under the care of the therapist, the mother's rage against her sons increased. The therapist reported that when it was clear to the mother that legally she would be sharing childcare with her ex-husband, she left the area and only saw the children infrequently thereafter. The therapist framed the problem in terms of the mother's need for exclusive loyalty from the children as the only love she could believe or accept. In other words, no matter how paranoid, dishonest, and distorted, it was still about achieving love according to this account.

It is in respect to the issue of love that I differ, which changes our understanding of the case.[24] Although there is no data concerning the parents' personal history, my assumption is that the mother suffered major disillusionments in childhood, almost certainly linked with the threat or actual loss of love. She lost any hope or belief in the reality of love. She stopped loving. Instead, she insisted on a total submissive harmony from her husband and then her children. When her boys dared to love their father at some crucial juncture, she broke with them. At that point, hatred, rage, and revenge were in the air. First, she tried to kill the husband off by having him declared a pervert and jailed. When this did not work, she turned her sights on the children and abandoned them. It was a symbolic infanticide and an expression of her hatred and omnipotent control. It also imposed on them the experience of a traumatic loss of love that I would predict paralleled her own experience in childhood. As such, the mother was in the zone of the destructive, which is a mind-set aimed at annihilation.

So how could anyone help such a person or family beyond what was accomplished by this skilled therapist? How might the family law system achieve greater success, and what would that look like? In this case, of course, the therapist did help the boys and their father, and the mother was not able to sabotage it. However, the children effectively lost their mother. Moreover, the therapeutic work was very intensive, occurring inside and outside the office, and beyond what can be provided to most families in this situation.

[24] Reinterpreting cases where one is not the clinician should be done with caution. My intention is to illustrate the destructive element and should not be read as criticism of the author's work.

What if the mother's destructiveness had been confronted from the moment it became clear? What if she did not have the easy option of seeking an aligned therapist and attorney because these people were not accredited to work with high-conflict cases? There would have needed to be a clear, unequivocal container—legal, judicial, assessment, and therapeutic—in which the family could have been "held" and treated. In confronting the mother's destructiveness, the therapy in her case would have focused on the traumatic history of disillusionments and its "return of the repressed" in this current encounter. Her false accusations would not have been used to disqualify her but to focus specifically on the destructiveness that was aimed at her children and ex-husband.

The problem for the therapist in this situation is the problem faced by all practitioners—legal and mental health—with such destructive high-conflict families. There is no containment because there is usually no knitted, integrated system that can be brought to bear on the real issues. The mother in this case hired aligned professionals to support her destructive intent. She would have used these like-minded supports to attack and destroy by denying these boys a father and seeing him pilloried by the criminal and family courts. Under the guise of love and protection, she would have then attacked her sons by denying them a father for defying her and for "betrayal." In the end, her destructivity went unchecked, despite the help provided the boys and their father, and she took the one route open and acceptable to her, which was to abandon them all. This could have salvaged some sense of omnipotent control in her mind although at a huge personal and familial cost.

One can hopefully see that "conflict" is not particularly relevant to what ails this individual and family. There is a traumatic and destructive core that coalesces in the dynamic to wreak havoc on the family unit and the system designed to resolve these problems. Ideally, there would be an interdisciplinary team intervening, along with judicial guidance and oversight dedicated to dealing with these families. The professionals would be included for their expertise, knowledge, and capacity to cope with the challenges presented by this population. This would be supported by the relevant regulatory colleges or boards. The supervisory judicial role would be essential to ensuring fairness and competence. With these changes, the system would be integrated and capable of withstanding destructive attacks intended to destroy it and preventing the right help being delivered to the afflicted family.

Of course, we have these systems in place, including judicial oversight in severe mental illness, where afflicted people who lack insight and rationality but who are very destructive to self and others can be protected and helped. Something similar is needed in family law. The moment these high-conflict individuals and couples can split the professionals, undermine the legal process, break the container, and wreak havoc on each other, they will. This destructiveness may not be fully conscious, with perceptions twisted by hate, threat, and fear, but the overall motive is destructive at its core, not just its impact.

So now you have the beginning to this reimagining of high conflict, the family law system, and how to frame and respond therapeutically to these complex family issues. What follows is a treatise on severe high-conflict divorce as a societal problem greatly affecting children and families. It is also a call to ethics and the need to restore an ethical perspective in the realm of divorce and high conflict. Further, it is a reflection on the problem of the destructive in human nature, how it is triggered, and what can be done to address its serious challenges.

Conclusion

The concept of "high conflict" in divorce needs a framework in which to understand its particular dynamics. In this regard, I posit that high conflict represents a radical breach of ethics, in which ethics is understood as a fundamental and irresolvable responsibility to the other. In this regard, high conflict splits this indivisible ethical link with the other, which accounts for its ferocity and the degree to which it overturns the legal and mental health systems available to divorcing couples. Further, I propose that conflict is not the problem in high-conflict divorce. It is destructiveness. The individual or couple turn on the family, either in the form of the ex-partner, the children, or the relationship between a parent and a child. The motivation for the behavior is the destructiveness rather than the destructive being a secondary consequence or collateral damage of conflict. My premise is that unless the family legal system creates a strong container with professionals attuned and trained to deal with this demanding population, there will be no real solution beyond attempts at case management. These services help, but heavily burdened family law courts everywhere speak to the need for contribution in this area.

2

The Nature of Destructiveness

Once destructiveness is unleashed, divorcing couples will escalate to higher ranges of conflict. This destructivity might reside more in one ex-spouse than the other but generally plays a part in both. *Destructiveness* needs to be defined internally as an emotional or motivational state within the individual rather than by behavior alone. It is first and foremost intent rather than action. Of course, verbal and physical aggression can be destructive, as can threats and emotional withdrawal, but the term *destructive* is best reserved for a pattern of personal and motivational characteristics that seek to attack links and undermine or even destroy the family. It is internalized destructivity, a mental state, that is compulsively enacted externally in dysfunctional, high-conflict divorce.

There are four main characteristics:

1. a fundamental breach with the other, leaving a bunch of projections without any authentic acknowledgment or recognition of the other
2. the destruction of the intrapsychic representation of the couple that leaves the other existing only externally
3. a lack of a self-observing capacity
4. a huge degree of self-justification while convinced of one's innocence and the other's guilt

There is simply no end to the grievance and disillusionments that boil in the destructive broth of the couple. At the same time, the lack of a bridge between the two becomes a chasm filled with projections of each other's worst fears and perceptions. Episodes with the former partner—and there are many—reinforce the dynamic of grievance. The lack of self-reflection and often complete refusal to examine one's own behavior make it a closed system, where no new learning occurs. Even if this is driven by one ex-spouse, not both, the pattern is usually chronic. From the perspective of mental health intervention, there is no easy entrance.

Optimally, a mental representation of the family must survive divorce in order for children to go back and forth between homes. This representation reflects the creative union of the parents in generating the offspring. The destruction of this inner representation in one or both ex-partners has profound consequences for how the divorce will ensue. Obliterated within the mind, the other then only exists externally, with no mental representation to support sharing, communicating, and cooperation. Conflicts then quickly escalate. High conflict marks the catastrophe and builds on earlier traumatic life disillusionments.

As much as the destructiveness is obvious to others, it is not apparent to the afflicted individual or couple. They presume that the children are unaffected, or if they are aligned with one parent's cause, then it is because they are showing good sense and clear minds. There is a profound discordance between the claim of loving protection and the actual damage being done to the family members and the family ideal. The costs are, of course, psychological but also social; economic; medical; and, in the case of children, a stressful problematic life.[1]

Destructiveness, then, is not really about anger or hostility any more than it is about conflict. It might reduce vulnerability in the short term, despite extreme negative consequences, but the price for such an illusory solution is very high. In cases where police and child protection services are recruited, which is frequent in high conflict, it reinforces the sense of power when it seems to succeed. This is not power as agency, however, but power to inflict destructive blows. When police fail to charge or support charges or when child protection agencies label the problem as divorce stress and not child abuse, the rage only increases. Negative evidence is anything but comforting. It aggravates the wish to attack and destroy.

As much as the discourse of high conflict rests on claims of justice, fairness, and especially the welfare and love of children, the intent is to break every link with the former partner and sometimes to directly

---

[1] Felitti, V., Anda, R., Nordenberg, D., Williamson, D., Spitz, A., Edwards, V., & Marks, J., (1998), Relationship of child abuse and household dysfunction to many of the leading causes of death in adults: The adverse childhood experiences (ACE) study, *American Journal of Preventative Medicine*, 14(4), 245–258; Hetherington, E., Cox, M., & Cox, R., (1982), Effects of divorce on parents and children, in M. Lamb (Ed.), *Nontraditional families: Parenting and child development* (pp. 233–288), Erlbaum; Hoyt, L., Cowen, E., Pedro-Carroll, J., & Alpert-Gillis, L., (1990), Anxiety and depression in young children of divorce, *Journal of Clinical Child Psychology*, 19, 26–32.

attack the partner. When links are destroyed, the other ceases to be a subject worthy of recognition. Aside from the radical delinking with the ex-spouse, there is also a delinkage with thinking itself. It is action without a mentalizing capacity, where issues could be thought about or worked through.[2] In the zone of the destructive, thinking does not really exist; this then places the whole burden on the family law system, which works hard to contain the chaos and make sense of it. The court itself or its experts are required to mentally process what has happened, with little actual contribution from the high-conflict couple themselves.

Nicole and Henry

Nicole had given up hope that she would ever marry and have children. Hence, she was delighted when contacted by Henry on a dating app. He lived in another city but was eager to meet her outside the internet and to deepen their ties. Inexperienced and cautious, Nicole insisted on a long correspondence before meeting Henry in person. She had never had a serious relationship, and there were few sexual experiences either. She had a strong Christian faith and did not support casual sex outside marriage.

Henry had a checkered past: two failed marriages and four older children between his two ex-wives. He was certainly more experienced and worldly and expressed himself well. Nicole was wary when he borrowed a friend's house in her city and arranged for them to be alone. Touching led inevitably to sexual relations. What he did not tell her was that he was infected with herpes, which she discovered only when the burning symptoms of an outbreak occurred.

Nicole was completely thrown for a loop. As much as she believed that she should immediately end the relationship, Henry rationalized his behavior, emphasizing that he thought he was asymptomatic. Nicole was also drawn to Henry's charm and his capacity to mollify her. He made promises of a future and expressed the wish to have a child with her. Nicole overcame her screaming doubts and eventually relocated and cohabited with Henry.

They married quickly, although the union lasted only two years before imploding on all fronts. Nicole became pregnant, and a

---

[2] Bouchard, M., Target, M., Lecours, S., Fonagy, P., Tremblay, L., Schachter, A., & Stein, H., (2008), Mentalization in adult attachment narratives: Reflective functioning, mental states, and affect elaboration compared, *Psychoanalytic Psychology*, 25(1), 47–66.

daughter, Sabrina, was born. Nicole described having to contend with Henry's other children, who seemed to have the inside track with their father. They were aided by one of his ex-wives in particular, who readily interfered and put demands on Henry that left Nicole and Sabrina on the sidelines. When Sabrina was considered, it felt more like she was an offering to his former wives and children. Nicole felt deeply threatened and negated.

Catching Henry absorbed in internet pornography horrified the conservative and spiritual Nicole. Further, she perceived him to be overly interested in their daughter's vagina when changing her diaper, which put Nicole into a state of alarm. Her anxiety and mistrust soared. She was then sure that she saw Henry put his finger in the child's vagina, which pushed her over the edge.

As the union collapsed in a storm of accusation, Nicole reported Henry to the child protection authority, and the police became involved. Indeed, she turned on Henry with a vengeance. Humiliated; stuck with a sexually transmitted chronic infection; and, in her mind, played for a fool by Henry and one of his ex-wives, Nicole clung to Sabrina and spurned Henry. Her inclination to label him a sexual predator became a fixed idea that she pursued relentlessly. Henry fought back legally, but he was required to see Sabrina under supervision, and with passing time, she learned from her mother never to trust her father or to see him as someone positive in her life. By five years of age, Sabrina was resistant and rattled when attending visits with her father. It was as if she looked through him.

Nicole saw herself as the only source of protection for their daughter (whom she would only refer to as "my daughter"). She blurred the distinction between how she, Nicole, felt about Henry and Sabrina's relationship with her father, as if they were one and the same. He was a predator to Nicole and would be no different with their child. In turn, Sabrina became increasingly confused and phobic. Nicole chose to homeschool her, which cut the child off from external influences. This isolation was extremely harmful. Henry was mainly frozen out of their child's life apart from minimal, supervised access. The whole situation was deeply destructive. Nicole had a complete incapacity to examine her feelings and perceptions. She enacted a vicious campaign to have Henry arrested, jailed, and vilified in the courts.

Understanding more of Nicole's family background shed some light on her predisposition. A child who had lost her mother to cancer at a young age, she had idealized her own father growing up and considered their relationship during childhood idyllic. However, when she was a teen, he withdrew considerably from her. This sense of loss was worsened when she was a young adult and he chose to move to another city, ostensibly to enjoy a better climate. The growing emptiness seemed to have hurt Nicole deeply, especially as she had lost her mother. She could not understand why her father would make the choices he did when there was just the two of them. It was in this state of void and feeling alone in the world that Nicole registered on the dating site.

On the one hand, it is difficult not to feel sympathy for Nicole. On the other, her enmeshment with Sabrina was clearly destructive to the child and placed an insurmountable barrier between father and daughter. Nicole's disillusionment and bitterness ran deep: the unfairness of losing a mother; a self-absorbed, disappointing father; and, in her mind, a perverse ex-husband who tarnished her forever and whom she perceived as a real danger to Sabrina. Nicole's fury knew no bounds when it came to Henry, and there was no real capacity to understand how this thirst for vengeance was affecting their child.

The origin of Nicole's destructiveness can be traced to the core ingredients of helplessness, powerlessness, and severe disillusionment. Henry's irresponsible disregard for Nicole's sexual health, his failure to maintain boundaries for Nicole with his older children and ex-wives, and his penchant for making hollow promises fomented the toxic brew. But he was not the immoral predator and reprobate that Nicole alleged, and he was sincere in his wish to be a father to Sabrina. Nonetheless, Henry had so invalidated himself in Nicole's eyes that Sabrina was obliged to see her father through her mother's lens, which created major impediments that took sizable court and mental health intervention to address, although imperfectly.

It is relatively easy to link Nicole's destructiveness to her attack on Henry. It is less apparent that her destructiveness was also directed at her child. Sabrina was made to endure the effective loss of a parent in lockstep with Nicole. Of course, Nicole would not have accepted any responsibility for what she was doing to her daughter. Destructiveness works under the surface and often lacks words and even conscious thoughts. It is a force that manages to destroy even while it loudly claims love and protection.

There was no firm, containing structure and process in place to enforce the ethics of responsibility on Nicole and Henry. The destructiveness was allowed to fester, increasingly encroaching on Sabrina's relationship with her father as she grew up within the horrific turmoil of her parents' divorce. The court could help manage the legal process, but investigations and legal defenses do not ultimately protect children and families in real time. The forces unleashed have no regard for legalities or the measured pace of justice. Nicole's deeply destructive rage hid behind the image of loving protectiveness. It was neither confronted nor addressed. Henry did not face his profound lack of respect for the woman with whom he chose to partner and have a baby.

False allegations of sexual violation of a child are rare in typical divorce but not so much in high-conflict divorce.[3] It is an expression of destructiveness intended often to destroy the other or, as in the current example, the child's relationship with that parent. Certainly, it is paranoid: The other is treated as an enemy or dire threat. The fear of being controlled, hoodwinked, colonized, and forced to passively serve the needs of the ex-partner makes any type of shared parenting beyond consideration. The conflict itself serves as a protective shield. The destructiveness, though, is denied. The false accuser clings to a self-image of protective love. Meanwhile, the destruction is incontrovertible.

When it comes to false sexual abuse allegations, "Daddy touches my bum" takes on an entirely new meaning when the father dries his five-year-old daughter with a towel after her bath. There is always indirect plausibility; incestuous abuse of children does occur, which makes these attacks on the other parent especially unsettling. What is often not perceived in these unfortunate cases is the attack on the child. It is masked by a protective delusion. Nonetheless, the child is often exposed to multiple interviews, intrusive physical examinations, exposure to police. Further, the child is effectively denied a parent and forced to share a traumatic fate with the accusing parent or to participate in the parent's vengeance.

---

[3] Saini, M., Laajasalo, T., & Platt, S., (2020), Gatekeeping by allegations: An examination of verified unfounded and fabricated allegations of child maltreatment within the context of resist and refusal dynamics, *Family Court Review*, 58(2), 417–431; Sheehan, E., (2019), Using Rule 11 sanctions to punish accusers who make false allegations of child sexual abuse in custody and divorce cases, *Family Court Review*, 57(1), 121–135.

Thoughts on an Ethical Divorce

Unethical divorce costs individuals, families, and society alike. It is not a small matter. In a dated but still poignant study, Wallerstein and Kelly determine that 30% of divorces with children involve high levels of interparental conflict for three to five years after separation.[4] Children can recover from their parents' divorce, as long as they are not exposed to unmitigated destructiveness and conflict. Decades of research demonstrate a distinct psychological vulnerability to harm in both children and parents in high-conflict scenarios that can drag on for years.[5] High conflict is by definition unethical. It is sad to see parents fighting, presumably for their children's future, in what is a decimating, often multiyear struggle of attrition that handicaps their future.

The need to put ethics at the forefront of divorce education is a crucial step. It should not be taken for granted. Separating adults with children need to be conscious of these choices and held accountable. This could take the form of divorce education that emphasizes the effect on children and families—not of divorce itself but of how one chooses to divorce. Current programs targeting conflict management are particularly helpful to those on the margin of high conflict, but in my experience, they have no appreciable benefit for those in the deep grip of destructive dynamics.

As much as certain people misuse or even abuse medical or social services, high-conflict ex-couples often abuse the composite of services that support family law. Thus, they exploit ancillary services, such as police and child protection, to serve their divorce ends. In addition to overutilizing court and related services, they invert a system intended for conflict resolution to enact a destructive mind-set. Everyone involved is dragged into this mire in what might be described as a "pay to hate" system. Ayoub and colleagues found that in a sample of children whose parents engaged in a highly acrimonious divorce,

[4] Wallerstein, J., & Kelly, J., (1980), *Surviving the breakup: How children and parents cope with divorce*, Basic Books.

[5] Amato, P. R., & Keith, B., (1991), Parental divorce and the well-being of children: A meta-analysis, *Psychological Bulletin*, 110, 26–46; Brock, R., & Kochanska, G., (2016), Interparental conflict, children's security with parents, and long-term risk of internalizing problems: A longitudinal study from ages 2 to 10, *Development and Psychopathology*, 28(1), 45–54; Grych, J., (2005), Interparental conflict as a risk factor for child maladjustment: Implications for the development of prevention programs, *Family Court Review*, 43(1), 97–108.

52.4% witnessed interparental violence.[6] This is a shocking statistic and reveals the pervasiveness of violence in high-conflict divorcing families. The impact of witnessing violence is often no less than experiencing it directly as a target.

This destructive behavior comes in many forms, not just overt violence. It is destructive because it attacks the family envelope, the container in which children are supposed to be held and protected. The possible list of such actions is as endless as imagination, but the following come to mind:

- sharing court documents with children
- devaluing the other parent to the children
- using transitions to stare down, devalue, fight, or argue
- interfering with communication between children and the nonresidential parent
- holding up or preventing travel for the children and the other parent
- holding on to information, distorting, lying, or otherwise obfuscating to make it harder for the other parent to be a meaningful part of the children's lives
- creating scenes at children's activities
- redirecting important mail that is inadvertently received
- bullying, intimidation, threats, coercion, trespassing, and other abuses of power and control
- refusing to share expenses or meet financial obligations
- taking no parenting responsibility for how the children treat the other parent, including subtle or overt messaging that encourages children to disrespect, dishonor, and disobey the other parent
- coveting children to bolster security and relieve the pain of divorce rather than representing the needs of the children for both parents
- creating mutually exclusive bonds with children while taking no responsibility (e.g., maintaining that the bonds are due only to the good judgment of the child)
- using e-mail or other web-based platforms to attack, criticize, devalue, and demoralize the other parent
- making plans unilaterally with children that interfere directly with the other parent's time with the children
- using shared legal custody to make every decision a marathon of energy and expense, so that it amounts to "no custody" or paralysis

[6] Ayoub, C., Deutsch, R., & Maraganore, A., (1999), Emotional stress in children of high conflict divorce: The impact of marital conflict and violence, *Family Court Review*, 37(3), 297–315.

- undermining the rule of law by ignoring agreements, court orders, and judicial advice
- using police and child protection authorities to persecute the ex-partner through false allegations

These actions can sabotage, destabilize, punish, hurt, or nullify the other parent. Sometimes these actions carry severe consequences for either parent and almost always strikes at the core of a parent's relationship with their children, who pay the price. These situations are depleting and destructive.

Once a divorce has spiraled out of control, no degree of education or reorientation will return the individual or couple to ethics. The destructive impulse aims to destroy links and negate the legitimate rights of others. It resists mental representation and claims to be something else, such as self-defense or reactive anguish. The destructiveness rests on a pathology of disillusionment: devastation, broken hopes, and failed dreams that seem too great to mourn. It is an emotional catastrophe that freezes time and narrows the life space. It must be faced directly.

Conclusion

In high-conflict divorce, the problem is destructiveness, not conflict. It is an inversion of values and cannot be reduced to a question of personality or hatred. The attack is both internal (intrapsychic) and external. Links are shattered until the other is viewed as alien, so "not-me" or "not-us," to be denied recognition or attacked with impunity. In this regard, high-conflict divorce is profoundly unethical because it destroys the fabric of care that makes families so vital, even in divorce. Painful disillusionment imperils hope and immobilizes grieving. Destructiveness takes over and fuels high conflict.

Ethics can be an important framework in which to understand the exigencies of divorce when children are shared. It is what gives impetus and context to conflict resolution. It is a way of being with another, even in divorce. High conflict, however, is situated outside ethics. In this state of mind, the destructive is in charge and guides behavior. There can be no return to ethics without confronting the effects of major disillusionment and the destructiveness that stems from it.

Divorce
A Crisis of Disillusionment

Codes of parental conduct are often found in the separation agreements of ex-couples least likely to honor them. These codes stipulate specific parental behaviors and attitudes that promote coparenting, such as:

* Speak respectfully and supportively to the children regarding the other parent.
* Support the other parent's relationship with the children.
* Function in the service of the coparenting, including communicating and planning in advance of speaking with the children.
* Acknowledge the children's right to contact the nonresidential parent when there is a request or need to do so.
* Respect the sanctity of transitions, which means no growling, feuding, hostile staring, or arguing in front of the children.

Expecting parents to follow these principles in supporting their children's best interests can be a challenge. This is especially true for the subgroup designated as high conflict, who are particularly resentful and unprepared to collaborate. Divorce for them is experienced as a traumatically disruptive, uncontrollable event that leaves them feeling helpless. Disillusionment runs deep, and their belief in the family as a sanctuary and symbol of safety, security, and goodness is badly shaken. This is far reaching in its consequences and brings a high level of tension to every personal encounter.

One sees a continuum of ethical conduct in divorce. Some people naturally adhere without having to be instructed. They are divorced, but there is little observable difference to the way they interacted when they were together. Others vary in their compliance depending on what they are feeling about the ex-partner at any given moment. It is always easier to be ethical when there is agreement. At the negative extreme, the low point of ethicality, the idea of continuing to be in a family, albeit a divorced one, feels intolerable. The family as a social and emotional construct does not necessarily survive the divorce.

Some people are naturally governed by internal precepts and values, while others have a more transactional view of the world and take their cues entirely from how they are treated. The latter mind-set, "quid pro quo," was cleverly captured by the late Canadian prime minister Pierre Trudeau, who famously said of his political adversary's style, "You scratch my back, and I'll scratch yours. You don't scratch my back, and I'll scratch your face."[1] High conflict is a chronic state of feeling raw, injured, and enraged by perceived unfairness. The impact on children or the family system does not really register in this group, and if it does, it is swept away by the retaliatory fury of the moment.

Much as premarital preparation classes often help the newly united, divorce education could put ethical thinking in clearer view. I am reminded of driving schools that use actual collision reports to teach good driving habits. Speeding, distracted driving, or failing to yield could have very real consequences. I think that this same principle could also apply to divorce education. Failing to meet basic ethical standards will destructively affect children and the couple.

Thus, what divorce education should promote is not so much good conduct but an ethical framework that favors reflection over reflexive action. This works especially well when there is some degree of foresight that gives preference to the family's overall benefit rather than a narrow, transactional mind-set in which one bad turn deserves another. But the problem with "theory" is that it usually fails to penetrate the closed, persecutory dynamics that saturate high conflict.

What is mandatory is the capacity to think before acting. It is a moment of reflection that occurs as a second look. The first response is always visceral and autonomic. Something has been lost or broken, ripped by disillusionment and discontent. The second look, though, makes all the difference. It provides an opportunity to reflect and interpolate core values that include the protection of children. Ethics becomes possible when there is a capacity for a second look.

---

[1] Trudeau, P. E., (May 1987), Oral communications, Meech Lake Parliamentary Hearings, quoted in Garfinkle, E. (1999), Quid pro quo: The inverse of talion, *Canadian Journal of Psychoanalysis*, 7(2), 245–270.

Emily and Brian

Emily had been mistreated, even beaten, by her mother, a single parent, and decided to "bury" her and never see her again. She was the antimother in Emily's eyes, and Emily felt lucky to have survived. Her father had not been involved in her life. Emily's marriage to Brian also left her feeling wrecked. There were moments of physical aggression between them, with each claiming the other as aggressor. Usually, though, she felt intimidated by Brian's scorn and derision. He was better educated and held this over her, at least as she described it. Perhaps surprisingly, they had three children. My impression was that not all were planned. She never felt that Brian valued or cared about her consent when it came to sexual relations.

Brian could see no merit in any of Emily's allegations. He described her as given to outbursts followed by regret in endless cycles. He could accept that she wanted to leave him but resisted her attempts to paint him as controlling, mean, and intimidating. Brian's problem seemed to be his completely defensive posture, in which he refused to acknowledge that Emily's complaints or feelings about him might have some validity. She experienced this as an impenetrable wall, where he refused to reflect on himself and his conduct.

Emily was deeply disillusioned. Despite three children, she felt that she lived with a man who despised and looked down on her and only valued her as a sexual object. Brian was also profoundly disillusioned and equally resentful, although he tried to hide this to avoid losing a court fight. If Emily was bitter regarding the hand she had been dealt in childhood and marriage, then Brian was furious that Emily was overturning his family dream to pursue a narrative of her own that did not accord with his sense of what was real.

Even five long years after this couple separated, they were still struggling to find some kind of balance. Their children suffered from living in a war zone of hatred, with each parent claiming victimhood.

The challenge for therapists and the legal system is to find ways to create an ethical space where the divorce can unfold without the push and pull of incessant argument over who is victim and who is aggressor. Once couples slide into the range of high conflict, they rarely reverse course. The dynamic builds on itself like a constantly fed bonfire.

The family law system is organized to manage conflict, and high-conflict divorcing couples are heavy users. However, case management and courtrooms often become further venues for conflict. It can be a site for struggle rather than resolution, which makes this population prone to relitigation. Mental health professionals lend what support and expertise they can, but there is no available, agreed-upon cure to return to ethics.

In the case of Brian and Emily, the issue of disillusionment loomed large. The crisis amounted to hopelessness that was handled poorly by each partner. In Emily's case, she retreated behind barricades reinforced by hostility and fear, vilifying Brian, summoning the child protection authorities regularly to control him, and using the courts to attack his custodial rights. It was a blistering assault on Brian as a person and, potentially, as the father of the couple's three children.

Emily had not married Brian and borne children to relive her catastrophe with her mother. It pained her greatly and left her feeling ashamed and guilty. She had deeply invested in the image of an ideal family experience that would heal her wounds. She would create what she did not have as a child. Her illusions were fundamental to her hopes and dreams for the future. When she experienced Brian as a wall of smugness and defensiveness, her disillusionment was profound. Her dreams crumbled, and she felt deeply bitter that he had done this to her.

Brian had believed that Emily would be grateful for what he did for her and for the children. He came from a successful family, with parents who had high expectations for their children. He was deeply ashamed of the marital failure and felt equally disillusioned by what he perceived as Emily's betrayal. Brian's defensive superiority hid aching self-doubts. Having Emily wear the mantle of the inadequate, failed one allowed Brian to sidestep his own deep insecurities, but this was extremely unfair to Emily, while it offered no real solution for him.

Emily's repetition of destructive relationships, mother and then partner, deserves some comment for its profound clinical salience. Freud was the first to describe this phenomenon as a form of remembering within the transference relationship.[2] It is an acting out of experience without any conscious awareness of recollection or insight. In this way, trauma is repeated in an unconscious drive to master what was passively suffered. It carries the force of what is unresolved and even what has not been symbolized or clearly represented.[3] In Emily's

[2] Freud, S., (1914), Remembering, repeating and working-through (further recommendations on the technique of psycho-analysis II), in *The standard edition of the complete psychological works of Sigmund Freud, Vol. 12, 1911–1913: The case of Schreber, papers on technique and other works*, 145–156, Hogarth Press.

[3] Scarfone, D., (2011), Repetition: Between presence and meaning, *Canadian Journal of Psychoanalysis*, 19, 70–86.

case, she certainly had very conscious hatred of a mother she wanted gone from her life. What she needed was something far more complex: to comprehend fully the impact on her, to reconfigure her life in light of what she knew, and to transcend the traumatic. This would include the self-knowledge of how this prior difficult and traumatic experience had sadly governed the choice of a mate.

The marriage between Brian and Emily unwound chaotically, and the divorce proved equally volatile and unstable. There was intimidation, violence, and reprisal. Brian hated Emily for ruining his dream. She painted him as a monster, holding her hostage, intimidating, and antisocial. He described her as delusional, evil, and unfit to parent. There were three children and two parents, but the family as the safe container of their lives was obliterated. It had been totally destroyed in the mayhem: intrapsychically and externally as well.

Divorce is a crisis of disillusionment. What was anticipated, hoped, or desired breaks down, leading to a loss of motivation and commitment. The notion that couples drift apart masks the pivotal role of disillusionment in the drifting. Of course, disappointment and even some disillusionment are inevitable in all relationships. Reality cannot live up to dreams, which is why relationships must be regularly renewed to keep them vital. Any disillusionment should happen slowly and never completely. We need our illusions because they are the stuff of dreams, and besides, they soften and personalize reality, which is very important to the richness of human experience.

Healthy, Creative Illusion

A long and robust marriage that sustains a couple is never achieved at the expense of illusion. Two elderly people view each other through the prism of their illusions, as this establishes the shared space in which romance initially sizzles and later prospers. As such, illusion is not the opposite of reality but its complement. It nourishes, energizes, excites, enlivens, and gives the relationship a very personal, playful, and subjective quality. When we think about illusion, we become aware that what we experience should be as much in our mind as in the external world. It needs to be both.

When a child plays with a favorite red fire truck, the toy comes alive in his imagination. Of course, the child knows that the fire truck is a toy, but imagination enriches the experience and makes this particular fire truck precious and very real. These are the precursors of creativity and are extended to what and whom we treasure.

Of course, there is a harmful form of illusion. This unhealthy form of illusion does not enrich reality but evades it. It is used to conceal the traumatic and has more in common with a fetish than a dream. It is not free and spontaneous but fixed and repetitive. The healthy illusion does not replace reality, whereas the fetish does.[4] The adolescent girl with an eating disorder, for example, who idealizes her thin body and equates it with magical power and control is fetishizing her body. So does the husband who can only feel desire for his wife when she is fully made up and in heels or the person who so idealizes money that it alone represents potency. This is very different, then, from the link between imagination and creativity, which is as important to healthy relationships as it is to art.

Disillusionment and Endings

Major disillusionments in relationships, whether this occurs after a few minutes, a few dates, or years of marriage, end relationships. They crumble in this instance, whether it happens all at once or over time. Hopefully, mourning eventually cleanses the spirit and restores the person to desire what will come next in life.

In severe high-conflict divorce, however, there is no capacity to bear the grief of actual mourning. As much as high-conflict divorce is so painful, there is a paradoxical refusal to experience loss. There is too much to endure. It would recognize the value of the other, who is now irretrievably lost, which would expose the subject to intense pain, loss, and vulnerability. The disillusionment, thus, is crushing and bears witness to an unhealable wound in the psyche, as if from an assault, which is how it is experienced. The result is a destructive mind-set that threatens to bring the whole house down: ex-partner, children, and anyone else identified with the other's cause. Destructivity, then, has full rein, and the consequences can be appalling.

Table 3.1 offers a checklist to help identify traumatic disillusionment and its divorce consequences. The clinician or researcher needs to consider both predisposing events and personality characteristics that are generally observed in severe high-conflict cases in one or

---

[4] Greenacre, P., (1969), The fetish and the transitional object, *Psychoanalytic Study of the Child*, 24, 144–164.

both parties. Of course, each high-conflict situation is unique, but the checklist provides features commonly observed in the disillusionment history and clinical presentation.

But why is there no healthy grieving and timely resolution for this subset who divorce and then struggle with each other, sometimes for years? Returning to the idea of illusion, I describe two forms: one healthy, which elaborates reality and is very much tied to creativity and subjectivity, and a second, which is more defensive and maladaptive,

---

TABLE 3.1 **Disillusionment Checklist**

Childhood Antecedents

- Parental divorce
- Parental high conflict
- Parental abandonment
- Parental mental illness
- Parental personality disorder
- Parental addiction
- Socioeconomic crisis
- Child abuse
- Gender inequality
- Extreme favoritism to another sibling

Childhood Clinical History

- Indications for aggressivity
- Poor social adjustment
- Low frustration tolerance
- Limiting physical illness or disability
- Learning and attention deficits
- Stressful family immigration
- Painful rejection in early romantic unions
- Sexual trauma
- Victim of bullying
- Frequently shamed and humiliated

Clinical Presentation

- Glosses over past history, presents idyllic family
- Fantasizes about idealized love
- Brief courtship, few indications of mutuality
- Relationship adversely affected by first major life demand
- Harmony until disillusionment, then conflict in all interactions
- Police and children's services attend home frequently
- Union ends traumatically with or without violence
- Fails at mediation, presents self as wholly innocent
- Expects court to punish ex-partner
- Changes attorneys frequently

in which whatever is idealized defends against what is most feared—some perceived calamity. These defensive illusions, fetishized, foster the image of a couple in perfect unity. With this idealized fantasy, there is nothing to hold on towhen the relationship breaks. The love wound is inseparable from a wounded self that is inflamed by the hostility of blame. It is the unbearable that must be defended against by massive denial of loss. This is precisely the formula for high conflict. The greater the defense against loss, the more destructive the dynamic, which can then emerge behaviorally as intense, unremitting conflict.

Aishah and Allam

Aishah's marriage to Allam could never be described as a rational decision. She was warm, responsive, and willing to accommodate others as she had done all her life. Aishah was also perceived as beautiful, inside and out, in a natural way; it was simply part of the package that she neither exploited nor fully recognized.

In the beginning, Allam idealized Aishah. He saw her as the loveliest woman he had ever met. He felt complete in her presence. His father died when Allam was in his late teens, but the relationship had not been good. His father had been extremely critical and harsh with his only son, although Allam was not an only child. There had been physical violence. His father seemed to equate disappointment with betrayal, as if any letdown must have been purposeful. Scenes of his father's angry tirades were etched in Allam's mind.

Allam put Aishah on a pedestal and took every occasion to publicly praise her. He looked like a man deeply in love with the woman of his dreams, but in retrospect, it was more adoration than genuine affection. She was like a figurine on a mantel; an image of perfection itself; or, as Allam put it, "only slightly below Allah." Aishah believed in her partner's adoration and felt both flattered and loved.

If the truth be told, Allam felt relief when his father died. He was free and, by succession, the man of the house. He had always appreciated his mother, who, curiously, seemed to defer to him after his father's demise. He was put on a pedestal, which was not what he needed. It twisted his expectations of how others should treat him, especially women. He was now beyond disappointing anyone. Allam, therefore, expected Aishah to defer to him, which she initially accepted as a cultural standard but soon came to resent. It was based on an unhealthy illusion that concealed Allam's shaky sense of manhood and inner security. In hindsight, their union was a series of adorations that could not support the travails of real life.

When Aishah showed independence, as she increasingly did, Allam saw this as "un-Islamic" and criticized her harshly. When he received an unfavorable review at work, he lashed out at Aishah for being unsupportive and stressing him so that he could not concentrate in his job. When their one child was born with a congenital leg problem, he blamed her. He was slow to warm up to the baby and only softened when the problem was addressed orthopedically. Nonetheless, Allam became extremely devaluing and denigrating of Aishah. She was no longer the image of perfection in his mind: the most beautiful woman for the most important and entitled man. It became intolerable for Aishah.

After much anguish and many painful episodes that were spiraling into dysfunction, Aishah left Allam, which he experienced as a catastrophe. He launched into immediate blame and began a campaign to destroy her reputation in their shared community. He demanded custody of their child and started a court action to this effect. His communications with Aishah were horrid in their aggressivity and contempt. He took every opportunity to withhold financial support and made every coparenting moment an ordeal. When Allam found out that Aishah consulted a psychotherapist, he wrote to the professional, blaming Aishah and devaluing her as a person and sexual partner.

When judges admonished Allam for this conduct, he brushed it off and continued in the same vein. He seemed impervious to new learning and self-awareness, as if his contemptuous rage was entirely warranted. It was only when his access to their child became supervised and support payments deducted at source that there was any slowdown of his assault on Aishah.

I use this example to illustrate the type of defensive illusion often behind what is called love in many high-conflict cases. There is something or someone defensively idealized: It could be the partner or a child of the union. In this regard, the other is an image more than an actual person, known and loved in their full humanity. Aishah was a representation in Allam's mind of feminine perfection that kept all his fears about himself at bay. She was more fetish than person. When this idealization was tarnished and reality came into view, the illusion shattered, and Allam's full destructiveness emerged. His single-minded theory was that Aishah profoundly betrayed everything to which she had committed, including their marriage, common faith, and him.

This example speaks to the extent to which high-conflict-prone individuals enter marriage for the purpose of controlling distressing emotional states or feared realities. Here, the other is not perceived as a person in their own right but as a fantasy of salvation or repair that would validate one's life and undo past disillusionments. The breakdown of illusion is thus intolerable and often perceived as a terrible betrayal or state of madness.

Examples abound of these illusory and defensive foundations:

- A man who believed in the image that his wife and he were like a prince and princess—a magical couple—which would allow him to emerge as the person he wanted to be.
- A woman whose belief in her husband was demolished when he allowed a child of a previous relationship to be adopted by the child's stepfather.
- A man harboring a deep wound to his pride for having been, in his eyes, a physically unappealing adolescent who grew up to marry a woman whom he saw as exquisitely beautiful. It was a magical undoing—frog becoming prince in his mind. Founded on a bed of illusion, however, the marriage collapsed when tested by real life, and interminable conflict quickly flared and continued for years.
- A lesbian couple bore a male child through a sperm donor. It was a celebration of their love, although, of course, only one was the biological parent. What was an idealized construct of a couple fractured severely over who the real mother was. The birth parent insisted that the other was effectively in the role of father, reformulated as "other-to-the mother." This was deeply injuring to the nonbirth parent, who claimed equal maternity. There was no mending this rupture, and the union broke into very high-conflict and aggressive litigation. When the child was interviewed at four years of age, however, his preoccupation was with fathers and not whom his mother was.
- A gifted student, adored by her teachers as a child and elevated above her siblings by her parents, married in her late 30s. She became pregnant quickly and gave birth to a daughter, whom she identified as an even more perfect emanation of herself. She treated her husband as an afterthought and excluded him. Conflict erupted when he resisted his fate. She left with the child, and this intensified the conflict. Forced to share the parenting with the dad, she reported to the police that he was molesting the daughter. Further, she attacked him at every turn, using every vehicle to separate him from the child. An assessment revealed that she spoke often to the girl about her father in very negative terms and formed an exclusivity with the daughter that was deeply alienating.

What is the fix?

Let us return to the case of Emily and Brian, where this discussion began.

Emily and Brian: One More Look

Brian's filibuster against looking at himself was not helping at all. He appeared arrogant and defensive to the core and denied his obvious aggression toward Emily about parenting. It took time for him to open the door to self-reflection and some greater awareness of his motivation in the relationship. In the end it was clear that he was deeply humiliated and felt an overriding sense of failure. Divorce simply did not happen in his family, and his parents were shocked and disappointed. He felt their searing judgment, including that he married Emily in the first place. It was deep source of shame.

Emily had looked up to Brian and admired his worldly ways when they met. Brian thought that her admiration would last forever, but alas, when children came, Emily demanded much more of him, simply out of need. But he saw her as assuming the dominant role, and he felt devalued whenever she was critical or expressed disappointment. He reacted angrily or imperiously, projecting arrogance and superiority. His assumption was that she should have been grateful to be with him and accept whatever he offered. He expected to be idealized by her rather than loved.

Brian wrestled with his own disillusionment. Emily had spoiled his dream, and he could not forgive her. His mother had always deferred to his father. She had become depressed during his adolescence, and his parents attended couples therapy. Nonetheless, Brian wanted the same ascendant role that his father seemingly enjoyed, even if this idealization was at his mother's expense. This theme of entitled patrimony seemed the source of disillusionment much more than anything Emily actually did. It was the deconstruction of an entire mythology around maleness, including the fantasy of his father, masculine entitlement, and his own sense of diminishment within the paternal relationship. Only then could he begin to see that if Emily did bark at him, it was because she was feeling overwhelmed with three young children, not because she was devaluing him.

Hence, the first step was for Brian to acknowledge his disillusionment and to begin to understand its origins. His internalized model of relationship, deeply chauvinistic, was a sure formula for failure. Emily wanted a partner and not an overlord. He also had to confront his defensive arrogance and acknowledge the ways his self-esteem was hurt by high expectations and shame next to his aspiring parents.

The second step was for Brian to implement more mature values based on self-understanding, to turn to ethics, and to stop regarding Emily as the cause or source of his behavior. In other words, he needed to bring ethics into view and use these precepts to guide him in the divorce. This could only be rooted in self-responsibility for his conduct and continuing accountability to Emily as a coparent and mother of his children. It was an unequivocal responsibility for which there was no way out.

Gradually, Brian came see the failure with Emily as a veiled attempt to regain what his father had lost, a distorted vision of a man as someone whose authority is unrivaled. It had been an idealized, unrealistic fantasy; it was man as fetish more than a three-dimensional person with strengths and weaknesses. He had expected Emily, who came from so little in terms of family wealth and education, to confer this lofty, inherited status on him. He was peddling the wrong kind of illusion, which was damaging to Emily and to him. It was not a dream about Emily at all but a dream about himself as some form of lord of the manor.

Emily railed about Brian's conduct, using her as a sex doll, controlling and debasing her. Yet, her disillusionment did not begin with the marriage. Its roots were in her own childhood. She had been given a raw deal, shortchanged on the parent side, and left to learn lessons of life on her own. Emily gradually acknowledged her envy for those who had able parents who loved and protected their children. She could only imagine what that must be like. Indeed, she was trying very hard to provide this environment for her children, which made the disillusionment in her husband even harder to bear.

Emily had been deeply impressed with Brian and admired his obvious intelligence, education, and culture. She expected him to be gracious and patient but was shocked and dismayed when he seemed so smug, demeaning, and exploitative after they had children. Instead of being a confident resource and companion, she felt humiliated and devalued. She felt his scorn and derision. In many ways, he turned out to be worse than her mother. However, her bitter recriminations went nowhere, and her wish for vengeance only added to her despair.

It was when Emily understood that she was pursuing a hateful vengeance against Brian that she could also appreciate the damage this was doing to her children and her. She was constructing another layer to the legacy of disillusionment and exporting this to her children to bear. For their sake as well as her own, she had to disengage and confront her despair and the destruction of hope and find a path forward that had some place for forgiveness. She could not vilify Brian in her children's lives and represent him simultaneously as someone to love and respect as a parent. Emily had to find a principled middle ground that allowed her children to have a father to love, though not at her expense. She did not dismiss or negate her experience of Brian as an ex-partner but learned to allow him to shape his own relationship with their offspring.

Fixing the Problem

When conflict becomes uncontainable, spilling over and flooding the family field, there is usually no space or time to think. It is a timeless zone of destructive reactivity, where all efforts, personal and legal, lead to conflict. There are two narratives, furious soliloquies, that are completely discordant with the other. It can be experienced as a psychotic splitting, with neither recognizing anything valid about what the other is saying. In this regard, there is no shared space, something that is third or coconstructed, on which real communication and recognition can occur. Every interaction is defined as push and pull, do and done to, in which each feels victim to the other in what becomes a chronic impasse of high conflict.[5] What is needed is a framework for divorcing couples to begin to understand the layers of illusion, disillusion, and destructiveness that seed the high conflict and keep it churning.

Situations differ, but there is often something fundamentally unrealistic at the core of the union, an idealized fantasy that can never replace two mature partners whose affection survives the adjustment of inevitable compromise. This illusion is of the defensive type. Hence, the expected disillusionment rocks the foundation, and the fragile union crumbles. Destructiveness emerges, fracturing, splitting, attacking, and undermining. The turmoil has a centrifugal effect, ripping through the fabric of the family, which often fails to survive.

[5] Benjamin, J., (2004), Beyond doer and done to, *Psychoanalytic Quarterly*, 73(1), 5–46.

Coping With the Disillusionments of Everyday Life

Children need to perceive their parents' humanity in small stages so that they can still feel protected and defended while building their own competencies. In this regard, tolerating disillusionment is important, and this is much easier when it arrives slowly as the individual matures. The first disillusionment in life might be weaning, but it is likely much more complex and has to do with all the ways, often minor, that the child experiences frustration or when needs remain unmet for too long. These are the disillusionments of everyday life.

Whenever major disillusionment happens precipitously, there are likely to be problems adjusting. It is a risk factor for depression and personality difficulties when the experience of disillusionment is major and traumatic. Much is made today of narcissism and narcissistic personality disorders. These are problems of disillusionment. The narcissist-in-making experiences the human world as unreliable or untrustworthy. This leads to a defensive illusion of grandeur and fosters an arrogant defense, a pushing away from dependence toward total self-sufficiency and a lack of regard for others and their needs.

In divorce, one can see the effects of disillusionment in children who lose faith in their parents and experience them as abdicating their protective role. They might feel that they have either to fend for themselves or take over. It is common, for example, for children of conflictive divorces to be almost perfect kids, despite the divorce storm raging around them. In other cases, an older child might believe that they need to take charge, judge one or both parents, and control them. There are also children who become frightened, anxious about the future, and unable to concentrate and who develop symptoms in response to the lack of a holding family environment. These children become ill in the midst of their parents' stormy divorces because they cannot emotionally tolerate distracted, chronically upset, and warring parents who give their children no peace or containment. Severe anxiety, attention deficit disorder, obsessive-compulsive disorder, and depression can all be found in children rocked by unremitting high-conflict divorce.

There are also children, especially the more naturally resilient, who develop a social maturity well ahead of their time in the midst of regressed, destructive parental divorces. They seem to be well adjusted, smart, and capable. The warring parents take comfort and feel less need to curb their destructiveness because the child seems unaffected. When I have seen these children as young adults in psychotherapy, however, they often struggle with a disbelief in relationships, unexplained anger, pessimism about the future, and depression. When these adult children of divorce confront their resentments and the deep unfairness that marked their earlier lives, they resent the expectation that they should live normal, productive lives when their parents made such a mockery of their childhoods. Self-defeat becomes a way of punishing those parents, even though it is at their own expense. Vengeance can become the tool of the disillusioned.

In marriage in general, some disappointment and disillusionment are inevitable, although this should arise slowly and moderately, giving time for intimacy to take hold and for the give-and-take of mature relationships to develop. What actually helps weather disappointments is the component of illusion, and what curbs an excess of illusion is tempering disillusionment. Each is the corrective for the other. There is no love without illusion and no mature adjustment without some disillusionment.

Sophie and Terry

"My heart is broken," exclaimed Sophie. She spoke on two levels, as she had been referred by a cardiologist, who discovered an underlying heart abnormality. When the physician asked whether she had any cardiac pain, Sophie replied that she was suffering from a broken heart so she could not differentiate. She was recovering from a failed marriage to Terry, a man she had once adored, even idealized, before discovering his hidden proclivity for strip clubs. There was a son born from this union, and this created major complications, as Sophie feared the influence her once-perfect man would have on their young boy.

Disillusionment was dramatic. One piece of evidence led to a string of discoveries on Terry's phone and credit card statements that made her aware that he was living a double life. Sophie alternated between grief over the loss and deep scorn and contempt for a misleading, deceptive man who had kept his secret life well hidden. The suddenness and extent of disillusionment proved crushing.

Prior to this nightmarish collapse of her marriage, Sophie would have said that she lived an ideal life. She was very close to her parents, who were protective and caring. Sophie adored her father and depended on him emotionally. He was a wonderful grandfather and had moved seamlessly into the picture now that her husband was so discredited. Sophie was a gifted pianist, and her parents had supported her education. She was now a successful teacher and soloist.

When we looked at what transpired in the marriage, Sophie acknowledged that she had willfully ignored warning signs. They had each concealed from the other. Sophie's romantic vision had retained a childhood, fairy-tale innocence that whitewashed the complexity of adult sexuality. It was too much based on parental love and left no real space for adult passion. In turn, Terry complied on the surface, offering a pretense of wholesomeness while pursuing an illicit, erotic world behind the scenes. The sacred and profane vied for dominance. It was a formula for disastrous, traumatic disillusionment. Indeed, Sophie could not imagine her son getting anything good from this man after the truth came out. She obliterated him from any recognition and acted as if he did not exist, which is precisely how the boy behaved in his father's presence. There was totality to the exclusion that belied its violence.

There are moments of major disillusionment at the bedrock of every divorce. Perhaps this explains the predominance of scorn that is often evident in the attitude of one ex-spouse to the other, as if scorn would prevent ever loving or depending on this person again. Some would say that it is inevitable to despise the person once loved, as if this is the sign of an authentic marriage. If so, then this also speaks to the significant role of illusion and disillusionment in divorce. It is common for people to say that their partner "changed" or that they hid their real character and created a masquerade. This is simply another way to frame the disillusionment, as if it would be better to be a victim of deception than to accept that the partner's flaws proved too much for love to endure. In high conflict, disillusionments are experienced catastrophically, which is what distinguishes this category from the rest.

One beleaguered man spoke of the image reflected in their wedding photos, "as if we were a Hollywood couple feted on the red carpet." This marriage ended in tatters, with much depleting litigation and stalled, immobilized lives. Another, an enraged, litigious woman with an allied, colluding therapist, saw her marriage as an escape from the depravity of her childhood, a scheming mother and a father who was willing to offer her to his friends. Her marriage was unconsciously framed as a rescue plan but turned into a violent repetition, with her playing the destructive role, dragging her husband into the mud of her inner life, and forcing him to live this trauma with her. What possible place can children have in such a morass? They are put through the wringer of their parents' turmoil, twisted by parental projections, and so burdened that they lack the needed emotional resources to grow up. They might be empowered in the short term, but the situation is dismal, and the negative consequences, lasting.

Conclusion

Lawyers, judges, social workers, and psychologists spend endless hours trying to comprehend and handle the damaging and depleting complications of high-conflict divorce. This comprises a group of people, at least one and sometimes both, who cannot cope with the traumatic disillusionment that ends marriages and sets in motion the divorce. One might say that they fail to divorce because the wounds of disillusionment prove crushing. Instead, they rage, struggle, foment, and blame repeatedly in a self-perpetuating cycle with no endpoint. In this regard, high conflict differs qualitatively from other forms of divorce conflict. It is unresolvable as conflict and cannot be reduced to any specific point of contention. The essence is an attack on the frame that holds the family together, even during the painful rupture of divorce.

All divorces follow major disillusionment, the realization that the status quo cannot continue. The dream is extinguished, and this usually means that the union should end. Mourning is necessary, not simply for the union that is lost, but also for the fantasy ideal that inspired the union. Marriages are made as much of dreams as reality. This is why they are so special.

In high conflict, the loss is disavowed by obliterating its significance. This powerful negation of loss sets in motion a very persecutory and destructive dynamic. The high-conflict couple and family law pull in different directions: The couple lashes out destructively at a family ideal, while the family legal system pursues resolution and anticipates better times. It is a vicious circle that stymies grieving because the experience of loss is repudiated and supplanted by an endless conflict.

In the high-conflict dynamic, the disillusionment is traumatic, and the conflict is unmoored from any specific issue or dispute. The destructiveness that erupts bears witness to the depth of injury. It knows no bounds and does not respond to legal or mental health efforts at containment. Reflective capacity is usually poor, and the conflictive situation is lived entirely externally without any appreciable theory of mind to distinguish psychic from factual reality.

There is no route to remediation that does not involve naming the destructiveness and linking it to the disillusionment experience. The analysis of disillusionment can become a handle onto which the individual or couple can begin to see themselves and catch some glimpse of the other. If we do not know what we have lost, then it is impossible to mourn. The extent of catastrophic disillusionment must be addressed to acknowledge or face loss. Otherwise, loss is disavowed, and in the gap, persecutory anxieties and destructiveness can take hold, with very damaging results. High conflict, in this regard, can be seen as a chronic state of disintegration, with the family in pieces, destroyed from within, and the ex-partners unable to end a nightmare.

4

Disillusionment Therapy

Could there ever be such a thing as disillusionment therapy? Probably not if one thinks of a dedicated process focused solely on disillusionment. Nonetheless, it can be extremely helpful for those in the grip of destructive divorce to identify and work through the core illusions and disillusions that ignite and fuel the negative process. The goal would necessarily be one of promoting ethical divorce.

The usual approach in high conflict is aimed at creating precise parenting plans to keep the parents in clearly defined silos of separateness while favoring alternate dispute mechanisms. These mechanisms are certainly necessary because they offer some degree of conflict management, which is essential to containment. These parenting plans, though, often prove insufficient to defuse conflict that needs little or no justification. A more lasting solution requires that the individual or couple account for their destructiveness. Each feels so much at the mercy of the other that they completely lose sight of themselves as behaving subjects. From the observer's perspective, there are bizarre moments of clear complicity, in which the destructiveness generated is totally denied or never psychically registered.

In the blame/attack mind-set, even offering to think about one's role or responsibility is interpreted as an acknowledgment of fault and an act of self-negation. The initial therapeutic interventions need to dislodge this deeply defensive war footing and shift the paradigm to a model of triggers and, especially, disillusionments: the shaky pillars on which the union was built and the events and experiences that triggered its collapse.

Some high-conflict sufferers cannot "think" in the sense of reflection in any interpersonal context of their life in which conflict enters. They are too lacking in mentalization skills when under intense emotional pressure, at least when it comes to the divorce. Some meet criteria for a personality disorder but not all. Most in the high-conflict range are simply too threatened, hurt, or under attack to think. They are in the grip of a catastrophic disillusionment that builds on earlier painful catastrophes.

It is not just a lack of conscious reflection or resistance to thinking but also a lack of reparative potential and a frozen temporality, in which the virulent rupture of the union remains raw and unhealed. Anyone who has worked with these individuals and families can attest to the interminability of the morass. It is as if the couple registers neither time passing nor the impact on their children. Fury does not abate. It is not a quenchable hate. Rather, it is a wheel of endless conflict that sticks to issues but does not need them for animosity to rein.

Statistics show that second marriages are even less successful than firsts, with 67%–80% failing. The chance of third unions working is even less than seconds.[1] This does not bode well for those in the high-conflict range, even if they are able to extricate themselves sufficiently to form a new union. It is my impression that many in the severe range of high conflict do not liberate themselves enough to repartner. High conflict is a full-time job.

Severe disillusionment is about much more than disappointment. The buildup of major disappointments, though, can tilt the balance toward disillusionment. Whereas disappointment is part of an accommodation to reality, major disillusionment is always unexpected and marks a crisis. Though the inevitable disappointments of life have a positive side in facilitating adjustment and maturation, severe disillusionment can reveal a shaky foundation that makes facing painful feelings destabilizing and emotionally risky. The psychological defense against grief and despair is radical in the high-conflict population and can approach delusional proportions, as seen in bizarre allegations, profound unmoored repugnance, extreme actions, and hatred. High conflict can serve as a tutorial in the creation of enemies. It is a mix of inner tension, anticipatory anxiety, fear, humiliation, self-doubt, and repudiated grief. The paranoia of high conflict at least creates clarity as it substitutes inner calamity for a state of external war.

Divorcing couples often look at each other through the lens of their disillusionment. If disillusionment is severe, uncushioned, and

---

[1] For interesting statistics on divorce in the United States, see Health Research Funding, (n.d.), *55 surprising divorce statistics for second marriages*, retrieved April 13, 2021, from https://healthresearchfunding.org/55-surprising-divorce-statistics-second-marriages

experienced as betrayal, then identity can become shaken. Thinking gets very concrete, raw, and unmetabolized. There is a traumatic quality to the constant repetition of antagonism in every interaction. It is depleting. The only possible reparation in the subject's mind is a return to an idealized state, which is impossible.[2] This becomes the source of hopelessness, as it feels like there is no escape: a vicious circularity of conflict that stands apart from time and resolution. It is this nightmare scenario of feeling helplessly controlled in which destructiveness gets unleashed, and the divorce can take on an entirely different hue from what is expected. It transforms into another genre that bears little resemblance to regular divorce variants.

A failed marriage is very different from a failed divorce. The former can be a solution whereas the latter is often tragic in its consequences. It can be important to differentiate between them.

Danny and Pat

Danny and Pat were separated when their legal mediator suggested that they address a maladaptive dynamic between them that was interfering with the resolution of their divorce. Anticipating two upset, highly conflictive individuals, I was surprised to face two very despondent and matter-of-fact people who spoke in monotone.

The marriage faltered a year after they relocated for a job. It proved to be a very stressful time. They had financial problems from the move that proved to be much more costly than expected. Additionally, not long before moving, Danny had been flirtatious under Pat's nose with a coworker at a company party, and this left her feeling empty and humiliated. Their communication had been poor for a long time, and after a decade of marriage, they were distant from each other. Their marriage did not survive the move.

As I came to understand, the impasse in mediation was less a matter of open conflict than a simmering reciprocal disillusionment that made it very difficult for them to address anything. They both had shut down but needed to get on with their lives for the sake of their two primary-school-age children as well as themselves. It was a lot at once: new city, divorce, and children who had to adjust to new lives on two fronts.

---

[2] Steiner, J., (2018), The trauma and disillusionment of Oedipus, *International Journal of Psychoanalysis*, 99(3), 555–568.

Pat and Danny shared their personal histories in the flat, emotionless way they both used to describe everything. When Pat was 17, getting ready for her first year of college, her mother died suddenly from a pulmonary embolism in the hospital after a hysterectomy. It was a wrenching loss that cast a prolonged shadow of grief over her life.

Danny's father, much older than his mother, had suffered a debilitating stroke when Danny was in his senior year of high school. After graduation, Danny put his university studies on hold to help look after his father, as his mother was obliged to work to support the family. Subsequently, his father went to a nursing home and died after a few years.

Despite the gravity of these disruptive and painful life events, Danny and Pat related these respective histories without any real emotion. They had each felt a commonality with the other due their shared experience, but this was as far as it went. My attempts to raise the important implications of these traumatic events met with their combined silence. These were distant happenings, according to both Danny and Pat, irrelevant to what they were now contending. They looked at me incredulously.

Pat became vocal when she related that Danny always criticized the children and took out his bad mood on them. She felt that she unfairly had to defend them from their father. Danny shot back that Pat was a spendthrift and showed no concern for the financial pressure that he was bearing alone due to the move, as he was the only one earning a salary. He felt totally on his own with these pressures. Danny's identification with his mother's plight came more clearly into view.

To stem the tide of blame, I reflected on the burden each must have been carrying and how painful it would have been for them to feel so alone. Indeed, they felt isolated from each other and were unable to provide the support needed to succeed at making this major move. When Pat began to cry, I asked her to reflect on what she was feeling. She did not really know and, curiously, might not have been aware that she was crying. The echo of old grief came into clearer view.

I asked Danny what he experienced when he saw Pat's tears. He related that he had felt the same helpless, powerless feeling that he used to experience when they were together. He worried, he said, that she would become an invalid or, worse, suicidal and be completely gone. Danny did not make the connection to his father, who had become an invalid due to stroke and the responsibility this placed on Danny's shoulders alongside his beleaguered mother. He had lost years of education and effectively lost the vital father on whom he had always relied.

I commented that they had both faced severe losses and disruptions in their youth and that this experience of depressive rupture had been repeated at crucial moments in their marriage. Indeed, neither had what the other needed to help them not feel so alone and unsupported. Sadly, the marriage had reiterated and then prolonged their sense of isolation and aloneness, which led eventually to the breakup.

Given their psychological mindedness, Pat and Danny were able to face each other, deal with the disillusionments of the marriage, and link their respective unhappiness with the depth of loss and dislocation that each had experienced earlier in life. They could then mourn not only for the loss of the marriage but also for what each had painfully experienced as teens when illness and death intervened and effectively ended their childhoods. It might have actually brought them together at the beginning but, in the end, also drove them apart.

What might seem obvious to an observer does not necessarily mean that the individuals themselves will see or appreciate its significance. Denial is powerful. Both Pat and Danny seemed to select the other for a common experience that, at the same time, they both denied. This shared project of disavowal protected them from having to contend with the emotional repercussions of what had occurred in their young lives, but it made them less resilient as well. Hence, in the end, their togetherness only amplified the aloneness each had been feeling for far too long. It repeated the pain of loss and aloneness that neither was ready to handle. They needed help with mourning, but at least with help, they were able to mourn.

Disillusionment therapy would apply to failed divorce and its corollary, escalating high conflict. It is aimed at connecting past and present through these moments where dreams are broken and life feels unbearable. It is the analysis of the layers of traumatic disillusionment that opens the door to healthy mourning and relief from the intense persecutory blame that often permeate high-conflict divorces. Perhaps we could say that high conflict marks radical disillusionment in double temporality, past and current, forcing the subject to face painful loss or defend against awareness through the unmitigated violence of high conflict. It is the facing that is so difficult in high-conflict divorce, and anything that can facilitate this important task deserves consideration.

Capacity to Say Sorry

If there was to be a disillusionment therapy, it would somehow involve the capacity to say sorry. Being able to authentically apologize is one way that a person can meaningfully relate to another. It can be extraordinarily important at crucial moments of empathic rupture. When someone essential to us apologizes, it relieves the pain of private suffering and offers healing human connection. Being able to apologize is at the heart of being ethical.

Whether an apology helps or fails to make a difference seems to have little to do with whether the hurt caused was intentional or unintentional. What the victim needs from the offender is recognition of the damage inflicted and a shift in their position or a change because of it. They must understand it, which means taking responsibility for the hurt caused.

Psychiatrist and psychoanalyst Lawrence Kubie published a remarkable article in 1955 regarding a 5-year-old girl who had been hospitalized after she acutely stopped talking, eating, or communicating.[3] The case was very puzzling. There was concern that this was due to childhood psychosis or even a brain tumor, but neurological tests were negative.

Kubie and his hospital colleagues attended a case conference, and per the style of the time, the child was brought into the room with them. After the girl refused to answer any questions, they heard her making a series of strange sounds. Dr. Kubie asked the attending nurse whether this was the first time the child had made these sounds, and the nurse answered that she had heard it before. The nurse added that it seemed like the child was uttering, "Say you're sorry."

This provided the cue for Dr. Kubie, who took the child's hand and said sincerely to her, "I am sorry, very, very sorry." The little girl looked at him closely; it clearly resonated with her. After this prompt, all the doctors and clinicians in the room stood one by one and offered their apologies. The child began to speak.

Whatever the specific causes and dynamics of the case (and there was an intensive child therapy process that followed), we might say

---

[3] Kubie, L., (1955), Say you're sorry, *Psychoanalytic Study of the Child*, 10, 289–299.

that this little girl had lost her faith in humanity and needed those responsible for injuring or treating her to accept responsibility for what she had endured. The apology reconnected her to the human world.

Apologizing is probably the main way that couples make amends to each other and repair damage to their relationship. In saying sorry, there is acknowledgment that our words or actions were hurtful. It is a moment of strong empathy for the pain and damage caused. It does not mean necessarily that causing pain was intentional; at the moment of apology, this is not important. The crucial ingredient is the capacity to comprehend cause and effect and to perceive the benefit of making amends. Whether love is being able to say sorry or never having to, sincere apology has a profound capacity to heal and lower tension in divorce.

Ex-couples in the high-conflict range lack the capacity to say sorry, or if they do apologize, it is often not sincere or unqualified. There is an association, it seems, between the capacity to be sorry and the capacity to be thankful or grateful. Being grateful requires acknowledgment of what only others can give us. Those prone to high conflict often have as much trouble being grateful as being sorry. Gratitude requires emotional freedom and openness. It is very important to adaptation and mental health.

In the best divorce circumstances, one might hear that although the union ended, there is still gratitude for what was good between them and, of course, for the children. Gratitude is an acknowledgment of what has been freely received from another. Shame, guilt, hurt, and vulnerability, all common emotional states in divorce, work against developing feelings of gratitude. Denial of gratitude in high conflict follows the refusal to acknowledge the worth of the other and, especially, the depth of the loss. This would be much too validating of the ex-partner to ever seem feasible. Where the narcissistic dimension is strong, gratitude is always problematic because it is associated with dependency and weakness. This was the essential insight of Melanie Klein, who contrasts gratitude with envy and the wish to spoil or ruin what the other gives.[4]

Psychoanalysts have long studied people whose ingratitude is built into their character. These are the same people who tend to blame as

---

[4] Klein, M., (1975), Envy and gratitude, in *The writings of Melanie Klein: Vol. 3, envy and gratitude and other works, 1946–1963* (pp. 176–235), Free Press, (original work published 1957).

a matter of course, push away from reliance on others, and justify every failure as one of being failed. They are incapable of really saying sorry, as this would mean, in their eyes, being discredited and unworthy. There is no gradation or nuanced way of understanding responsibility that can still preserve dignity and worth. In this mind-set, one must be blameless to be worthy, heroic to be respected, and faultless to be adequate. This sets the stage for monumental struggles that consume lives and courtrooms to achieve this untarnished state. It is an omnipotent goal to be blameless, and yet this mind-set permeates high conflict.

Hence, it would be essential in disillusionment therapy to help each partner locate the "goodness" of the union, at least in terms of what brought the couple together and what they were able to share. It would acknowledge the positive benefit that was freely given and received, linking this with the dream of love and, using this foothold in gratitude, fostering some recognition and eventual reparation to allow the two to parent together. The refusal to acknowledge gratitude is itself destructive, as it destroys the goodness in the other.

Indeed, there is no worse violence than nonrecognition, which is a hallmark of high conflict. Thinking and feeling what the other might be feeling is replaced by a penchant for coercive action and externalization. Conflict fills every interaction, and the only recourse is a type of phobic avoidance, which makes cooperative parenting impossible. The other cannot be seen apart from projections, which becomes the focus of therapy.

Monique and Pierre

Monique stood out in a crowd. Her high style and vivacious persona reflected strength and purpose. She had been divorced from Pierre for several years. The couple had failed to contain conflict, which spilled over and flooded the family field. Mediation looked at one point like it might succeed, but both Monique's refusal to follow agreements and Pierre's curious pattern of submission one moment and confrontation the next derailed the mediator's process. With an 8-year-old and 6-year-old to raise jointly, there was limited capacity for coparenting, as tempers easily flared.

In this regard, Pierre and Monique related through the discourse of power. Monique clearly saw herself as the leader and responsible parent. She underscored the toxicity of the situation and attributed all the "aggression" to Pierre. Moreover, she castigated him for lying, exaggerating, and misleading everyone about how controlling and domineering she really was. She insisted that he hid his true self, especially the belligerent, sadistic part of his personality, and that he had abused her during their union, including sexually.

Monique grew up in a family where there was a profound asymmetry in power and influence between her parents. Her mother was the leader, and her father occupied the periphery. Monique's father held a modest management position in a retail store, while her mother was a senior manager with a dynamic high-technology company. As an only child, Monique followed easily in her mother's footsteps. This was not to say that Monique did not love her father, but he often appeared in her memories as irrelevant. Only her mother's opinion really mattered.

Pierre envied Monique's strength and assertiveness but also feared being taken over by her. He often felt irrelevant and turned to pornography to soothe his wounded pride. His fantasies tended to the domination/submission genre, which was a source of embarrassment and shame. He admitted wanting to enact sexual scenarios in his marriage that he had watched online, and this offended Monique, who wanted no part of it. Pierre also acknowledged undermining Monique with the children, which he connected to his resentment. He denied hating Monique, though, but certainly went out of his way to antagonize her.

Neither Monique nor Pierre could be vulnerable in the face of the other during the marriage and, as expected, much less so after the breakup. They seemed permanently defensive, spitefully ungrateful, projecting the traits they feared most in themselves onto the other. I had the impression that their children were not front and center for them. They seemed to tag along, with the main show being the interminable fight between their parents.

It was slow going working with them, but then Monique surprised me by offering a quick and seemingly superficial "sorry" when she clearly misinterpreted a logistical text from Pierre. It was the first time I had ever heard this sentiment from her, especially directed at Pierre. I asked her to focus on her apology and what she might have been feeling. Was this what she really wanted to say? Monique became uncomfortable, initially deflecting with a laugh, but finally managed to convey that it felt weakening, almost humiliating. She added, giving sway to blame, that this was Pierre's habit, using what she told him in trust against her. There was truth to this accusation, but Monique's descent into blame would scuttle any opportunity for meaningful self-reflection.

Hence, I urged her not to go there. It was important to redirect to her moment of vulnerability and hope that she could stay there, even briefly.

THERAPIST: I wonder, Monique, if you have memories of your parents apologizing to each other?

MONIQUE: My father said he was sorry a lot. All the time. I think my mother expected it.

The absence of reference to her mother apologizing spoke volumes. Monique's mother seemed to be above any such requirement. It was impossible for Monique to integrate the influences of a mother and father who occupied such extreme polarities of power in her mind.

I told Monique that I thought that she was trying in her own way to apologize to Pierre but that this was linked with being weak and devalued, like her father. Monique acknowledged that her father was low on the totem pole in the family's power hierarchy and that she had never respected him or his authority as a child. She had the impression that her mother functioned as a single parent and made all decisions, major and minor. Monique added, "When I say I'm sorry, it feels weak, spineless, like I'm admitting something terrible about myself."

There was no covenant between her parents that they would respect each other and take responsibility for their actions. Her father's constant apologies were reflexive and hollow; they did not mean anything. He may have just submitted as a way of bypassing his wife. In this way, he was more abstaining than weak. I suspected that Monique was actually deeply hurt by her father's abdication, which amounted to self-protection or plain disinterest.

I suggested to Monique that this was her real fear with Pierre: that he would be uninvolved and absent from her and their children's lives—a repetition of what she had experienced with her father. In actuality, she was apologizing for superimposing this template on him and treating him as abdicating, weak, and disinterested.

Pierre was quiet during this part of the session, until he spontaneously added that he knew it was hurtful to Monique to constantly compare her to her mother. He apologized to Monique for stereotyping her, even though he knew that she was trying to be different. He admitted that it was a sure way of poking and punishing her for how he felt treated. He referred to it as "low-hanging fruit." He raised what we had discussed previously, which was that he grew up with two very critical parents and could not take what he perceived as Monique's overriding judgment of him as a complete failure.

Of course, it would have been wonderful if at this moment of insight and vulnerability, the power of the apology would have been enough to have them throw their arms around each other. Sadly, it would not have been realistic. Their lives had moved in different directions, and disillusionments had eroded anything romantic. Nonetheless, I was aware that they had, for the first time, related outside their conflictive dynamic. It was a sign that they could improve significantly as a divorced coparenting couple.

The example illustrates how deeply significant apologies can be. They provide an essential route to building an environment of reparation and gratitude. In this sense, apologies are very ethical and a vital part of what can make a couple or ex-couple work. Divorce might seem a strange context in which to speak about apology, yet divorce ethics require that the couple retain a capacity to responsibly attend to the impact of actions and words on the other. It concerns having the conditions for a mutual forgiveness or viewing forgiveness as a coconstructed process. As much as parenting agreements can be written with ironclad certainty, there remains a vulnerability in the interparental relationship that cannot be eliminated. This becomes very significant when children are shared.

The capacity for apology coincides with the capacity for gratitude. Therapists should take note of whether either or both can express gratitude to the therapist for the therapist's efforts to help them through this crisis or the assistance of relatives, even if they are not capable at the moment of experiencing or expressing gratitude or indebtedness toward each other. This can provide a useful window into the relative capacity for gratitude and the reparative potential for mutual recognition in the couple dynamic. Even when apology and gratitude seem undeveloped in one or both ex-partners, it is important to distinguish between trauma-induced regressions common in stressful divorce and chronic patterns suggestive of personality disorder that go well beyond the divorce context.

Vulnerability is never safe in high-conflict divorce because destructiveness is so pronounced. There is a constant dread of attack, which is a formula for endless turmoil and emotional constriction. It is not that the "good object" is completely absent. It is, however, very unstable; seriously weakened by the buffeting of disillusionment, both historical and marital; and resulting paranoid antagonism. So much was invested in this other, the ex-partner as a representation of some ideal, that the disillusionment is overwhelming.

The Couple Mentality and the Couple Quotient (CQ)

In pursuit of a disillusionment therapy, it would be helpful to know whether this ex-couple ever had or has retained some relational capacity. We might call this mentality "coupleness." It is the implicit understanding that the couple and what it represents and needs from each partner is separate from the individuals themselves. Successfully married couples often share this capacity. Each naturally tends to the needs of the relationship, and this keeps them together through good and not-so-good times. Indeed, this is the basis for couple resiliency, flexibility, commitment, and overall relationship security. It is not that the two are selfless, nor are they necessarily emotionally dependent. Rather, they can rely on each other to represent the best interests of the couple; they acknowledge its central place in their lives and take the necessary steps to foster its vitality.

I have seen many situations where there is strong chemistry and shared interests but little coupleness. The couple does not emerge as a third perspective that transcends either participant to become a shared point of reference or focus. When the effort to have a union collapses, there is no precedent of a shared space in which to resolve matters together. If they have children, then the problems mount quickly because, without coupleness, there is no basis to collaborate when breaks occur. In high conflict, there is a fantasy ideal rather than coupleness that shatters and leaves two fundamentally alienated strangers who easily become enemies when they realize that they must share precious offspring.

There is very little written about couples who have a deep tenacity to overcome obstacles, differences, and sources of conflict in order to stay together. They have the couple mentality, coupleness, but their relationship is certainly not smooth. Nonetheless, they identify the marriage as something separate from themselves; designate it as very important and a source of identity, security, and intimacy; and will defend it even in the face of major impediments. They love even when they do not get along.

Marriages, like all institutions, should never be idealized. These are very human enterprises and are never perfect. Disturbing emotions, fears, sensitivities, and traumas find their way into the marital field. These are the toxins of everyday life that bubble up within couple interactions, vulnerabilities from childhood as well as from life in general outside the marriage. Marriages need the capacity to contain and process these inevitable intrusions. In its absence, the marriage will splinter, often when the couple faces a trying moment or major demand.

What is heartening is the successful couple who has the capacity to soften the blow, soak up the toxin, mitigate damage, and offer security and safety. The two people will demonstrate their couple bond and working capacity at crucial moments, which is especially evident when they are dealing with difficult feelings and burdens. This could be called the "couple quotient" (CQ): a measure of the couple's capacity to contain, process, and overcome stresses by all means open to them—talking, joking, lovemaking, sharing activities, socializing, counseling—or whatever adaptations and skills they have developed to foster and maintain their intimacy.

High-CQ relationships do not trigger regression in each other, destroying the very bond that they most need to meet the challenges of family life. Their relationship can handle a lot, and there is no need for a dense filter. Low-CQ couples must keep most of what ails them under wraps, as their relationship lacks this capacity to contain and process tensions. They can have low conflict before things turn sour. When tensions do erupt, the low-CQ couple has little means to resolve anything. They go from getting along to eruption and emotional distancing. It is either calm and neutral or viscerally rancorous.

Divorced ex-couples with low CQ are those most likely to end up in high-conflict divorce. Their marriages fail, but unlike the usual breakups, which tend to solve the problem of misalliance and disillusionment, these divorces trigger destructiveness. When the relationship breaks, there is no external referent, such as a shared sense of family, to absorb tensions or mitigate hostility and blame. Everything that was once good between them is obliterated by the negative. The ideal shatters and, with it, any positive regard toward that person. If not friends, then they must be enemies, and enemies are prone to start wars with each other, which is precisely what happens.

As one woman related about her experience with her ex-partner, "The worst part in him triggered the worst part in me." They engaged repeatedly, she noted, in an interminable argument "about cause and effect." In other words, they were consumed about who was right and who was wrong—a binary conception ensuring that each felt like the victim of the other. In her case, safety and security had eluded her from childhood onward. Each of her failed relationships was an echo of her childhood—parents who were unable to provide a reasonable base of love, belonging, and protection. Thus, we encounter layering disillusionments from childhood onward, each new layer increasing the likelihood of further painful repetition.

Low CQ also complicates attempts at postseparation mediation in the hope of developing a workable, attuned parenting plan. If there is no internalized transcendent value shared by the parties other than what each thinks or believes, then there is no basis to mediate. There must be a third perspective, something that is neither one nor the other, something that becomes the place where mediation occurs. Paradoxically, this cannot be the children's best interests, in major part because parental identifications are so strong that there is often too little psychological distance between parent and child to separate interests. It would have to be a reimagining of the family, in which each parent contributes to a shared though revised concept of the family container. This would be implicit in what would make mediation work.

For example, consider the divorcing, low-CQ, high-conflict couple who are in mediation. They are in separate rooms with their attorneys, and the mediator is shuffling between them. They are working on a parenting plan. One ex-spouse wants an equal sharing arrangement, while the other insists on an eight overnight/six overnight division. There is only one overnight in a two-week stretch separating their respective positions. It does not matter. They remain entrenched, and no variation or rationale offered will budge either party from their fixed views. The whole morning passes, and there is no progress. Each will go to court if necessary, despite the expense, time, and emotional costs to themselves and their children. There is a standoff precisely because neither can imagine a value that does not equate with their own position.

The following important qualities, in no specific order, are associated with a high couple quotient:

1. Provide a safe atmosphere for the other
2. Are passionate and fully engaged as a principle
3. Accept responsibility for the effect of actions and words on the other

4. Prefer to listen and understand versus defending
5. Place a high value on the relationship and be ready to act to protect it
6. Treat conflict as a stimulus to deepen communication rather than needing to win an argument
7. Value consensus and work toward this goal in any joint endeavor
8. Treat the partner the same—respectfully and affectionately—whether alone or in public
9. Hold the other in their mind as a source of love and comfort
10. Accept inevitable disappointments without discarding what is precious
11. Elevate the ideal of family in childrearing as being more vital to collective well-being than any particular position

Couples seen in a clinical practice, either together or separated, could be plotted on a continuum of CQ, although there might be individual differences within the pair, not just between pairs. Can these skills be taught? These are mainly personal qualities, but there is certainly a place for helping individuals and couples to transcend solipsistic positions and view themselves as contributors to a single functioning family system that is more important than either of their views.

Being aware of these high-CQ qualities can thus offer an ethical road map for divorce. Naturally, there is no expectation or likelihood that the ex-partner would remain a source of love and comfort in divorce, but safety, accepting responsibility, listening versus defending, communicating, and working to consensus and a notion of family are all highly relevant to divorce—as much as they are to marriage. Paradoxically, then, some of the same qualities that would predict a successful marriage also predict a successful divorce. As such, it is worth noting that a high CQ is no guarantee that a marriage will or should survive. A high CQ, however, will certainly make it much more likely that the couple as individuals will survive their divorce and not turn it into destructive turmoil.

Something Versus Nothing

The point of rupture of a marriage usually occurs at the apex of disillusionment. This might accrue slowly or occur suddenly due to some dramatic episode, such as discovering an affair or other betrayal. If the relationship was based more on illusion than tested reality, then disillusionment could shatter the union, effectively leaving nothing.

Major disillusionment leads to partners losing the essence of what linked them. Loss of other and loss of dream can translate into a loss of identity, which is why it is so traumatic. Ex-couples in high conflict fail to recognize the other's pain or the legitimate needs of the ex-partner. The crisis can be short lived or follow a prolonged and tortuous trajectory for years that severely affects children. In order for divorce to succeed, there must be a process of mourning that is long enough to recover a sense of self and the relational adjustment to engage effectively with the ex-partner. Grief is not the only emotion in mourning. There is also anger, regret, guilt, shame, disappointment, and disillusionment. Where healthy mourning does not occur, however, destructiveness can emerge full bore, often in proportion to the degree of calamity. What is calamitous is the degree to which identity is rocked in the emotional turbulence of loss and disillusionment.

As much as disappointment can be difficult to bear, major disillusionments change the way the world is seen, including trust in others and trust in love. This complexity adds to the burden of grieving broken marriages. When children are involved, the burden is amplified. Parents can be frightened and preoccupied, emotionally unavailable, and with diminished parenting capacity.

In healthy mourning, there is a retained awareness that the ex-partner was loved, and this puts some cap on hatred and conflict. Mourning is not averse to anger; it is just not overrun by toxic negativity. It retains a sense of the good and what was valued, loved, and sadly lost. High-conflict divorce, on the contrary, bypasses sadness, grief, and mourning. The catastrophe of disillusionment destroys any representation of what was good, and in its wake the individual feels victimized, bullied, tricked, cheated, and betrayed. Survival is in jeopardy, and in response, destructiveness takes over, driving an entropic process, which can then feed hostile, prolonged strife, fueling litigation that can carry on for years. Mentalization is impaired in the area of the high conflict. These people who were one-time lovers and partners can be surprisingly ruthless and even sadistic. Instead of being proactive, the high-conflict mind-set is reactive, contemptuous, retaliatory, and potentially violent.

Adult children of high-conflict divorce often present with the imprint of unresolved mourning. The emotional residue of their parents' divorce continues underground, emerging in sometimes surprising ways but often casting a shadow of sadness over their lives and interfering with life progression and relationships. In therapy, they can express a sense of missing, sadness, loneliness, and lack of self-cohesion. This suggests that not enough was done to help these children mourn or cope with unsettled, interminably conflictive parents who took years to adjust to the breakup.[5] In this regard, mourning in divorce is a transgenerational issue with cumulative impacts. The more dysfunctional and high conflict the divorce, the less the children can process what is happening in real time. It is a matter of survival during childhood years, which then requires the child as a young adult to do the work of mourning. This involves not only acknowledging what they lost but also coming to terms with the destructiveness of their parents' conduct.

Serena and David: Healthy Resolution

Serena and David had a long marriage on paper, but their relationship had long lost its romantic luster. They raised their two children cooperatively and without major difficulty. It was a busy household dominated by soccer and hockey.

As a couple, they seemed to endure each other unhappily. Serena was sure that David did not value her due to his constant wandering eye when they were out in public. It offended her deeply. Besides, David could be harsh with Serena, and he did not seek her out. He wanted her effectively to leave him alone and stop ordering him about. However, he was a very responsible man in terms of duty but was clearly unwilling and perhaps unable to love Serena as she longed to be loved.

The problem between them had a long history. A crisis occurred about a decade previously, when Serena reported to David that she often felt very alone and unsettled following physical intimacy. David would leave her quickly to do other things and seemed moody and irritable, which made her feel bad. She refused to have sexual relations until this was addressed. David, however, responded critically to Serena's unilateral decision. He felt that she was trying to control him and make him behave according to her rules. He denied moodiness and stated that he would have welcomed her communication about her feelings rather than the unilateral action that affected them both. It broke something crucial between them—his trust in her emotionally and her sense of safety with him. An impasse took hold.

Indeed, they were both disillusioned and, curiously perhaps, could never really recover from this rip in the fabric of their relationship. There

---

[5] Gunsberg, L., (2019), Separation and divorce: Reverberations through the life span, *Psychoanalytic Study of the Child*, 72, 1–4.

was an ongoing, low-level struggle. Serena viewed David as withdrawing from the world, and David saw Serena as pushy and controlling.

It was clear that David wanted out of the marriage but had hung on because he felt responsible for Serena and did not have the inner freedom to leave. Serena knew that David wanted out, but she had convinced herself that his problems were his own rather than anything particular to her. If only he could resolve his own life, she insisted, they might have a marriage again.

Disillusionment was nothing new to either Serena or David. Her mother had been a liability in her life, and there had been no contact in the last five years. As a child, she had also feared her mother physically and felt unsafe and untrusting of her mother's commitment. David's father had descended into abusive alcoholism, and as the oldest child, David felt responsible for his mother and siblings. This weighed on him greatly.

As much as this couple had difficulty parting ways, there was a mutual realization that this might be the best solution for what had ailed them for too long. It was a door that they had long ago gone through, and there was no real path back, even if they would have wanted it. Serena had to accept that David's sadness was not a depression affecting his total life. He wanted to end the marriage and did not know how to do this. David had to accept that feeling responsible is not loving and that he was doing a disservice to Serena and himself.

The marriage ended amicably, and the couple managed to continue to share friends and to coparent. They were able to grieve because they could bear the loss without having to destroy what had been good between them. Divorce proved to be a solution that paradoxically improved their link by reformulating it in a shape they could both use. In this regard, they could be divorced while still remembering what they loved.

In contrast to divorce being the solution, as it was for Serena and David, high-conflict divorce intensifies the problems between the couple. There is not necessarily more disillusionment in this subgroup, but the response is particularly catastrophic and traumatic. This can be evident as much before the breakup as after.

Carol and Daniel: The Road to High Conflict

Carol and Daniel were both active in their careers, although both were quite psychologically vulnerable, even brittle. Together they had three intelligent and engaged children, despite a raucous marriage. Carol and Daniel's union did not just end; it imploded. Their marriage lacked the core assets of communication and mutuality. It was an abominable divorce with acting out on both sides and very upset children rocked at every encounter. One accused the other of assault during an exchange; in reality, it was an exaggerated version of what happened and left out the accuser's provocative behavior. The other surreptitiously took photos of the ex-partner's messy house and sent them to the child protection authority. Their offensive text messages bounced between them with no filter and no limits. Automobiles were frequently used to block driveways, spy, and shield from attack. Their lawyers struggled fruitlessly to achieve containment. The couple fought about childcare and money for years. The children either left home early or became estranged from one or the other parent.

In the end, of course, the children grew up, mainly on their own. The parents, however, remained hobbled. They were drained financially and psychologically. What had transpired between them was destructive. Curiously, they always expressed a residual affection for each other, but there was no accountability, no secure frame on which they could count, and no limit to their actions. There was no safe space to be found.

Mourning seemed out of reach for both parties. When Carol was seven years old, her mother walked out and joined a man she had met at a gym. She eventually left the city, and although Carol saw her at least twice a year, it was a hugely rejecting and disillusioning experience that cast a shadow on her life. Carol's attachment to her father was certainly sustaining, but this did not erase the wound and vulnerability she bore.

Daniel was also no stranger to childhood loss. His father died suddenly of cardiac failure without any prior hint of underlying heart disease. Daniel was only five years old at the time and the youngest of two children. His mother was obliged to return to work as a teacher. As Daniel related, he could recall playing under the kitchen table when his mother was informed of her husband's sudden death. He remembered the LEGO set with which he was playing at the time. It was as if a pall descended on him that had never lifted. His mother did her best, but she was not a naturally warm, nurturing person, according to Daniel, and he summarized his life as being orderly but empty.

Carol and Daniel met by a lakeside on a holiday. They had many common interests, and their relationship ramped up quickly. They both adored hiking and took this as a sign of compatibility. They had little history of being able to resolve issues when they married. Sadly, the wedding planning itself became a source of significant conflict. There was no common vision.

After they settled into married life, it was not long before they were insulting each other regularly. Their quarrels, however, did not stop them from having three children. It was a peculiar combination of chemistry and strife that might have appealed to them at some level but wore them out and certainly drained their children. The marriage eventually collapsed under the strain, although not before all the children were well into school age.

In this case, though, divorce did not stem the tide of conflict. It fueled it. Carol insisted that Daniel's behavior alone was overwhelming the children and forcing them to choose one parent over the other. She noted that he loved them but otherwise provoked disaster in their lives. She castigated Daniel as a dreamer who refused to wake up. Daniel portrayed Carol as an insatiable flirt and an unreliable caretaker who falsely depicted herself as the children's primary parent.

There was no boundary that the two would not cross. Reading their children's private journals, trespassing in the other's home, using every communication device and social venue to rail about the other, whether their children were privy or not. They discussed and eagerly showed legal documents to the children. The children followed suit, refusing to obey any schedule with regularity. The parents vied for the children's favor.

Notably, Carol and Daniel were unable to mourn. In their noisy divorce, they hung onto each other in a fitful battle. The marriage did not really terminate; it simply morphed into a free-for-all marked by intense, open struggle. They could not get on with their lives even if they met other people. This clinging through conflict meant that they would never have to mourn, as if to grieve would have opened the door to all the losses and disillusionments in their lives. Of course, to the lawyers, courts, mediators, and parent coordinators, it was baffling. Perhaps their children grasped the essence: two emotionally fragile people afflicted by childhood trauma, who are in one way repeating their traumatic histories and in another preventing it from ever happening again.

Disillusionment and Same-Sex Unions (LGBTQ)

Traumatic disillusionment has no gender. It can be an important factor in same-sex and heterosexual partnerships and a trigger for destructivity. This should not prevent clinicians and researchers, though, from studying conflict and severe high conflict in same-sex unions specifically.

One of the most welcome consequences of changes in marital and family law pertaining to lesbian, gay, bisexual, transgender, and questioning or queer (LGBTQ) individuals and couples is their capacity to marry, become parents, and raise families. Access to diverse and effective reproductive technologies offers further advantages for LGBTQ couples who want to be parents. Of course, this opens the door to the custody and care implications of breakups, and in this regard, there is no appreciable difference between how the courts in the United States and Canada, among other progressive jurisdictions, treat heterosexual unions and same-sex unions. The best interests of the child provides a common and overriding precept for custody and access, no matter the sexual orientation or identity of the committed adults providing care. No sexual or gender orientation has a monopoly on love and commitment.

Research supports that sexual orientation has no relevance in good parenting and that children raised in same-sex families are no worse or better off than children raised in heterosexual unions.[6] This does not mean that LGBTQ individuals and parents could not personally face discrimination, even within the courts. Nonetheless, children are increasingly being raised in lesbian and gay households, either because the couple sought to become parents or because at least one of the couple previously was in a heterosexual union, from which there are children.[7]

Nonetheless, there may be differences between same-sex and heterosexual unions, as well as between gay and lesbian relationships, that could affect the dissolution of these relationships and implicate childcare. With heterosexual unions, the historical division of roles between the sexes continues to pervade family law when it comes to

---

[6] Allen, M., & Burrell, N., (1996), Comparing the impact of homosexual and heterosexual parents on children: Meta-analysis of existing research, *Journal of Homosexuality*, 32, 19–35; Crowl A., Ahn S., & Baker, J., (2008), A meta-analysis of developmental outcomes for children of same-sex and heterosexual parents, *Journal of GLBT Family Studies*, 4, 385–407.

[7] Tye, M. C., (2003), Lesbian, gay, bisexual and transgender parents: Special considerations for the custody and adoption evaluator, *Family Court Review*, 41, 92–103.

divorce and custody. When young children are involved, the maternal claim for custody, for example, can be or at least appear to be stronger than it is for men. Males and females are raised with specific and often different expectations about themselves and gender roles. These certainly enter into the equation when couples divorce.

One obvious difference between same-sex and heterosexual unions is that same-sex couples will inevitably require reproductive technology or a surrogate if they want to conceive and gestate a baby. This leads to an unavoidable triangle, even if the third is an anonymous sperm donor. My impression is that this has effects when it comes to the child's identity and how conception and parenthood is understood within the couple. This would, then, have consequences if the union ends, especially when the biological parent asserts primacy over the other. The nonbiological parent might feel less protected legally or less represented as a valid parent and caregiver. There could also be inconsistency between jurisdictions in how the nonbiological parent's claim is treated.[8]

I suspect that the majority of high-conflict same-sex divorcing couples who come before the courts are lesbian, as many more lesbian couples than gay couples have children, which accords with my personal experience with custody litigation.[9] Also, maternity is multifaceted as an identity intricately connected with the reproductive function in women. Maternity is the purview of all women, whether they choose to or are able to conceive. It arises from a positive feminine identity and has nothing to do with sexual orientation or whether the woman actually births a baby. The capacity to grow life within one's own body and to sustain it is central to feminine gender identity.

In contrast, men have a very brief biological contribution, and fatherhood can be mainly defined psychologically through identification and commitment. The capacity to inseminate is too abstract to become an essential ingredient of masculinity. As such, fathers are inclined to view parenthood more as a role and act of devotion or duty than as a destiny bestowed by nature. Boys generally think of parenthood later in development, while this often evolves from an early age in girls. Hence, there is seemingly less distinction made between "the father" and "a father" than between "the mother" and "a mother." Motherhood, thus, goes well beyond role, implicating the

[8] Moalemi, L., (2018), Blood will not justify my relation: Same-sex couples and their battle for standing as de facto parents, *Family Court Review*, 56, 490–505.

[9] Bala, N., Queen's University faculty of law, (2019, December 15), personal communication.

woman's body, her womb, and her capacity to nourish and keep alive her baby with her own lactating breasts.

Beyond childbirth, the maternal involves an intimate reciprocity between mother and infant, for which each is defined by the other. The baby exists within the body and then on the body of the mother. It is a shade of difference from which a psychological remnant persists. As such, there is no baby without a mother.[10] Human survival depends on primary care linked to maternity. What happens, then, when two women share a child and only one is the birth mother? This is certainly a dilemma that can affect lesbian divorce in a unique way that is not shared by heterosexual unions or those of two men where a surrogate or adoption is required. While one man could certainly be the birth father, this may not represent the same identity predicament as when both parents claim motherhood. The sharing of maternity can seem anathema to a birth mother. It can become fertile ground for intense conflict. Whether this devolves into high conflict, however, would follow the same formula as in other divorce situations: radical disillusionment, imperiled hope, psychic trauma, and release of destructiveness.

Denise and Pauline

When Denise and Pauline got together as a couple, Pauline had already taken steps to have ova extracted and frozen for any future decision on whether to become a mother. She had long pondered this dream, but as a lesbian woman, single and busy in her family's fabric business, she had not really considered having a baby in the context of a committed couple. When she met Denise and became romantically involved, a baby quickly became a shared vision. Denise embraced the idea, and Pauline was swept into the enthusiasm of the moment. They agreed to be joint custodians of their future child. Denise was present when the implantation occurred.

Yet by the time Ben arrived, a gregarious, charming son whom they both adored, the relationship was already fragmenting. Pauline found Denise unappeasable, demanding, volatile, and destructive to her relationships with her own family. Denise demanded an exclusivity that rocked Pauline and created enormous strain. Whenever the liaison was

---

[10] Winnicott, D. W., (1965), Transitional objects and transitional phenomena, in *The maturational processes and the facilitating environment: Studies in the theory of emotional development*, International Universities Press.

close to fracturing, Denise would beg to be forgiven, only to begin the cycle once more after the briefest of reprieves.

Pauline's essential reasonableness was evident on meeting her. She described herself as a mirror image of her accommodating mother, whose kindness and devotion were exemplary. Like her mother, Pauline would almost certainly put her own needs aside to achieve peace. Unfortunately, this did not work with Denise. Pauline felt constantly bombarded and put off balance by the emotional Denise. When the breakup finally occurred, Ben was about six months old. The police were summoned to break up the melee. Denise moved out after tense, acrimonious negotiations.

At five years of age, Ben was bonded to both women. He called one "lama" and the other "ama." He seemed to be adjusting, although he was extremely secretive about his relationship with Denise and would not answer any of Pauline's questions following visits. Tensions between the women remained at a high pitch, which affected Ben's personality development.

Denise insisted that she was a legitimate comother to this little boy. Pauline refused to accept parity. From her point of view, she was the mother who had conceived and grown this child within her own body. It was a long-standing wish that well preceded her liaison with Denise. Motherhood, Pauline argued, was indivisible, and while Denise was certainly a parent to Ben, she was not his mother. Denise found this preposterous and an insult as well as devaluation of her relationship with and feelings toward Ben. She attacked Pauline, and each lobbied their mutual friends for support in the struggle. Denise used social media to rebuke Pauline and destructively implicate Pauline's family's fabric business.

Curiously, while Denise and Pauline feuded over the issue of what defined motherhood, Ben was interested in superheroes and masculine heroics. When he was asked to use dolls to represent his family, he chose a father, mother, and boy doll and insisted that this was his family. He was trying to adjust to his specific reality but was declaring his own concerns.

Denise insisted that she was a mother to Ben in all ways equal to Pauline. Even if she was not the lactating mother, she had lovingly fed Pauline's pumped breastmilk to Ben. In other words, Denise refused to accept that Pauline was first among mothers. She was absolutely determined to safeguard her place in Ben's life. Any hint of differentiation in role, identity, or status sent Denise into a tailspin.

Ben was increasingly unable to remain outside his parents' conflict. He became hostile toward Pauline and seemed to blame her for trying to take him away from Denise. He also asked Pauline repeatedly why he did not have a father like other children he knew in kindergarten and read about in storybooks. Pauline blamed Denise for recruiting Ben as an ally in her fight. Denise denied this accusation vehemently and attributed the whole problem to Pauline's refusal to accept her equal maternity.

On the surface, there were three angry people: a child demanding a father, a birth mother demanding her due as the "real" mother, and a second maternal parent whose sense of threat and legal insecurity within the family system was eroding the middle ground.

It was clear that Pauline's insistence on maternal primacy was deeply injuring to Denise. She felt negated, shut out of a crucial aspect of her own identity. It was as if Pauline was destroying something precious for Denise that amounted to a dream about herself and, of course, her chance to be a mother. It did not seem to matter whether she shared equally in the care of Ben. The focus was Pauline's refusal to acknowledge her maternity. Denise's attack on Pauline and inability to protect Ben from her emotional pain and vulnerability ricocheted through the family system. Underneath the rancor, Denise felt broken and in despair. She raged at Pauline, whether Ben was present or not.

There was nothing particularly noteworthy about Pauline's life. She had progressed seamlessly from childhood to adulthood within the protective confines of a close-knit business family. She had studied accounting after high school and joined the fabric business. Pauline had always known that she was lesbian, and this was accepted by her family without issue.

Denise was raised in a religious family. She went to church regularly and was very invested in sports growing up. It was a close family who promoted a virtuous, Christian ideal. Thus, her parents' divorce when she was 15 smashed her childhood. Her mother did not spare Denise and let her know that her father had been caught in an affair. The father was banished, and Denise saw him infrequently after the breakup. Her mother shunned her ex-husband and his new partner, the woman with whom he had the affair. Denise's father also became tainted in her eyes. It was all deeply disillusioning and shattered her worldview.

Denise threw herself into competitive gymnastics as a way of coping. The disciplined routine appealed to her, and she attended college on an athletics scholarship. In contrast to this success, she related that when her parents' marriage ended, it was like the death of her childhood. Denise's flight into athletics helped her get control of what had been a complete rupture in her world.

Adding to the complexity of her youth, Denise became infatuated in her senior year with a female classmate, whom she idealized. Everything about this friend appealed to Denise, and she lived for the moments they were together. In retrospect, Denise realized that she must have acted like a lovestruck fan of a movie star. It likely became too much for the classmate, who precipitously broke off contact and thereafter refused to acknowledge Denise. In the aftermath, overwrought with shame, Denise drank so much alcohol that she ended up in the emergency room. She struggled again with the loss of hope.

It was sometime after this event that she chose to explore her own sexuality. Although she had several brief liaisons with young men in college, her intense emotional unions were with women.

Though Pauline certainly accepted Denise as a coparent, Denise's preoccupation was with what Pauline would not acknowledge: her parity as Ben's mother. This fomented in Denise's mind and incited a toxic stew of emotions. Her bitterness was palpable and spilled over into her care of Ben. The two developed a kind of mutual exclusivity that was especially alarming to Pauline. Ben had difficulty transitioning from Denise to Pauline and was often defiant in Pauline's care. Ben was empowered but also ignored for what he needed. Motherhood was not his issue.

Denise took no responsibility and blamed Pauline totally for pervasively undermining her link with Ben. Denise spoke of Pauline's "betrayal" in language that recalled Pauline's own mother's diatribe against her father for his infidelity. Denise's identity was shaky, and her mental health suffered. She required sick leave from work. She was too distraught to concentrate. She refused permission for Ben to get therapy, and it took a court order to put this in place. Denise insisted that Ben did not need help for what was Pauline's problem in allowing Ben and her to have the loving relationship that they both wanted. The furor surrounding his young life left Ben struggling to find some middle ground between these two warring halves of his family. In many ways, it made it hard for him to have a mother, even though on paper he had two.

This case illustrates what could be an important element of high-conflict divorce in general: psychic trauma. Clearly what is destructive externally, attacks on the other parent or a parent-child relationship, is internally perceived as a reaction to an attack on the self. Idealized relationships become totally devalued, good becomes bad, and identity is shaken. As much as I highlight the destructiveness of these individuals and couples, we should not forget the pain and trauma experienced by those broken by disillusionment.

Conclusion

In the case of marriage and family, the whole must be greater than the sum of its parts. When couples decide that they must split or at least accept its inevitability, something of this ideal, the couple and the family, must remain to help them bridge living as a committed couple to living as autonomous individuals with shared offspring.

There is no contradiction, then, between ending a marriage and keeping this residual element intact. It is the coupleness of the couple that makes this possible, no matter the fate of the relationship. They must be able to conceptualize beyond themselves to something more. As much as the union ends, this must shift to family as a shared ideal and ethic. It is the extension of the "good" that was and can continue to be.

Destructive divorce arises from two people lacking this capacity for transcendence. They have a conditional contract more than intimacy, which depends solely on getting along and being aligned. Indeed, it is differences that expose their lack of capacity to function together. They are extremely prone to disillusionment, as their union is hinged on shaky idealizations. Without agreement on issues or values, they have no capacity to pull together and quickly become enemies. Each is too exposed to the other, which creates a permanent vulnerability. In fury, they attack each other as well as the family ideal, exposing it as a mockery of invention, a false idol that failed to deliver what was promised. It is the destructivity that gives rise to conflict rather than the converse. The destructive is an ever-present risk in the human psyche, an entropic force that once triggered engulfs the field. When turned on the family, the symbol of human security, the results are legion.

One consequence of the usual view of divorce destructiveness as a symptom of high conflict is that it tends to lead to services aimed at case management. These take substantial court resources and clog the family law system due to high demand. If the legal system took the contrary view—that it is a destructive process at the core of the problem—then the objective of the intervention would change.

Therapy could be approached from a different perspective without conflict management being the central theme. It would need to include, though, an understanding of the layers of disillusionment linking past and present in the lives of the ex-partners. Ultimately, there must be capacity to mourn, with its roots in a residue of gratitude, accountability, and atonement. Something must be retained that represents an ethic and way of being together, even in divorce. Coupleness, in this regard, may be an aptitude, but it is also a value that can guide judicial and therapeutic intervention with high-conflict ex-couples with children, so they can find their way out of a destructive spiral.

The opportunity now exists for adults with varying gender and sexual orientations to marry and have families. This underscores the importance that civil society gives to equal opportunity and the ascendance of love and family. How the family is constituted, whatever blend of gender and sexual orientation, is much less important than its internal functioning. High conflict is a people problem that has nothing to do with sexuality or gender. Nonetheless, each situation must be understood in its specificity for the voices of children to be heard.

5

Love in the Age of Divorce

Marriage was never intended to be an idle promise. Indeed, the phrase *tie the knot* carries with it much of the history of marriage itself. Marriage was conceived as an indissoluble bond that connected families and communities, creating extended families and clans.[1] *Indissoluble* meant that marriage was intended for life. "What therefore God hath joined together, let not man put asunder" (Mark 10:9) captures the early Jewish and Christian value that marriage was never to be a reef knot, easily undoable, but a Gordian knot that would be next to impossible to undo. If marriage conveyed status even in God's eyes and was a means of transferring property, then it needed to be permanent. On the other hand, if marriage was for love and subject to human frailty, then some means to undo the vow would be needed. This tension between permanence and transience defines the history of marriage and its corollary, divorce.

Whatever the legal and cultural dimension, the moment society placed women and men together in lifetime contracts, relationship factors emerged as important. Enlightenment thinkers in the 17th and 18th centuries reinforced the individuality of people, including women, and the values of liberty, reason, and self-determination. Children were expected to respect both parents, not simply their father, even if property and money was transmitted through the paternal line. In other words, whatever the asymmetries of power and role between the sexes, there was regard for the soft virtues of love and partnership.

As much as the knot was meant to be indivisible, divorce was inevitable, and governments made provisions in extreme cases, such as impotence, desertion, adultery, and bigamy. As Enlightenment values took hold, society made divorce easier. Initially, it took legislative acts to end a marriage, but this was later transferred to the judiciary.

[1] Ury, C., (2018), Narcissism and its discontents: The fall of the marital institution and the postmodern malaise, oral presentation, Ottawa Psychoanalytic Society, April 13, 2018.

The progressive emancipation of women, facilitating ownership of property, education, employment, and voting rights, added to the impetus for divorce liberalization. Marriages, which were always voluntary, did not have to be for forever. The shift in the 1970s from fault-based to nonfault divorce in the United States and Canada, among other jurisdictions, opened the door fully to divorce while concomitantly changing what we understand of marriage and romantic relationships.

The advent of the birth control pill in the early 1960s also created much more sexual freedom for women, but the erotic gain was minor compared to the huge dividend in allowing women more control over their lives and the right to make choices about when to have children.

The remarkable shifts in society's appreciation of the role of divorce to help remedy troubled, unhappy, and sometimes dangerous liaisons has also changed how marriage is understood. Whereas marriage began as a means to organize society into social, biological, and politico-economic groupings, love seems to be the ever-present counterstory. Shakespeare's *Romeo and Juliet*, first performed around 1596, highlights the idealization of romantic love as an ultimate human experience. It reflects the high status allocated to love relationships and the power of love to move families and propel human history. People will die for love, whether in a duel fighting a rival or by self-starvation due to melancholic despair after love is lost.

In this regard, marriage exists in a paradoxical space where it is both permanent and transient, blessed by God, as well as primal, visceral, and deeply emotional. It is also a secular legal institution governed by the state. Those who work with couples in therapy are keenly aware of this complexity, in which early unmet childhood needs mix with adult motives, demands, and responsibilities to create a complex amalgam called marriage. It is an interpenetration of selves and motives within a legal context, transactional at so many levels, that is built by tradition to last a lifetime but increasingly does not.

Once handled by legislatures and later given over to judges, divorce is now often handled by mental health professionals and mediators, who clinically specialize in the twin institutions of marriage and divorce. I can foresee the progression in this tendency to where marriage and divorce will be managed by specialist practitioners with decreasing reliance on courts and litigation, which are simply becoming prohibitively expensive and slow due to demand on resources and the enigmatic complexity of the cases.

Love is now the principal reason to marry or partner. Why else would one marry? It is not essential for procreation, as reproductive technologies are making even partnering optional. The inclusion of same-sex couples within marriage laws has only reinforced the primacy of love as the essential reason for people to get together in committed unions. Indeed, gay and lesbian marriage was introduced and broadly accepted by civil society as a testament to love and to the societal value that no one should be excluded from this opportunity to tie the knot before one's chosen community.

Of course, there are people who abuse the institutions of marriage and divorce, much as there are those who abuse other state-sanctioned and controlled endeavors, such as alcohol and gambling. These are serial spouses who partner repeatedly and lack the means to establish or retain a stable, adult relationship with anyone. Research points to unstable, insecure attachment histories; egocentricity; and a persecutory mind-set dominated by strong feelings of victimization and alienation.[2] Such people might marry to be rescued from themselves. It is a plan that fails very quickly. They do not usually learn from experience and need in-depth psychotherapeutic work that can be increasingly hard to find or access.

Kenneth and Irene

Kenneth was in a panic when he sought help for a spiraling nightmare of a marital separation. His wife, Irene, the mother of their three-year-old son and love of his life for the past four years, ended the union. She accused him of emotional abuse, controlling behavior, and tyranny. From Kenneth's perspective, Irene seemed to be describing herself while ascribing dysfunctional behavior to him.

Irene had a complicated but unclear relationship history. She alleged that her parents were controlling and abusive and that her first husband had been alcoholic and violent. Her second husband and father of her nine-year-old daughter was described as serially unfaithful and a cocaine addict. Irene left the city where they lived when her daughter was a baby. The daughter had no idea who her father was or that he had actually been trying to secure a place in her life.

Kenneth stated that he was very close to his stepdaughter, who, since the separation, was refusing any contact, which hurt him deeply.

[2] Epözdemir, H., (2017), Echoes of the serial murder of the psyche: A psychoanalytic approach to serial marriage, *Couple & Family Psychoanalysis*, 7(1), 59–80.

The daughter acknowledged that her relationship with Kenneth had been positive, but her mother subsequently briefed her on how mean Kenneth actually was and why she needed to avoid him. Mother and daughter had a pejorative code word so that they could speak about Kenneth in front of the 3-year-old brother without naming him. Kenneth emphasized that he adored his stepdaughter, and although he realized that he was not her father, he was prepared to play a significant role in her life and was committed to serving as her parent.

Irene had simply dumped him. She told him that the marriage was over and that she had no hope that they could make it work. From that point onward, he found her incredibly cold, hostile, and determined. Their young son was managing, but the stepdaughter was clearly suffering. Kenneth sought assurance from the court that Irene had no access to the children's passports, as he had good reason to fear that she would simply flee.

Irene's marriages had all been unstable, with her as the common denominator. Kenneth had been swept off his feet by her beauty and charm, but he had seriously misjudged Irene's emotional immaturity, her lack of authenticity, and the extent to which she would not protect her children from relationship chaos. There was no self-control or accountability for her behavior to expect ethical conduct.

Irene was required by the court to tell her daughter in the presence of a therapist that she had been much too upset with Kenneth after the breakup to support her daughter's relationship with him and that this had been a mistake. Kenneth and Irene shared the care of their son. Gradually, the daughter's wall came down, and she allowed Kenneth into her life, with the help of the therapist. However, their relationship remained fragile and unstable.

Although Irene was instructed to seek individual therapy and to accept responsibility for her problems, she chose a counselor who reinforced in Irene's mind that she had been defamed and victimized by Kenneth, despite the court's assessment. Irene continued to blame Kenneth and learned nothing from the thorough and expensive court process.

Whatever Irene's personal and character limitations, these were two people who, beyond the child they biologically shared, had little else in common. They might both have married for love, but there was no joining of families, transfer of property, or religious sanctification and fellowship with other faith adherents. There was no external structure that watched over, guided, and held them. They did not surrender to a higher force, idea, or value that might act as a container, authority, and beacon for ethical conduct. In this regard, apart from Irene's obvious lack of integrity, they were typical of many romantic partnerships today.

There is often a huge underestimation of what it takes to succeed in a marriage, particularly when there are children involved. There are those with minimal history together but who still manage to partner in what becomes tenuous unions: people who get together in their middle to late 30s; likely meet through social media; become pregnant before they have achieved a stable, working alliance; try their best to make it work, to no avail; and then separate in less than five years. They then struggle to achieve in divorce the bare minimum of cooperative parenting that they never achieved as a united couple. Their struggles effectively feature two strangers who share a child but little else.

The urge to have offspring provides the impetus in these cases, but it is a wish that only makes sense when there is a secure holding environment, the support of extended families, proven emotional compatibility between the adults, tested ability to solve problems together, and a capacity to tolerate disappointment and achieve mature compromise.

High conflict is more likely in these transitory unions because the impetus for coming together is often illusory. When the fantasy crumbles, which is usually after the first real test of their partnership, the disillusionment can be dramatic. It is never the first serious letdown, and the consequence can be explosive. When all that is shared in the end is a young child, the prospect of being tied forever can foster a claustrophobic terror that then creates a destructive process.

Norman and Kayla

Norman was infatuated with Kayla and taken with her sweet nature. Theirs was a love story. However, he drew a blank when pondering the insights he had gained from understanding Kayla's relationship history and whether he felt assured that she had deepened her self-knowledge and was taking responsibility for her previous missteps.

Although Norman's father was particularly involved and supportive of the union with Kayla, Norman's mother had cautioned her son and openly expressed concern about Kayla's suitability as a partner and parent. Norman had never met Kayla's mother, as Kayla was estranged from her. Her father had died a decade before, but her parents were separated at the time of his death. Kayla had already married and divorced twice. There was a string of relationships. Kayla was rarely alone, but she had not really succeeded in any intimacy for very long.

Kayla and Norman agreed to have a baby together, or at least she became pregnant. This, though, was not only a life decision; it also had ethical implications. Implicitly, they agreed to the ascendancy of parental responsibility independent of what happened between them personally. They undertook to guarantee that they could raise this child together. Whether they were aware or not, there were limits to parental rights, and society would impose its own moral authority if it was determined that they could not protect their child from harm.

As an ethical decision, Kayla and Norman were bound by this moral obligation. It could not be undone by making exaggerated complaints to a court that one or the other was unworthy, derelict of duty, or otherwise deficient. In this regard, neither could be excused from the moral contract inherent to bearing a child by insisting that the other was making it impossible.

The relationship was essentially in tatters by the time their child was two years of age. Kayla blamed Norman for being controlling and abusive, but in truth, she had stayed as long as she was capable. Her tolerance for the other's needs was minimal. Unfortunately, Kayla also had little sense of personal ethics, particularly regarding Norman and coparenting.

In Kayla's view, she was entitled to have her way, to hire and fire men at will, to force them to own responsibility for the failure, and to treat their mutual child as a narcissistic possession. It would be accurate to regard her as a narcissistic personality. This had implications in her capacity to love and her willingness to act ethically when not in accordance with her personal needs or preferences. Whatever rationalizations she could muster, Kayla had minimal capacity to be aware of anyone else but herself and her needs. When the union ended, she expected Norman to disappear and was furious when he resisted her wish to severely minimize his involvement and even eradicate him from their child's life.

This case does afford us the chance to consider the concept of narcissism, particularly with ethics.

Narcissism and Ethics

Narcissism is a word bandied about loosely in today's parlance as a pejorative synonym for *being selfcentered, entitled, and insensitive.* It is actually a complex and poorly understood term. Narcissism relates to the self: the sense of aliveness, coherence, and affective coloring of the self.[3] Optimally, identity and self-esteem are nourished by healthy, empathic, loving, and caring relationships with parents that lead to a graduated sense of individuality. This is "healthy narcissism."

In the case where the child experiences the parent(s) as unavailable, unloving, or unreliable, dependency becomes painful. Disillusionments are very important to the etiology of narcissistic problems: sickness in a parent, the birth of siblings, parental depression, divorce, or other fracturing events that instigate a rupture in a parent-child bond at crucial moments of development.

Instead of developing a healthy reliance on others, the subject develops maladaptive strategies to avoid painful disappointment and disillusionment. This includes fantasies of specialness and callous disregard for others. There is often an endless pursuit of praise, of which there can never be enough to overcome feelings of inferiority and emptiness. Instead of pursuing ideals, the individual conceives of him- or herself as the ideal person, someone lacking nothing. This is "pathological narcissism."

Unhealthy or pathological narcissism exists in two forms. One comprises people who suffer from excessive narcissistic vulnerability. They are easily shamed and feel inferior and brittle. They crave praise, but its benefits are extremely short lived. They often harbor feelings of being special but simultaneously worry endlessly about what they lack. They go to great effort to conceal what haunts them as inadequate in themselves. In their vulnerability, they tend to live from hurt to hurt and demand to be treated with special care. It is hard for them to genuinely care for anyone other than themselves, and they are hypervigilant about being injured.[4] Relationship problems are to be expected.[5]

The other type are those individuals with grandiose personalities. Some reach the level of a personality disorder, which entails a series of

[3] Stolorow, R. D., (1975), Toward a functional definition of narcissism, *International Journal of Psychoanalysis*, 56, 179–185.

[4] Gabbard, G., (1989), Two subtypes of narcissistic personality disorder, *Bulletin of the Menninger Clinic*, 53, 527–532.

[5] Kohut, H., (1971), *The analysis of the self*, International University Press.

fixed, maladaptive traits.[6] These narcissistically disordered individuals are ruthlessly exploitative and denigrating of others. They are unable to tolerate any form of reliance. They do not appreciate and recognize others as separate people with their own entitlements. Empathy and concern for others is shallow or nonexistent. It is a challenge for narcissistically disordered individuals to admit any need for the other's love. Thus, they reject or push away before they can be rejected. They would prefer to be admired than loved.

Excessive narcissism is a limiting factor in relationships generally and an important contributor to high-conflict divorce. The fundamental issue is not the self-centeredness necessarily but the fragility of self-esteem and the extent to which the needs of the hypersensitive self will govern action. In this regard, the narcissist can easily be brought to rage and destructiveness. The partner will often recall that initially they were treated as very special, even exalted and idealized, and could do no wrong. Disillusionment is always traumatic, after which the partner will complain of being ruthlessly devalued and treated as worthless. The demarcation can be dramatic.

There is much in common between the two variants of narcissism, even though they present differently. For instance, both feature egocentricity, and neither type can easily empathize and represent the other's needs. Fragility and impermeability can fluctuate in the same person: one moment haughty and aggressive while at another vulnerable and fragile. An important element is the refusal to allow the other to have an independent viewpoint or subjectivity because this is experienced as intolerably threatening.

As much as narcissism is an important subject, with its links to fragile identity and destructive aggression, there is little benefit to using a diagnostic label unless one can offer psychotherapeutic treatment. In other words, it makes sense in a health or treatment context but not in a legal forum When it does get used in family law, it is generally employed as an insult and to convey the sense of hopelessness. It is better, in my view, to eschew labels and look for the specific disillusionments, both historical and marital, that have decimated trust and left the individual feeling empty and betrayed. Frightened and

---

[6] Bernardi, R., & Eidlin, M., (2018), Thin-skinned or vulnerable narcissism and thick-skinned or grandiose narcissism: Similarities and differences, *International Journal of Psychoanalysis*, 99(2), 291–313; Kernberg, O., & Caligor, E., (2004), A psychoanalytic theory of personality disorders, in J. F. Clarkin & M. F. Lenzenweger (Eds.), *Major theories of Personality Disorder*, 2nd ed. (pp. 115–156), Guilford Press.

ashamed of needing others, hostility, rage, and destructive attacks can erupt against the once-idealized ex-partner as well as against the children, whose love for their other parent smacks of betrayal. These are the roots of unethical divorce. The goal is to confront the destructiveness in a way that minimizes shame, allies with healthier parts of the personality, and leaves the possibility of a strengthened identity and greater capacity for empathy and intimacy.

Donald and Jill

Donald was an impressive man: tall, strong, and forceful in his personality. He was much admired by Jill, his wife, and he expected to be, even though he had his share of rebuffs and disappointments. Generally successful in work, he was a good provider but controlled the family money and was insensitive to Jill's need for autonomy. Donald seemed to suck out the available oxygen, and even the three children existed within his shadow. It was oppressive and overwhelming for Jill, who experienced her husband as a bottomless well of need. She did not trust that he could deal with their children as separate from himself. Her initial admiration had long faded, and with it went her tolerance.

After a series of incidents, mainly involving Donald's insufferable egocentricity, the marriage imploded, and Jill initiated a family law action through the courts. Jill had endured enough. She had concerns regarding Donald's oppressive impact on everyone in the family and how he would respond to her initiative to separate. He was flummoxed by Jill's allegations and resisted acknowledging any merit to her complaint. He could not take criticism and exploded with self-justification when challenged. His identification with the children was excessive, to the degree that he would inappropriately and embarrassingly leap to their defense if he perceived any criticism. There had been inappropriately aggressive behavior with a teacher, who had raised concerns regarding one of their children, and an altercation with a child therapist whom another child was seeing.

Donald's contempt for others would peek out from under a thin guise of civility and superficial respect. His imperious behavior and lack of sensitivity underscored the degree to which he was ethically challenged. He was simply too self-admiring and devaluing of the legitimate rights of others to feel accountable for his behavior. Although mortified when I confronted him, Donald finally accepted to speak about his situation and how, from his point of view, he was constantly misunderstood. I had gotten his attention.

Helping Donald understand his part in the family problem required a detailed analysis of the times in his life that he felt deeply disappointed, either with those close to him or with himself. These had a cumulative disillusioning impact and included the following:

- disappointment when told by a teacher that he would unlikely reach university
- disappointment in his father, who claimed to be exceptional at his job but whose performance and success he discovered was middling at best
- disillusionment with his mother for her seductive message that he was the perfect antidote for her husband's lack
- disillusionment with Jill because he had always been her champion, and this changed dramatically after they had children
- disillusionment with his oldest son, whom he was sure was destined to be a great baseball player but who failed to make the competitive team Donald was coaching
- disillusionment with Jill for failing to appreciate how hard he was trying to fix their marriage and harshly rejecting him as if he was worthless in her eyes

Donald did not as much want a partner as a mirror reflecting his specialness, as if this would protect him from ever having to face his failings and disappointments. At times he was deeply insensitive and blind to his impact on others, while at others, he was hypersensitive to any hint of criticism. He was hard to live with, either feeling on top of the world, as if he had answers for everything, or deeply despondent and self-pitying when life did not confirm his distorted judgment of himself as ideal.

When Donald grasped that he was oscillating between states of illusion and disillusionment, trying to know his real value and stabilize his self-esteem, he began to see more clearly his own history. He had always risen to the top, and his mother in particular had taken huge pleasure in his prowess. In his mind, they were a team, in which he felt like her special child, as if he was succeeding for both of them. Indeed, Donald felt his mother preferred him over his father and older brother. It did not take Donald long, though, to acknowledge that there were moments when he had let his mother down and she had coldly turned away from him. He described one incident in which he had received a lower grade than usual on his report card. His mother's chilly withdrawal left him feeling shaken, humiliated, and alone. In another episode, where his grade on a high school physics exam slipped below A+, she made him apologize. Underneath Donald's arrogance and haughtiness was a child fearing that his prowess was illusory and that his value in the world solely resided in being the best and most important.

When the haze of illusion lifted for Donald, including the degree to which he felt manipulated by his mother for her emotional ends, he was able to begin to understand himself better and consequently to see Jill more clearly. It was not a complete metamorphosis, but he could start to envision his obligations as a divorced husband and father. This included seeing his ex-wife and children as separate people, with their own rights and needs and to whom he had a duty to listen. In Donald's case, it was an important turn to ethics. It was an ethics based on respect for others in his family and for their wants, wishes, and opinions.

Why Ethics?

Ethics inserts itself in human relations from the very beginning of life. There is something profoundly ethical about maternal care, grounded as it is in an abiding responsibility for this new life that supersedes any other motive or concern. It is an exercise in oneness: mother and baby as a unity, from which the self emerges.

As development proceeds, there is a process of internalization. The baby takes in the world, beginning with the parents, and gradually constitutes a self. Existence is owed to these parents, not because anyone has asked to be born, but because it is their loving connectedness that sustains life, shapes vision, and anticipates becoming. This care creates a lifelong obligation. Hence, what we call morality, the ethics of living, is founded in the encounter of child and parent at the outset of life.

Development is not without its deep ambivalences. "I hate you, Mommy/Daddy" is a common refrain from young children frustrated with being denied some anticipated pleasure or want. Every child wants to be free from control and longs for the very autonomy and richness of individuality that will later spark feelings of loneliness and anxiety. Still, if things go well enough, the result is a sense of trust, confidence in the world, respect for others, and capacity for mutuality. As such, we never fully resolve our debt to the other.

There is much to atone for in life. I could list a few that affect me personally:

- the health professionals who have betrayed patients and harmed them
- the profit made from a land of opportunity stolen from the indigenous people who were here before European colonialism
- the enjoyment of visits to landmarks and beautiful cities created by slave labor
- the too-comfortable life in a society that tolerates income inequality and creates opportunities for the well-off not available to the poor

Atonement, an act of reconciling with the other for whom we are entrusted to care, affirms that ethics is very much about delivering on this responsibility to others. But what does this have to do with divorce?

There is a strong sentiment in society suggesting that once one leaves a spouse and becomes "ex," there is no longer any responsibility to care. What obligations remain are only those specified by law and pragmatic necessity—child support, details regarding scheduling, and so on. It is a binary view of the world, as if ethics only applies when the two agree to be a couple and ends when they separate. This harmful misunderstanding and distortion animate many divorce battles. Both parties are deeply offended, even revolted by the ethical mismanagement of their relationship during and after the breakup. Whatever disenchantment existed before the breakup is magnified by the errant conduct afterward.

This binary categorization of ethics—"I am responsible" or "I am not responsible"—does not fit the realities of human interconnection. We are always responsible, and there is no escaping this duty to care. When politicians refuse to accept responsibility for serious ethical lapses, they add to the problem of a society that sees ethics as the domain of the guilty rather than of the responsible. Our responsibility is socially constructed, but it cannot be separated from the basic encounter of parent and infant that is steeped in ethics.

Of course, there is a time in life that concern for others does not rationally apply. Toddlers, for example, are immune from caring about the impact of their actions. They do not have the emotional maturity to understand consequences. This capacity will, however, develop in time. A child of five years, in contrast, often becomes sad if they feel they have hurt someone unintentionally. This emergence of empathy coincides with the development of morality. It builds on a rudimentary conscience but has more to do with sympathetic identification with the other founded in love and attachment than internalized self-judgment.[7]

This evolving concern for others is an integral part of human relations and is essential for being able to have a healthy adult partnership. Here, I also follow the line of thinking of philosopher Emmanuel Levinas, who includes ethics as an absolute part of human subjectivity.[8] It is present before we even know it is there.

What I find useful about Levinas's take on the human project is that he sees something beyond pleasure seeking or attachment. Of course, it is important that marriages, for example, meet relational needs for intimacy, an important aspect of attachment, but there is something more fundamental. Levinas would say that we are hostage to the responsibility for the other and that this precedes any rights or privileging of self-gratification.

I have in mind a young man who, in his youth, acted callously, self-indulgently, and defiantly until it led to a decade-long schism with his adoptive parents. He had no sense of ethics. Drugs, alcohol, and petty crime were his passion. Along the way, however, he met a young woman, with whom he connected, and after several years, she became pregnant with twins. She had a decent and stable job. It fell to him to look after the babies. The transformation was remarkable. He could not escape his absolute responsibility for the life of these children. In discovering this responsibility, he found ethics. At its core, the parent's devotion and acceptance of overriding responsibility for their baby is inescapably ethical. He changed, matured, and reconciled with his parents.

If ever there was a time that ego interests should be put aside, divorce would seem to be such a moment. Ironically, perhaps, it is often a phase where people tend to be most self-centered and least able to accept responsibility for the other. This is natural. Divorce occurs in a bed of hurt, anger, disappointment, and especially disillusionment. It is not a relational context where one is driven to kind

---

[7] Sagan, E., (1988), *Four contributions to the theory of the superego, guilt, and conscience: Freud, women, and morality: The psychology of good and evil*, Basic Books.

[8] Levinas, E., (1985), *Ethics and infinity: Conversations with Philippe Nemo* (R. A. Cohen, Trans.), Duquesne University Press.

thoughts or charitable actions toward an ex-partner who has caused such life disruption and wounding. However, those who are most self-possessed, blaming, oblivious to the children's needs, and undermining of the ex-partner are the same individuals who suffer the most despair and who are most prone to high-conflict divorce.

This is certainly not to say that taking responsibility for the other is easy even at the best of times. We are not selfless creatures and can be forgiven for not wanting to represent the interests of another who has hurt, upset, and deeply disappointed us. Nonetheless, many problems in divorce can be traced to a radical severing with the other. It is then a much smaller step to deem this person a foe and take actions that would only be saved for an enemy.

Of course, it can be a struggle to be caring of others. It does not always come easily. This is especially true in divorce. However, those who take defensive refuge in their wounds, bitter disillusionment, resentment, and blame miss the heart of what justice is about. It will never be achieved through vengeance, even if legally sanctioned. Ethical reflection, though, focusing on remembering one's debt to the other, even one who has hurt or denied us, allows for real justice to emerge. It can reduce suffering and increase hope when there is conscious awareness that one's debt to the other survives divorce. It is not a sign of weakness or lack of closure. Rather, it is an indication of an ethical approach that does not make an exception of an ex-spouse.

Conceptualizing divorce pathology as an ethical problem rather than one reducible to psychopathology or a wicked character can serve to focus efforts on overcoming hurt and anger as well as offering a constructive framework for the divorce process. Mental health professionals frequently see divorcing patients who are entrenched in the divorce, holding on to grievances and rejecting any responsibility toward the ex-spouse. The lack of an ethical framework leaves the individual focusing on attribution of fault, for which there is never an answer, rather than adaptively viewing the divorce as a reworking of responsibilities to others, including, in particular, the ex-partner.

Simply helping people manage their endless conflicts does help but does not amount to a longer-term solution. Children are dragged down by such chronic divorces, and the courts are burdened by the volume and intensity these couples place demand of the family justice system.

In what I frame as a return to ethics, we would look for the following vital achievements in a divorce involving children:

1. Acknowledge and accept the very real guilt and shame one feels for what went wrong in the marriage and the harm done to the other.
2. Examine all the ways that this culpability applies personally, even when one is sure that they are the victim and did nothing wrong to deserve this sad fate.
3. Reflect on one's moral record, the extent to which responsibility to others has been a guiding factor in life.
4. Meaningfully confront the tendencies to selfishness, exploitation, self-preoccupation, and self-protection over and above caring for the people who should matter most in life.
5. Change the inner conversation from what will make one happy to what one must do to discharge our duty to others, including, in particular, the ex-spouse.
6. Reflect on what is correct about what the ex-spouse is saying rather than looking for ways to counter and refute.
7. Monitor the impact of this new way of thinking. See how it affects the family situation and what benefits occur. Dig deep to experience divorce as a solution guided by respect and not contrary to caring for the ex-partner, even when the breakup was initiated by the other.

It takes resolve to care for someone in marriage and even more resolve, as well as courage, to do so after divorce. Marriage takes a capacity for mature dependence, an ability to maintain intimacy in spite of disappointments and in the face of inevitable loss at the end of life. Divorce frees one from having to confront the fundamental ethic of marriage—"till death do us part." I think of how many people explain their disenchantment and subsequent divorce based on the realization that they did not want to grow old with that person. There is a responsibility to love, which only increases over the years. How many people bail on their partner, frightened by the prospect of aging and loss? This is an example of how the finitude of life enters into the couple narrative and can inspire greater intimacy or divorce.

Although my evidence is clinical, the crisis of narcissism, so often referred to today, is in many ways a flight from responsibility for others. If divorce is conceptualized as a means to free us from this duty to care, then it is misunderstood. There is no easy exit. Indeed, the responsibility to the other must survive divorce in order for children to be raised. Those who eschew all responsibility for their ex-partner, who are willing to treat them as a stranger, if not an enemy, are unlikely to love successfully the next time.

Conclusion

In this age when people often meet outside the context of family and community, love seems to be the main motivation for partnering and as a basis to start a family. This accounts for its power to move human society but also for the fragility of these relationships, especially those founded on illusory lines that have not been tested by the exigencies of life. Add children to the mix, and it will take more than fanciful, romantic love to shoulder the emotional demand on the couple.

A surfeit of illusion often predicts divorce pathology, including high conflict. This is perhaps why narcissism as a character trait features so large in the self-help and professional literature trying to make sense of the high-conflict mind-set. The grandiosity, entitlement, and fantasy of self-sufficiency of problematic narcissism is itself an illusion that conceals shame over inadequacy and insecurity in the connection to others. There is a fundamental denial of responsibility for the other in the solipsism of narcissism, which makes it very much an ethical problem.

Ethics is founded in the primary encounter of infinite responsibility between parent and baby. This fundamental relationship of care informs other close encounters, including those with intimate partners, even following couple separation when there are children to rear.

Illusion mixes well with love, potentiating love's protective and inspiring powers. Although inevitably modulated over time, illusion should never be fully dismantled or prematurely crushed, undermining the sense of security and cohesion of the growing self. In narcissistic pathology, illusion is excessive, supplants love, and eschews the capacity for trust and intimacy. In its stead emerges a grandiosity that fundamentally denies otherness and can only visualize itself. Understandably, then, excessive narcissism in one or both parties in a union amplifies the risk for high-conflict divorce. There is too much shame and underlying inferiority to tolerate relationship breakdown. The stain of failure cannot be mourned.

The goal of "disillusionment therapy" is the turn to ethics. This requires an appreciation of the intricate link between early attachments and the capacity for ethics. Breaches in trust and safety, experiences that left the subject feeling alone, wronged, insecure, and anxious, can be the source of destructiveness when the marriage repeats the same pattern or when it traumatically ends. The therapy requires a form of reverse engineering to trace destructiveness to its roots in disillusionment and, in the working through, to chart a path for ethics to return.

6

Those Who Cannot Love
Destructive Personalities

Some people, especially those in high-conflict divorces, contend that their ex-partner is evil. In rare cases, this is true, although the term should be limited to highly destructive behavior, to which the majority would experience a sense of horror. In other words, it is hard to define *evil* without resorting to moralism. At the same time, one viscerally knows when confronted by its effrontery to everything decent and human. It is important, though, to clarify that everything destructive in human relations is not evil, although everything evil is certainly destructive.

Negative personality structures come in a variety of styles. The most flagrant is the sociopathic or psychopathic. This is the form most likely to reflect evil. Others include narcissistic, paranoid, and sadistic personalities. Whether evil or destructive for other reasons, there is one overriding attribute: the inability to love. This makes marriage especially risky for such individuals and, almost always, complicates divorce.

Psychopathy has traditionally been understood as an absence or even a disease of conscience. Film portrayals are often chilling, such as Hannibal Lecter, played by Anthony Hopkins in the 1991 film *The Silence of the Lambs*.[1] In reality, psychopathy or sociopathy (I use the two interchangeably) is on a continuum. We are all capable of deviousness, but in some cases, ruthless deviousness and cold exploitation describe a way of living and relating. Lack of empathy is profound; self-serving rationalizations for abominable actions and behavior are typical. The chilling lack of love can be devastating for an unwitting, often naïve partner who finds out too late to avoid the adverse impact. These are the real sociopaths.

---

[1] Demme, J., (Director), (2001), *The silence of the lambs* [Film], MGM Home Entertainment.

The current psychiatric lexicon combines these traits under the heading of "antisocial personality disorder." However, not all psychopaths are overtly antisocial or have histories of conduct problems. Nonetheless, they lie, manipulate, and deceive, although superficially they can be socially smooth and even beguiling.

In "Outsiders to Love: The Psychopathic Character and Dilemma," Elizabeth Howell views the psychopath as employing the power of deceit in a world that is geared to trust.[2] These individuals function outside love but have a knack of interacting with the needs, desires, and fears of others. They insinuate themselves into domestic situations but exploit, violate trust, and easily break norms of social behavior. Their ruthlessness is always shocking.

In a world where people meet online for the sole purpose of gauging romantic interest, the risks are higher that someone will meet and become involved with a sociopathic personality. Charm; pseudo-authenticity; and an energetic, appealing façade opens doors with others. Once on the inside, however, it is not long before a diabolical intentionality becomes obvious.

Jerome and Sylvia

Jerome felt desperate when he came for help in his broken marriage to Sylvia. They shared a son of two years. Jerome related that he had fallen deeply for Sylvia, thrilled to be in her vivacious company. He considered her the most wonderful person in the world. He felt passionate about her. They were married one and a half years after meeting online. He felt blessed and considered his union made in heaven.

In retrospect, Jerome saw red flags, but in the umbra of her glow, he skipped over any misgivings. In particular, Sylvia had no contact with her family of origin. She explained this away glibly and without detail. It was only much later, when he dug deeper and eventually made contact, that he learned that her mother and father had cut off contact with her out of self-protection.

Sylvia had been a troublesome child. Her parents had to be constantly vigilant. She found many ways to cause upset and pain to those closest to her. As a teenager and young adult, she stole from her parents' bank account, forged a parent's signature on purchases, abused drugs, shoplifted, and got into regular trouble with school authorities.

---

[2] Howell, E., (2018), Outsider to love: the psychopathic character and dilemma, *Contemporary Psychoanalysis*, 54(1), 17–39.

Sylvia would raise her parents' hopes, only to dash them repeatedly, until they could not tolerate it any longer. Although they suffered guilt over their decision, her parents decided that severing contact was the only way to cope.

Yet the Sylvia whom Jerome met had none of those characteristics. She was charming, open, and insightful about him, if not herself. He had no idea that this was her background. She was intelligent, held a prestigious job, and did not fit the picture of anyone antisocial.

Following their son's birth, however, Jerome saw a different side of Sylvia. She hated being pregnant, giving birth, and being a mother. There were ugly scenes that arose out of nowhere. She accused him of infidelity and erupted especially during moments that he felt were special between himself and their baby. It was as if Sylvia could not allow him to have anything sacred in his life. Her envious attacks were worsened by the demands of nursing their infant. She resented his lack of functioning breasts. Soon after, she refused to nurse, and they switched to bottle-feeding to even the score. Sylvia demanded that Jerome get up at night and claimed that she was too depressed and anxious to tend to their son.

Much to Jerome's chagrin and dread, Sylvia began to regularly leave their home. She insisted that she needed space to breathe and could not cope. He realized that she was going to bars and partying and came home late, saturated in alcohol. Jerome had to take leave from work to care for their child. The marriage came to a vicious end after one fight when Jerome expressed frustration at Sylvia's lack of commitment to him and childcare. She came up behind him and delivered a sharp blow to his head. Nonetheless, it was Sylvia who summoned the police.

Sylvia's version of events put the blame squarely on Jerome, whom she accused of infidelity, assault, and bullying control. Her accusations became bizarre, alleging outlandish and cruel acts of vengeance. She had absolutely no regard for Jerome or their child but might be brought to tears by an injured animal. In this regard, Sylvia was not completely cold and ruthless, but whatever goodness she could muster was never directed at family, whether her family of origin or her family with Jerome.

Sylvia was most certainly on the psychopathy spectrum. She had a deceitfulness and capacity for menace that was shocking and destructive. In her mind, it was a matter of survival, but it was others who were in fact in jeopardy. She had no sense of the cumulative harm she was causing to her child and the people who cared for her. The divorce, as is routinely the case, mirrored the marriage. Her accusations bordered on the bizarre and reflected a deeply sadistic way of thinking that was projected onto the hapless Jerome.

In this regard, Sylvia accused Jerome of perverse behavior and called the police and child protection services on multiple occasions. She fashioned "truth" to achieve her legal ends. Her hostility was not defensive; it was a means to an end, which was to gain total control over their child, even though she had no actual interest or capability in parenting. She demanded custody and open mobility to move anywhere she chose in the world.

The incapacity to love is a troubling phenomenon, especially when it involves someone with antisocial traits. Incapacity to love, however, comes in various forms and usually features the inclination to divert blame entirely and attribute to the other the negative traits actually displayed by the individual in question. Morality is viewed as weakness, and empathy is absent. If there is underlying emotional trauma from earlier life, it is reenacted, with the other serving as victim. There is a sadistic intent, which means that the other's suffering is welcomed and encourages more of the same.

At the same time, psychopathic personalities can arise from diverse backgrounds with little antecedent causes. Sometimes their cruelty and sadism are apparent in childhood but not always. There is a continuum of psychopathy with those in the divorce context, who are often less antisocial than scheming, superficial, Machiavellian, and self-serving.

John and Melissa

John's wife, Melissa, was unable to bear his browbeating domination, cruelty, and constant complaint that she was not earning her keep. He resented having to support her, even though they shared a child with special needs who required extra attention. It was an impossible situation for Melissa, whose tolerance and energy were drained by having a special-needs child on the one hand and a debasing husband on the other. He wanted to spoil everything for her.

Melissa had a strong capacity for love; she benefited from two loving parents and caring siblings whom she adored. In contrast to

Melissa, John had been given up for adoption as an infant but was raised in an orphanage and then in foster homes. Adoption never happened in his case. There was certainly some kindness during his childhood but never love. At the same time, John was smart and versatile; he could adapt and learn. He paid for his own university and graduated with a professional degree that led to a thriving career. There was so much to admire in John. Yet, unfortunately, he could be brutal, caustic, demanding, and bitterly attacking. Although generous at times, it would only be on his terms, and he was mainly transactional with everyone. He expected Melissa to earn whatever money he gave her by way of service, as if she was an employee.

John was damaged by the lack of love, and he could not transcend it. However, he was not psychopathic or even antisocial. He was simply severely limited by an incapacity to love. It was complicated, though, because he had married Melissa and, one can presume, aspired to be her loving partner and to gain a loving family himself. His treatment of her, however, was deeply offensive and bordered on violent. Physical intimacy was very unsatisfactory and selfishly oriented. He had a fondness for pornography that allowed him to avoid a live person who might want his love and support. Of course, he could not acknowledge any of this, which made remediation impossible. Melissa felt like his slave at times and lived in fear of his constant rebukes, physical intimidation, and pressure.

When John proved irritable and punitive with their son, himself burdened with learning challenges, Melissa could not take any more. She felt she had to leave for her child's sake. The marriage broke apart, with Melissa taking refuge in a shelter until she could arrange temporary support through the court. John was enraged and turned vengeful. I suspect that he put Melissa in the camp of the ungrateful and exploitative who wanted to bleed him dry. He saw it as another "mother" who refused to love him. This was unfortunate for Melissa because she had tried hard to love John and would have welcomed any acknowledgment from him that he was struggling to deal with his deficits. She only left to survive and to protect their child from continuous exposure to his father.

As much as John treated Melissa abysmally, he likely wanted her to survive his attacks and prove that she really did love him. Sadly, this is a story told many times, where someone born into unfavorable circumstances unconsciously puts their adult partner in the same miserable, loveless human environment in which they were raised. Melissa did understand what John had experienced, but as much as she tried to prove her commitment, he was never convinced. It was his targeting of their son, however, that broke her resolve. What she might have been prepared to tolerate on her own terms, she was not prepared to accept when it came to their child.

As Melissa anticipated, John continued to be vindictive. He accused her of manipulating and exploiting his goodwill, perpetrating a fraud, and planning all along to bail on him. He could not acknowledge how hard he had been on his partner and why she feared what it could mean for their son.

John's vengeance was never ending. Melissa had to rely on the court to guarantee financial support and to assess whether John could spend positive time with their son without supervision due to his fomenting bitterness. It was an ignoble situation for a proud man who had overcome so much in his life.

John's accomplishments, however, did not generalize to developing a self-reflective capacity, or what is often referred to as the ability to mentalize.[3] He had great difficulty appreciating what others might be feeling or, for that matter, what he was feeling. This very negatively affected his capacity to have a successful personal relationship, especially one dedicated to love and belonging. We can only speculate about John's early life, but shifting caregivers and lack of loving intimacy would have certainly affected his self-development. He did not have the benefit of a mother preoccupied with his care, attuned to his needs, and lending her mind to help him learn about his own. Reflective function is very much tied to meaningful attachments in early childhood. Mothers and fathers mirror what their children feel, and this fosters a reflective capacity. In other words, it is how children learn to think in a personal or emotional sense.

Hostility and threatening, cruel aggression would explode out of John. He had no trust at these moments, and his faith in human goodness and love was weak, if not absent. It would take him a long time to recover from these episodes. He needed Melissa to take concrete steps to appease him. Her words, soothing for the most part, would often not be enough. He would then send her on difficult errands and disrupt her schedule to force her to accommodate his needs.

There was no way out for Melissa other than to leave the union, which sadly only confirmed for John that he was destined to live in

---

[3] Fonagy, P., (2001), *The growing consensus in developmental theory: A review of attachment theory and psychoanalysis*, Other Press.

a world without love. His sense of persecution blocked any capacity for insight into himself and the impact of his behavior on his wife and child.

John is an example of someone unable to love, principally because he was never loved as a child. It does not mean, however, that everyone with a bad beginning is destined not to know love or to be aware of their own minds and those of others. It has something to do with constitutional factors, such as temperament and inherent resilience. In this regard, John reveals the complexity of personality development: street smart and very adept in business but at the same time inept, dysfunctional, and very destructive in personal intimacy. It underscores that to be autonomous and self-regulating, it helps to have had a healthy, good-enough dependency in early life.

It is not surprising that researchers are making important connections between neurobiology and psychological development. High stress levels in babies due to unsupportive conditions, for example, create excessively high levels of cortisol, a stress hormone. This affects the development of the orbitofrontal cortex of the brain, which is where emotional regulation processes are situated.[4] Such a background creates a psychological liability to states of alarm and stress. The emotional centers of the subcortex signal urgency and threat, which fails to be modulated by the adjacent cortex, leading to the type of reactions that in evidence in John. It is not surprising that John drank alcohol excessively and ate poorly for much of his life. These addictive tendencies often reflect unmet emotional needs, affect dysregulation, and a desperate search for self-control when there was no other whose loving presence could be guaranteed, used, and internalized in early childhood.[5] John's severe mistreatment of Melissa, effectively treating her as unreliable and absent, repeated this damaging and cumulatively traumatic early history. He could believe in food and alcohol's salutary benefits and control its presence. It was the human world in which he had been permanently disillusioned.

Being in love is a wonderful state of human fulfillment. Memories of intense intimacy, emotional, communicative, and sexual, remain

[4] Gerhardt, S., (2015), *Why love matters: How affection shapes a baby's brain* (2nd ed.), Routledge.

[5] Taipale, J., (2017), Controlling the uncontrollable: Self-regulation and the dynamics of addiction, *Scandinavian Psychoanalytic Review*, 40(1), 29–42.

etched in our minds for a lifetime. This creates profound gratitude to those who choose to love us, increase feelings of self-worth and esteem, and buoy a sense of optimism about life in general. This is very different from infatuations that do not survive inevitable disappointments or transactional "love," where anything positive is conditional, with strings attached. Mature love, in contrast, infiltrates life, fills in the cracks, and allows for deepening interest in the other and the other's ambitions and interests. Love helps get outside one's self.

Those with an incapacity to love are forever locked into their own needs, with very limited appreciation of the other. The formula for getting along is transactional—you scratch my back, and I'll scratch yours—and there is always careful accounting of the perceived balance. Imbalance, whether alleged or real, leads to scathing protest and retaliation. Inevitably, such individuals start to feel ripped off and abused. There is a paranoid orientation. The truth is often the opposite, as they often misuse and mistreat the one supposed to be loved. As in the example of John and Melissa, the partner is often a caring person who tries to provide the remedy for the other's aggrieved, emotionally deprived, and damaging childhood.

Sometimes the incapacity to love is less an emotional deficit than due to misguided and distorted fantasies that are idealized and unrealistic. Love needs to mature, deepen, and become more realistic to meet the challenges of these important relationships. Love that is better described as infatuation, more fantasy than tried and tested reality, collapses with the weight of real-life demands and problems. I noted this previously and its correlation with high conflict in divorce.

Susanne

Susanne sought help after her most recent relationship ended dramatically after only 18 months of being together. Sadly, there was a string of brief failed liaisons in her relationship history. The men she chose seemed to be of a type: superior in intelligence, superior in looks, but who gave very little and were entirely self-absorbed. They accepted her but on their terms, never meeting her halfway. This habitual surrender, putting men on a pedestal, seemed more like worship than love. Curiously, the relationships crumbled whenever the men broke ranks with this role and seemed vulnerable or fragile. Susanne could not tolerate the real person. She was infatuated instead with an ideal, an icon or fetish, that magically insulated her from painful realities and memories that she struggled to forget.

Susanne was raised with her older brother in a comfortable city suburb. Her father was a brilliant, charismatic, erudite university professor in the humanities. He seemed so much smarter than her stay-at-home mother, and as Susanne grew, she saw how little her parents shared. Susanne liked to think that she was her father's favorite, but in truth, she ached for his acceptance and only felt glimmers when he seemed to notice her. He was self-absorbed, insensitive, and probably narcissistic.

Susanne's mother was clearly the more available and warmer parent. However, she seemed diminished next to Susanne's dashing, powerful father. Susanne fought against identifying with her mother and disparaged her. Susanne was sure that she could have been what her father needed when compared to her lackluster mother. Underneath, however, Susanne felt lingering guilt with her mother and a conflicted sense of femininity. She leveraged her self-esteem on the love and recognition of a father who was illusory.

As an adult, Susanne was sure that only a gifted, superior man could fulfill her and give her a purpose in life. When on his arm, she felt complete and blessed to be in his arc of greatness. However, any hint of weakness, emotional need, or fallibility in the man filled her with contempt. She wanted to love and be loved, at least consciously, but whenever any of these men showed actual affection and care, she felt panicky, if not revolted. Indeed, she was better off when they continued to be self-absorbed and unavailable, as much as this also frustrated her.

In therapy, Susanne found herself focusing on her mother, who had gotten short shrift in many ways. Susanne's hypercompetitiveness with her mother and devaluation of her cut her off from the one parent who was emotionally available and responsive.

During one session, Susanne reported a dream. She was on an elegant sailing boat with a tall mast and blossoming sails. It was a boat built by someone special. The sea was calm, and the sun shone warmly, like a commercial for the Caribbean. Suddenly, the boat began to disintegrate. There seemed to be no explanation. The sails collapsed, and gashes opened up in the hull. She was soon in the water, witnessing the remnants of the boat disappear beneath the surface. Susanne recalled feeling deeply alone and miserable, as if her world had crumbled, but became aware that she was floating effortlessly. By all accounts she should be drowning, she thought, but wasn't.

It was the sea, *le mer* in her native French, but by association, *la mère*, mother, who caught our attention. Susanne was perhaps representing something about her mother's holding that she could not admit consciously or at least value.

> SUSANNE: I want to say that I feel badly about how I treated my mother, but there is part of me that sees her as weak and useless. Why did she put up with my father's self-centeredness? I saw him as such a hero, the best.
>
> ANALYST: You gave up love for the image of power and wonder how to find your way back.
>
> SUSANNE: It was so confusing. Mama always seemed to be in the background. She was content with her role. I remember her putting me to bed at night; it was very nice, warm. I knew she loved me, but I still wanted my father in the morning. I fought being her daughter, just wanted to be Papa's.
>
> ANALYST: You insisted on your love for your father, your specialness in his eyes, not to have to face how illusory this love was for you.
>
> SUSANNE: The boat just disintegrated. I knew that I couldn't test my father, so I never did. He was more like a dream than a person. My mother was so ordinary next to him.

Susanne's capacity for love was stifled by her fixation on a narcissistic father who drew the limelight his way. She had an understanding, caring mother but clung to her father as an ideal of power and mastery, much as she clung to impossible men, at least until any of them showed signs of loving her. In this regard, her self-esteem was linked to a powerful, idealized, masculine icon. It was emotionally precarious and left her feeling empty-handed whenever the current man in her life tumbled off the pedestal of her making. Susanne's identification with her mother had been tarnished by this false comparison of her parents: a mother who was the backbone of the family but was devalued, contrasted with a self-possessed father who enjoyed his own reflection too much and required his children and spouse to applaud him.

It was in discovering the real, authentic mother that Susanne was able to psychologically repair the link to her. There was a rapprochement in Susanne's mental world that set the stage for a firmer acceptance of herself. She could then recover her self-love that had been emptied into her idealized father. In finding her mother, Susanne also found a missing part of herself. It was also an anchor for ethics.

Individuals like Susanne love the partner at the expense of themselves. Indeed, the self is diminished in favor of the other, which creates a major risk when these relationships fail.

There is another form of narcissistic love when the individual adores themselves totally at the expense of the other. Instead of being reliant on others, especially the kind of reliance found in love, this type of person pushes away from dependence and exploits others solely to affirm their own greatness or to achieve selfish ends. The capacity for love is greatly impaired.

Melanie and Stanley

Melanie had fallen hard for Stanley. He was a triumphant figure, an astute businessman who seemed smarter than everyone else and more interesting as well. She had left an unhappy marriage, in which she was mainly bored and unfulfilled. Nonetheless, Melanie had a young daughter, and with a promising career, she had no concerns regarding her capacity to cope and even thrive on her own. Her attraction to Stanley was founded on how interesting she found him. Her biggest fear was being bored, and she knew that this would not happen with him.

Stanley had already made a lot of money in his career. He was also divorced, with two sons. It had been a fractious divorce, but Stanley achieved his goal of paying his ex-wife much less than she wanted while sharing the care of their growing family. Melanie joined forces with Stanley, which meant a family of three children when they were all together. The two boys were older than Melanie's daughter.

It was not long before Melanie was pregnant with the couple's own child, another daughter for her, who unfortunately revealed early signs of mild autism. Melanie showed her usual resolve and confidence. She was prepared to handle whatever hurdle this represented, and she was true to her word. Stanley, however, was a different matter.

He blamed Melanie for their child's problems and held her responsible. He could not accept having a child with special needs and attributed their autistic daughter's behavior to Melanie's poor parenting. Melanie was shocked at this development. Whatever efforts she made to engage him as a father for this child failed. He retreated into his offspring from the first union, cutting off Melanie's two natural children: her daughter from her first marriage and the daughter with Stanley. He idealized his sons from his first marriage and sang praises of their perfection, despite having ruthlessly devalued his first wife. He was pitiless in his cold disregard of the "unimportant" children in his eyes, and Melanie saw a very different side to Stanley that she abhorred. At the same time, she did nothing to protect either herself or the two children who were Stanley's target. When she finally accepted psychological help, she was depleted and in a weakened position.

Stanley's two older children rallied around their father, probably as much due to intimidation as desire. They understood their father's severely conditional love. He reveled in their accomplishments but could be painfully dismissive when let down. He had nothing to do with his sons' mother and treated her coldly, even though they were in a coparenting arrangement.

Melanie's idealization of Stanley wore thin but defied logic and common sense. She stayed with him much too long, and this affected her and the family. Finally, when Melanie was anonymously sent photos of Stanley draped over some woman, she ended the union. As occurred in his first marriage, Stanley paid as little as possible, and Melanie felt that fighting him would be more pain than profit. She was simply happy to get away.

Stanley serves as an example of someone in the personality-disordered range. He was incapable of establishing an authentic, caring relationship. Stanley was immersed in his own delusion of superiority, which he extended to his children, as long as they made him look good. He was an inveterate liar and exaggerator who created a fiction that fit the moment. His children, it seemed, had a good relationship with their mothers and understood their father's foibles. As a wealthy businessman, however, he controlled them financially, and for the most part, they fell into line. He was an intrusive man, transgressive to the core, who was extremely untrustworthy and fundamentally dishonest. There was no ethics nor any path that would have led to ethics.

Stanley was unable to love. All the essential capacities to love were notably absent in his case: a lack of basic trust; incapacity to depend on or need others; incapability of gratitude; poorly integrated morality or regard for truth; inability to admit mistakes; faultiness or failure; and an inability to respect others; their autonomy; and their right to secure boundaries.

Those like Stanley, however, are a minority. Nonetheless, this type of person can wreak havoc on children and adults alike. Their willingness to act unethically can be difficult to handle because the world works on trust and accountability. The lack of shame reduces the impact that authorities, laws, and ethics might exert in controlling such individuals or encouraging them to control themselves. Pathological narcissism and sociopathy limit the capacity to care, empathize, and even to want to do the right thing.

Ticking Biological Clock: High-Conflict Risk

As much as people want to live creative, fruitful, and meaningful lives, there is a tendency to equate this more general ideal with bearing children. It is not surprising that physiological fertility and psychological fruitfulness become linked. When having a baby is the main motive, mature love and couple commitment are likely to be afterthoughts.

It is a frequently troublesome combination, therefore, when a woman is in her middle to late 30s, wants a family, and finds temporary inspiration in a man she might idealize for as long as it takes to get pregnant. The man follows suit, either passively or actively. They speak from the first date about shared values of family, honesty, respect, and other cardinal virtues that suggest a wonderful partner. None of this, though, is ever tested, but for the moment, it is thoroughly accepted as truth.

If there is a union or marriage, it is very brief. Very often, the relationship collapses when it is tested by the demands of pregnancy, delivery, and early childcare. There is no getting around the heightened need of new parents for emotional and physical support. Without any demonstrated track record of meeting each other's needs, the relationship often fails as the two sides square off: a mother with an infant or very young child whom she is breastfeeding and a new father afraid that the woman will use her maternal leverage to oust him as a valid coparent. It does not take long for both participants to feel maligned, deceived, and let down. They have little or no capacity to communicate or work together. Clashes come to define the child's early life. These are often acutely antagonistic and disequilibrating. If either or both have a history of major disillusionment or past seismic events, even if not consciously elaborated, then destructiveness can potentiate the struggle and propel it into the high-conflict range.

Barbara and Jeff

Barbara was blown away by the well-spoken, handsome Jeff, whose big brain and six-pack abdomen were a winning combination. She easily accepted his explanation that he had decided on a career change but had yet to find his true calling. He had worked as public relations consultant in a large firm, but this had ended 18 months previously. Jeff did not declare to Barbara that he had been fired for an impetuous office romance that led to business expense improprieties and other unethical behavior. There was no forthcoming employment reference, and Jeff was trying to find a job that would not inquire about his work history. It was proving difficult.

Barbara did not ask many questions. She accepted Jeff at face value. His standoffish family was a little scary, but she very much wanted to meet someone who would be as interested as her in starting a family. Jeff seemed more than willing. He was charming and compliant and spoke about being "in transition" with his career. He concealed his past misconduct.

In contrast to Jeff, Barbara was well employed. She made a good living working in a trendy public relations and marketing firm, where her creativity and spirit were valued. However, Barbara did not have the best relationship history. She had little capacity to read behavior or to intuit the merits and personal values of someone based on her experience with them. She also had an impulsive side, and her inclination was not to go into depth.

Moreover, Barbara naïvely equated image with reality and believed what she was told, as if people were always equivalent to what they said they were. She did not learn easily from experience and had a particular blind spot when it came to romantic relationships. Barbara was raised by her mother and stepfather. Her birth father had left her mother when Barbara was an infant, and she had never met the man. There was never any interest in looking for him either. Her mother and stepfather had twin sons when Barbara was three years old. Barbara felt like the odd one out, at least until she had her own baby. She finally felt that she belonged.

Jeff promised big but delivered much less in the end. His social judgment was faulty, and his behavior was inconsistent. He became defensive when challenged and engaged in battling text wars with Barbara, who participated too willingly. There was never any resolution or improvement. When their son was born, Jeff was effectively gone from Barbara's life, offering neither financial nor reliable childcare support.

At the same time, there was a delightful child resulting from this encounter, and Barbara was thrilled. The single-parent life did not prove to be so doable, however, and she struggled without Jeff's support. One positive outcome for Barbara was a baby totally dependent on her for its very survival. She felt this responsibility deeply, and what previous psychotherapies could not accomplish, the presence of her child achieved. It was a call to ethics.

Domination, Submission, Sadomasochism, and Problems in Loving

Marriages take a large dose of mutuality to work, and this capacity to recognize and ally positively and meaningfully with others begins during childhood. If the parents socialize the child through age-appropriate negotiation and reasonable limits, then the capacity for mutuality tends to evolve. In contrast, a child socialized through fear, coercion, and threats of abandonment, even if this is more covert than expressly violent, has no experience of mutuality or love, for that matter. Instead, this child internalizes the dynamics of power, threat, and control as a way to negotiate with others, especially those on whom they would otherwise depend.

Sadomasochism is precisely this fixation to power in the service of control, whether the inclination is to surrender or dominate. Each position establishes a dynamic of power as the way in which the relationship is negotiated. It avoids the painful possibility of loss and mourning through the locus of power. This can become sexualized but is more often observed in the way relationships function. Sadomasochism as a way of relating is inherently destructive because it overrides any of the core values that committed intimate relationships need: mutuality, empathy, recognition, and respect. There is an attack on human trust and generosity that is replaced by the discourse of power, aggression, and often abuse, which is the testament to power and control.

Dennis and Lila

Dennis was raised in a cold, empty household apart from his father's alcohol-fueled rants and discipline that were infrequent but always terrifying. In retrospect, Dennis imagined that his father was severely frustrated by his very pragmatic wife, who seemed unable to provide physical affection or comfort. Dennis felt that he was in the same boat. He could not recall being touched by his mother. His father, however, touched him mainly by hitting him, and did so fairly regularly. The sharp crack of his father's belt and being pushed and shoved curiously felt better sometimes than the empty coldness of his mother's gaze and her seeming aversion to physical closeness. It was very confusing and disillusioning: a mother who could not hug and a father who took out his violent frustrations on him.

Dennis married Lila, a woman with a temperament that resembled his father's more than his mother's. This made sense, as nothing could be more painful than the emptiness and lack of affection he had endured growing up. However, it still represented echoes of past traumas and offered no exit or resolution. Lila's volatile side was not easy for Dennis to handle. There was an implicit pleasure, though, a glow of warmth and love that came over him when she would become physical and attack him. He would cower, but this hid the erotic charge of the moment.

When Dennis and Lila had a child, there was a noticeable shift in their dynamic. She became focused on the baby and was noticeably calmer, much less willing to engage with Dennis in their usual violent foreplay. The old violence dynamic ended abruptly for Lila, but Dennis experienced a frightening aloneness that scared him with its intensity. It was worse than anything he had ever consciously felt. He found it intolerable.

What had begun as a minor interest in beer after his work week or on holidays became a more frequent habit. Dennis felt constantly aggrieved, and his temper flared, often in front of their child. This led to sharp marital conflicts and a wife who demanded that he grow up and start acting like a parent. In his view, Lila had withdrawn completely, turning from a partner into a variant of his mother, who had no interest in him whatsoever. In Lila's view, he was an immature, selfish man who refused to accept that their lives had changed and that they had to change with it.

Dennis had no sense of love unless the word itself was prefaced by another qualifier: punishing love, beating love, controlling or dictatorial love. He fought with Lila and attempted to control her or induce her to control him. They would argue incessantly. His would provoke her to yell and curse so he could feel her presence. Dennis had no capacity, it seemed, to experience Lila's presence simply in the mutual project of raising a shared and loved child. Lila became exhausted and insisted that he leave to give her a reprieve. He refused, which led to therapeutic intervention when it became evident that the problem was more psychological than legal. Nonetheless, there was an implicit threat that unless he resolved his issues, she would take legal action to end the union.

Hence, as the marriage teetered on the precipice of separation, Dennis sought psychological help. It was clear that he loved his wife and child and wanted the union to succeed. He wanted presence, not absence. As much as Dennis defensively complained about his partner's unavailability, what emerged was the degree of his silent suffering in childhood. It was a matter of "strain trauma" growing up in an empty home environment, where his needs to be touched were only met by a fiercely assaultive, drunk father who beat him for minor infractions.[6] There was huge unfairness and emptiness.

It is likely not surprising that Dennis first viewed me as either uncaring or using my dominant position against him. He had no model of mutuality to guide him. Either he would need to control me, or I would be seen as controlling him. Gradually, however, Dennis was able to internalize a sense of a therapist who was committed without being either coldly hostile or out to bully and dominate him. He had to allow for something new, and it was only from this reflective vantage point that he could perceive the reverberations of what he had experienced traumatically as a child.

What had seemed so inevitable previously gave way to a new possibility of relating that could be more respectful and mutual. Dennis recounted that in childhood, when he would go to sleep at night, he would sometimes pinch himself until it hurt. He now understood that as much as he induced pain, what he really wanted was loving connection. This need was generalized then to the marriage: His mind registered being berated, pushed, or struck as love. He realized that it would be terrible if this was passed on to his child, another generation of confusion between love and pain. He could see a new path, and this gave him hope and a route to ethics.

There is clearly a connection between mutuality and recognition. Each germinates within the early coupling of parent and baby, in

[6] Khan, M. R., (1963), The concept of cumulative trauma, *Psychoanalytic Study of the Child*, 18, 286–306.

which the child is "held" in the mind of the parent. This is the first recognition. It is a relational process that involves two people from the beginning. It initiates a developmental trajectory, in which the child becomes gradually able to recognize the subjectivity of the other. This is linked to the capacity for attunement and tolerance for the other's differences.[7]

There is no capacity to recognize ourselves unless we are the recipients of recognition from the first others. Dennis looked into his mother's eyes and saw a vacuous stare—someone going through the motions of living but deeply hidden and unavailable. In general, we need the important others in our life to recognize our subjectivity, independence, and rights as a person and, in turn, to recognize the other, partner or child, as separate and worthy as well. This must be given freely. The act of domination by an adult in a marriage or union sidesteps recognition and forces the other to bend to his or her will. The risk is too great that there would never be recognition, linked as it is to profound disillusionment and emotional injury in childhood. Otherness is therefore denied and appropriated so that it is under the whim and control of the dominator. When one has omnipotent control, loss is not a possibility.

Nonetheless, in all cases where recognition is refused and domination is the mode of relating, what cannot be controlled must be eradicated. Sometimes in very sick circumstances, this can happen for real. Again, there is no path to ethics as long as this power and control dynamic is ascendant.

It is fair to say that such individuals are extremely emotionally abusive. The term *abusive* refers to aggression, injustice, and cruelty toward another human being, whether this is physical, sexual, verbal, or emotional. The cornerstone of all abuse is the denial of the separateness of the other as a subject with their own rights, needs, feelings, and thoughts. What all forms of abuse share is the abuser's inability to ask for recognition from the other. Of course, asking is uncertain and full of vulnerability. Subjugation, turning the other into a slave or victim, precludes ever having to be recognized.

In the example of torture, the torturer's recognition is guaranteed by the violence they perpetrate against the victim. There is no need to ask for recognition. The "other" in the paradigm of domination is an object, not a subject. This applies directly to the family

---

[7] Benjamin, J., (1990), An outline of intersubjectivity, *Psychoanalytic Psychology*, 7S(Supplement), 33–46.

context. Whether the domination is of the adult or the child, the other is reduced to an object under the all-powerful control of the dominator. This removes the need to experience the passive vulnerability of wanting the other's recognition. In the sadomasochistic mind-set, this is intolerable.

As a variant, the child might not be allowed to love another parent, which is child alienation, or the partner is not allowed to live outside the total control of the dominator. In every case, the dominated are forced to serve the needs of the dominator without exception.

Alienated Children: Power and Control

Alienation is rarely conceptualized within the category of those unable to love, but I believe that this often applies to the instigating or colluding parent. It is certainly a risk factor for alienated children, whose love capacity is seriously compromised. These children are inclined to idealize the preferred parent while they denigrate the targeted parent. It is an emotional evisceration that can have lasting consequences into adulthood.

The term *alienation* refers to a subcategory of children who refuse to visit the other parent. These are not children necessarily estranged for legitimate or plausibly legitimate reasons (justified rejection). They are children whose refusal is part of a systematic dynamic in which they seek to bolster and align themselves totally with one parent to the radical exclusion and devaluation of the other (unjustified rejection).

In many ways, these children are appropriated by a parent who cannot recognize them as separate, shared, and otherwise free agents with relationships to diverse others, including both parents. At times, this can be a result of a conscious, sustained manipulation on the part of the preferred parent, but most often it occurs as an unconscious collusion between a child and a beleaguered and troubled parent. In this regard, many parents convey denigrating or alienating messages to children in high-conflict divorces, but only a minority actually become alienated. In other words, parental denigration on its own is not sufficient to cause alienation.

Current understanding favors a multifactorial family-systems model of parent-child contact problems. Each case is different, often an amalgam of realistic and unrealistic estrangement dynamics that is not clear cut or simple. The court system and the professionals who contribute continue to struggle with a rising number of severe cases.[8] It takes skilled assessors and therapists to sort out abuse versus alienation or realistic versus unrealistic estrangement. Most cases are unlikely to fall into simple categories with a clear victim and villain. Moreover, the alienating dynamic can be very hard to budge once it is established. Usually the preferred parent and child or children make a huge investment to maintain it.

What is particularly grievous about this situation is that alienation damages a child's capacity to love in the future, which is its transgenerational impact. The child's willful denunciation, rejection, and exclusion of the targeted parent is empowering, but it completely distorts and confuses love with alliance, collusion, and splitting on multiple levels. These children tyrannize the targeted parent, rejecting them for sure, but often also attacking their worth and character. It can be heartbreaking for the beleaguered parent.

Research places the incidence of alienation between 11% and 15% of cases where refusal to visit occurs in a family. Among high-conflict cases involving disputed custody and intensive court involvement, the prevalence of child alienation can rise to 20%, although severe rejection occurs in less than half.[9] In other words, only a minority of children who do not see a parent do so because they are alienated. Many will refuse to visit for other reasons.

When it happens, though, it is a family affair, with mothers or fathers serving as the preferred, aligned parent and both boys and girls voicing rejecting or refusing messages. Whereas emotionally and even physically abused children tend to cling to parents, even in the face of despicable treatment, alienated children are usually categorical in their rejection and renunciation. The targeted parent cannot win for trying. The fact that the targeted parent is rarely blameless only adds to the dilemma. What distinguishes such targeted parents, however, is not their extent of faultiness but the radical consequence

---

[8] Fidler, B., & Bala, N., (2020), Conclusion: Concepts, controversies, and conundrums of "alienation": Lessons learned in a decade and reflections on challenges ahead, *Family Court Review*, 58(2), 576–603.

[9] See Eddy, B., (2010), *Don't alienate the kids: Raising resilient children while avoiding high-conflict divorce*, HCI Press; Fidler, B. J., & Bala, N., (2010), Children resisting postseparation contact with a parent: Concepts, controversies, and conundrums, *Family Court Review*, 48, 10–47; Johnston, J. R., (2003), Children of divorce who refuse visitation, in C. Depner & J. Bray (Eds.), *Nonresidential parenting: New vistas in family living* (pp. 109–135), Sage, (original work published 1993); Johnston, J. R., (2003), Parental alignments and rejection: An empirical study of alienation in children of divorce, *Journal of the American Academy of Psychiatry and Law*, 31(2), 158–170; Wallerstein, J., & Kelly, J., (1980), *Surviving the breakup: How children and parents cope with divorce*, Basic Books.

they face, which is either major reluctance or outright refusal to visit. Further, it is a consequence for which there is never a simple remedy or, too often it seems, one at all.

David

David insisted that his son and daughter were the sole priorities of his life now that his marriage had ended. However, he was adamant that he urged his 14-year-old son to see his mother, despite the boy's total refusal. The 12-year-old daughter seemed to have less difficulty and went back and forth according to the agreed schedule. The son, however, was seething in his apparent contempt for his mother and would run away, initiating police involvement rather than spending time with his mom. David shrugged and insisted that he reinforced the importance of his son's maternal relationship and was an innocent bystander. The ex-wife, the targeted parent, was not so sure.

David could not accept that he had failed as a husband in his wife's eyes. As far as he was concerned, he was married forever, even if it was her decision to end the marriage. Further, he could not imagine repartnering. It was a mix of pride, denial, stubborn refusal, and destructiveness. It was the son who would affirm his father's martyrdom. Indeed, the boy's choice of his father over his mother confirmed David's righteousness in his eyes and placed the son at the cornerstone of his father's defensive bastion. As far as David was concerned, the son served as judge and found his father innocent and his mother guilty. The son's fidelity undid the trauma of the breakup and mitigated the loss for David, even though it severely damaged the child's relationship with his mother and potentially his own relationship in the future. There was huge rancor and pain as the family envelope ripped. David, however, remained aloof, as if this circumstance had little to do with him and was strictly the son's decision.

The boy's split with his mother was very deep. He was dismissive of her grief and efforts to connect with him. He was also dismissive of his sister and resented her continued loyalty to their mother. He blamed his mother for having a boyfriend and not showing the dedication and devotion of his father. Scorn and hostility were his dominant attitudes. He insisted that his father met all his needs, and there was no requirement for another parent, especially his selfish mother.

Here is another brief example that links disillusionment to alienation and reveals the crumbling impact of an illusory union.

Mary and Henry

Mary's discovery that her husband, Henry, had a parallel life involving pornography and lap dancers overwhelmed her. She experienced it as a direct threat to their toddler son's welfare. At another level, Mary crumbled at the prospect that she was not enough for Henry.

The union ended abruptly. It was rancorous from the outset. In addition, their child could never part with his mother enough to enjoy an independent relationship with his dad. Mary's older brother, in particular, initially filled the paternal role, at least as far as Mary was concerned. He had a young family himself and often included his nephew in their activities. Mother and son both presented the uncle as a worthy alternative to the perverse and untrustworthy Henry.

Of course, Mary never explicitly held on to her son but in countless ways conveyed her horror about who his father was. Indeed, her abhorrence proved fatal to the father-son bond. The husband might discard her for a stripper, but their son discarded him in turn. In Mary's eyes, her husband was unfit to serve as a parent, and their son had nothing to gain from having him in his life.

What appears to be clear alienation, however, is often more complicated. Henry's mother had been destructive in the family and had damaged her son's image and sense of safety with women. His father was distant and submissive when he was around. Henry's retreat into pornographic sexuality and strip clubs protected him from dealing with real women and bolstered his flagging sense of masculinity. Discovering the split life was catastrophic for Mary, who was traumatically disillusioned by a partner who, on the surface, promised so much. Nonetheless, Henry's contribution alone would not be sufficient to cause the alienating outcome. Whatever destructiveness from his mother he had endured as a child was now repeated in the short but disastrous marriage to Mary.

The Fate of the Family in Alienation

In child development, identity is very much supported by a sense of family. Some remnants of the family that the parents constructed or at least tried to construct must survive the breakup in order for children to go back and forth between the homes. It is a residue of the love they had for each other that gave inspiration to the children of the union. To salvage this vital remnant, each individual must be able to mourn in a way that lets go of the painful part of his or her history but preserves a place for what was good as well. Of course, such mourning is precisely what allows an ex-couple to relinquish a wish for each other while maintaining a place for the children they cocreated and continue to share. The family remnant allows for the sharing of parenting duties as well as helping weather the absence when the children are in the other parent's care.

For alienated children, this family remnant does not survive. In David's case, as much as he was apparently married forever, his whole way of relating to his children, its totalistic and usurping force, was simply too much for the son to bear. His ex-wife was outside the circle rather than within a family crucible, despite the fate of their union. David could not mourn. He seemed to suffer pain but not grief. It was too threatening to his self-esteem and identity. Instead, he resorted to desperate means to hold on to as much as he could. The alienation undid the breakup by offering him an unlimited contact with his son, who identified with his father's cause and ensured that his father would not have to face what terrified him. The cost for the son and for the mother was high.

Likewise, Mary married a man she did not know in any intimate way. She had no concept of his prior identity struggles, nor was he ever able to express his feelings so she could know him. He had always lived a split and discordant life. The rupture of this brief union over Mary's discovery obliterated any potential for him to be included in the family. He might have been the birth father, but he was expelled from the family circle and blamed fully for his own exclusion. Mary simply foreclosed on the fact that there had ever been a marriage or family. It did not exist, except for the son, who did not acknowledge his father's existence or, for that matter, that his father was part of his family.

Note the same structural factors in both scenarios. There is a severing of the ex-spouse from the family unit. All responsibility is put onto the shoulders of the rejected parent, whose only recourse is to fight or submit, neither of which works as a remedy. For the preferred parent, there has been a shock, a broken marital dream. When this catastrophe occurs, there is insufficient psychological capacity to recover from it. Perhaps there was an original trauma from childhood or weak spot in the psyche, an old wound that is reactivated when the marriage disintegrates. It is not just that the marriage shatters, as the identity and equilibrium of the preferred parent threatens to collapse with it.

What happens next is sometimes hard to chart, but there are always clear signs of where it is headed as the alienating dynamic takes hold. At the same time, there is no single, defined scenario. Gradually, the preferred parent cultivates a permissive, all-embracing bond with a child, which squeezes out the other parent. In turn, the child, sensing the fragility, moves to shore up the vulnerable and rocked preferred parent. It can involve one child among others or all children in the family, especially when there is sibling pressure to ally in a common cause against the targeted parent.

In response and as a countermeasure, the targeted parent either becomes more "parental" and disciplinary to maintain a rational structure or retaliates legally and in any other way possible. It does not usually matter, though, what they do. There are powerful inducements for the child or children who sense that something far more important than parental competition is at stake. From the child's perspective, it is both empowering and sacrificing. The psychosocial cost to the child is enormous in terms of loss of a right to their own life and loss of a parent.

The alienated child's exclusive loyalty in many ways undoes the trauma of the breakup for the preferred parent and bolsters the parent's identity. It is a violent solution but one that occurs without insight, reflection, or self-responsibility on the part of the parent, even when there is some dim recognition of earlier trauma. This is what makes it so difficult to influence. The scene between preferred and rejected parent plays out endlessly in a confusion about who is the victim and who is the perpetrator. Each claims the victim role. The rejected parent is accused of bringing this fate on themselves, while the preferred parent is accused of a callous manipulation of the child's mind.

Of course, there are cases where children do need protection from personality-disordered, psychotic, violent, or addicted parents. These involve clear findings of endangerment, predictably requiring active intervention by child protection services along with the criminal and family courts. Moreover, these children's reactions tend to be more equivocal, agonized, and fearful that alienated children's, whose attitudes are often strident, callously judgmental, and hostile.

The destruction of the link with the targeted parent is a concomitant destruction of the family as it had been constituted. Such is the depth of disillusionment that the family cannot survive intact. The child is the linchpin in the drama, unequivocally choosing one and radically discarding the other. The preferred parent has an ally like no other in the alienated child, while the rejected parent may see a record of parental love treated as if it never existed or mattered. The choice of the preferred parent by the child speaks to the parent's specialness and undoes any sense of psychological alienation that haunts the parent. It is the parent's alienation that needs the fusion of the child. It is an omnipotent solution for child and parent alike.

Alienated children can go very far in their eradication of the discarded parent if they are in the preteen or teen years: name change; ruthless, poisonous, condemning letters; obliteration of contact with an entire side of the family; and severe resistance if there is any effort made to foster reconciliation. As already noted, the targeted parent is rarely blameless, although in my experience, they are not distinguishable in faultiness or lack of merit as much as how they are treated.

Phillip

Phillip finally broke with his father, but he had resisted the minimal access in place for several years. When he broke contact completely as a 15-year-old, he confided that the only reason he had seen his father at all was because he feared legal consequences for his mother if he did not. He hated his father, hated how he smelled, hated his house, and could not bear the sound of his voice. His mother was ideal in his eyes and the only parent he needed or wanted. The inexperienced father hardly knew his son, as the breakup occurred when Phillip was an infant. He was an awkward father, unsure, and at a major disadvantage. The mother hated him, but this word does not capture the depth of her enmity. He was shit in her mind, which corresponded to the son's aversion to his father's smell. He had been flushed. Yet it was the mother's own estrangement that also drew my attention. I was unable to imagine that there ever was a loving couple or to see her as part of anyone's life except her son's. The father had been effaced from the family envelope by the mother as much as by the son.

Who Is Dominating Whom in Parental Alienation?

The term *parental alienation* is problematic, as it implies a specific motive that would not be shared by nonalienating conflictive parents. This is not the case. Alienating behavior is ubiquitous in high-conflict divorce, although only a minority of children resist contact to the degree of total alienation. It has more to do with who the parent is and less with what the parent does or says to the child. There is a complex, triangular dynamic between the chosen parent, the rejected parent, and the child. Although I am not aware of studies looking for common factors in the targeted parent, I have observed clinically that, in relative terms, they are less fragile psychologically than the chosen parent. At the same time, the rejected parent's personality and place in the family system are not irrelevant. In many cases, the rejected parent's reactions and counterreactions amplify the problem and become part of the child's justification for the refuse/resist dynamic.[10]

The issue becomes more complicated with articulate, ascendant older children and young adolescents who intractably refuse contact for spurious reasons. These children are anything but weak and programmed. Yet they enact a destructive agenda with remarkable certainty. They still may be influenced or influenceable, but they are not blank slates or mindless instruments of their parents' projections and agenda. These refusing children can be very dominant, influencing younger siblings and assuming control, particularly if the favored parent is hobbled emotionally by the divorce process. Power dynamics and emotional immaturity, however, do not explain the severity of the attack on the targeted parent. The child marshals together enormous defensive vitriol from the preferred parent's inability to process or mourn the marital breakdown. It is the child who undertakes a "parentectomy," radically severing the rejected parent from the family. It is the court, on occasion, that will do likewise by removing the child from the favored parent's care, although this solution can also be damaging and traumatic.[11] The catastrophe that presumably takes place in the favored parent's mind, rupturing and beyond mourning,

---

10 Kelly, J., & Johnson, J., (2001), The alienated child: A reformulation of parental alienation syndrome, *Family Court Review*, 39(3), 249–266.

11 Mercer, J., (2019), Are parental alienation treatments safe and effective for children and adolescents? *Journal of Child Custody*, 16(1), 67–113; Polak, S., Altobelli, T., & Popielarczyk, L., (2020), Responding to severe parent-child rejection cases without a parentectomy: A blended sequential intervention model and the role of the courts, *Family Court Review*, 58(2), 507–524.

is visited on the targeted parent, who must bear their own version of the same irretrievable, traumatic loss.

Lena

"I don't need to be here, but Danny sure should be," 15-year-old Lena began, launching immediately into a sarcastic tirade about her father, Daniel, whom she insisted on calling by his first name and familiarizing it as well. "He screams at me for no reason, a real bully. He is a complete asshole. There is something wrong with him. He should never have been a parent," she added. Lena was the oldest of three girls. She was smart, articulate, and seemingly older than her years. Her mother and father had separated two years before. The situation was still volatile. Her mother railed at her father, desperately furious that he was to blame for the ruination of the family. She accused him of hiding income and plotting to abandon her all along. In Lena's mother's mind, it was betrayal and not incompatibility. Daniel struggled against the wall of fury and his own indecision. Acrimonious litigation was in process.

Lena had once thought that her parents would reconcile, but now her dad had a girlfriend, and there was no way Lena was ever going to accept her. This seemed to be the flashpoint. Her mother strongly suspected that this relationship preceded the end of the marriage. The girlfriend had also tried to speak with Lena and shared that she, too, had lived through an awful parental divorce when she was a child. Lena dismissed the girlfriend's effort as self-serving and manipulative. She was not going to be taken in by her father's "whore."

Lena's grades at school had slipped after her parents separated, and she was still struggling. Focus was poor, and study skills were weak. Lena assured me that she was content with breaking with her father. It was the best thing she had ever done. Her little sisters were still seeing their dad, but Lena was sure that they would come to the same conclusion as her: "Danny's a jerk." She made no effort to spare them from her diatribes, and they were confused.

Lena was not waiting for her mother's approval necessarily, but they were both livid with Danny, and this was mutually reinforcing. Yet her mother's brittleness and limited coping capacity was obvious to Lena.

When we met, Lena accepted the idea that life at her age was complicated enough without having to endure a family drama. I stressed that she was paying a high price. Lena, though, most wanted to attack her father in the session.

> LENA: Danny says that Mom cheated on him and that is why he left. He is trying to cover up what he was doing. He can't have me in his life and some silly girlfriend. My sisters hate her too; they are too scared to say anything.

Her father had not openly admitted his new relationship for a long while, afraid of his children's reaction and what his ex-wife might do. Lena had discovered a text, however, when her father left his phone open. This had incensed Lena and filled her with righteous vitriol. She refused to see him thereafter. It was hard to separate mother from daughter: Both were rocked by a conviction of betrayal.

I tried to find a way to turn her diatribe into a two-way communication, but she was very resistant.

> LENA: My mom says that you have to explain to me why my dad is such a fucking idiot.

> ANALYST: You want to be your parents' therapist—pulling every lever to push them to get back together.

> LENA: Oh no, no, I am much better off now. He doesn't care about us and never did.

> ANALYST: Perhaps, but your mother is having a hard time, and you seem nervous about leaving her alone. It's like you are watching over her.

> LENA: All she does is cry and drink.

Lena's disillusionment in her parents was severe. Her father had vacillated when the marriage ended. It was less that he voluntarily left than he was blown out by his wife's rage. There was no forgiveness on anyone's part, but the surfacing of the father's girlfriend proved to be catastrophic. Lena's attack emerged full bore, and her mother assumed no responsibility for what then transpired.

Lena's mother came from a dysfunctional family herself, with poor mothering in her background and lack of parental boundaries. She was both fragile and warring. The legal combat was also fierce, and the family field became an inhospitable, dangerous battleground. Lena was seemingly a soldier in her mother's army, but it might have been the reverse. It was hard to tell.

I had to keep in mind that beneath this omnipotent enforcer role, bullying everyone in the family by all accounts, was a young teenager who was herself suffering. At the same time, her ongoing contempt and ridicule were hard to bear, as she could be profoundly disrespectful. It was like an impenetrable wall that she was determined to keep between us.

I tried to find a way to get behind this barrier.

ANALYST: Lena, I think you worry what this will mean for you in the future.

LENA: I am sure that I will never get married. It is such a joke.

ANALYST: It's hard to accept how let down you feel.

LENA: It doesn't matter really. I will survive. Who cares if I am disappointed? I am not going to come here and feel sorry for myself.

ANALYST: Maybe, though, you are less sure about your mother surviving, which makes you feel responsible and resentful at the same time.

LENA: Yes, and Dad goes off and has a new life. Such a joke.

Lena felt abandoned by her father and left with a fragile mother who seemed buoyed by rage but also despondent, depressed, and consoling herself with alcohol. On the surface, it could well have looked that Lena was simply following her mother's destructive commands. Indeed, her mother supported Lena's rejection of her father and relished every morsel of scorn her daughter heaped on the besieged father. Her dad did not look that good, either, letting the children know of their mother's infidelity, hiding the girlfriend, and then seeming to hide behind her. Nonetheless, it is important to underline that Lena had her own sense of being failed by her two parents, who constituted a mockery of a family that could not fulfill its duty to her and her sisters. It was Lena who felt like the sacrificial lamb.

LENA: My friends have real families. I am not going to pretend and let my Dad do this. My family sucks. It's not real. He didn't have to leave. What are we supposed to do anyways?

If she was denouncing the family ideal, then it was her parents who set the precedent. She certainly bolstered her mother by taking sides and eliminating her father, but then she saw him as the more stable and reliable parent and source of greatest betrayal. Her refusal to contact her father softened somewhat after approximately one and a half years of complete refusal. Although she never did follow the parenting schedule, Lena began to meet one-on-one with her father for lunches or walks. Her sisters maintained the access without disruption, but the family mood stayed tense, and Lena's mother's adjustment remained an issue. Alcohol and tranquilizers were a ubiquitous presence.

Alienation is a taxing problem for which there is no easy solution. It is a lesson in the dynamics of power and control that interferes dramatically in child development. Sometimes the parent has a direct hand in cultivating this mind-set but more often than not, it is an unreflective parent, emotionally brittle and socially alienated, who finds huge comfort when a child rejects their other parent outright.

Indeed, the more regressed the favored parent, the more dramatic the alienation often becomes. A psychotic parent, for example, sure that the other parent can sexually violate their child faster than the eye can see, might gain the full support of a child at the expense of the rational, sane parent. It might look like the vulnerable child is being brainwashed by a delusional, mad parent, but the reality can be more complex. Children will prop up an ill parent, even a delusional one. It is not a rational calculus, of course, but children can be swayed by the compelling force of role reversal to sacrifice personally in order to bolster an unstable parent. It is the child who is caring for a parent who otherwise cannot cope with a deeply traumatic experience that cannot be mourned. The alienation represents a retreat from triangular relations by creating a fusional dyad that undoes or softens the traumatic rupture for the favored parent.

The fact that the refusal to visit is welcomed and celebrated by the preferred parent is reinforcing for sure, but it does not mean that it is the parent's direct, conscious manipulation that is causing it. Yet lack of reflective capacity and a narrow comprehension of complex social realities fan the flames. There is absolutely no empathy with the rejected parent. Everything bad is attributed to the other, and everything good, to themselves. The children understand this need for the preferred parent to be unblemished and free of any fault or responsibility in their own eyes. Thus, the children are loath to point to anything negative about this parent while heaping scorn out of all proportion on the discarded one.

It is a ganging up that occurs as the family is transformed into a battering ram aimed at the targeted parent. We can blame this dilemma solely on the destructive intent of the alienating parent, as is often observed in court proceedings, but perhaps alienation also demonstrates the extent to which children will go to buttress a parent in psychological peril, even if this means cutting themselves off from another source of love, support, and identity.

Alienated Child—Alienating Parent

Often these are impressive young people, articulate and successful in other parts of their lives. They are respectful of others except the targeted parent, about whom they will have nothing good to say. Their rudeness toward that parent can be breathtaking. Views are unchangeable, especially in the more malignant cases. The targeted parent, often referred to by their first name, can be described as useless, offensive, foul smelling, abandoning, disinterested, selfish, or other pejorative labels. There are often few choice memories or episodes used to justify the child's alienation. Sometimes the preferred parent tells these to the child, and the child was not even present. The discourse is extreme, unwavering, and lacking in nuance or perspective. Judgment is harsh, and the child's main message is that this parent is expendable without the child losing anything of value. The rejection often extends to grandparents and other family related to the targeted parent. In contrast, there is a wholehearted embrace of the preferred parent and the preferred parent's family, along with an inability to think of anything negative or critical regarding that parent.

Alienated children mirror the toxic, blaming attitudes of the preferred parent toward the ex-partner. This features a channeling of negative attitudes, beliefs, and perceptions regarding the targeted parent that demean, devalue, and even vilify that parent.[12] This does not have to be verbalized. There are parents who say little but communicate precisely these profoundly negative attitudes. Nonetheless, only a fraction of children whose parents engage in a pattern of scorning and vilification actually become alienated. In other words, alienating behavior is either a necessary though insufficient cause of alienation, or it is a red herring and not a primary factor at all. In this regard, clinicians should look for a common vulnerability factor in the preferred

---

[12] Johnson, J., & Sullivan, M., (2020), Parental alienation: In search of common ground for a more differentiated theory, *Family Court Review*, 58(2), 270–292.

parent's emotional functioning postseparation rather than focus on behavior, which is endemic to the high-conflict population.

Conclusion

Pathologies of love help us visualize the developmental origins of the capacity for love itself. It is a developmental achievement with optimal roots in early experience of parental responsiveness and attunement. However, in love we seek to refind not only what we once had from early caregivers but also what we never had. It is easier to understand why we hate than why we love. There is something mysterious and ungraspable about how it arises and why it ends. It is so important to human life that those who cannot love or whose vulnerabilities prevent love from developing in a healthy way stand out for the problems that evolve.

Those who cannot love are unable to tolerate the vulnerability of loving as well as its limits. Among pathological manifestations of loving, some resort to a scripted formula of domination and control that guarantees the other's presence, although on very narrow, restricted grounds. Some cannot love at all and occupy a very problematic zone, where they can cause serious harm to others. Then there are those who fetishize the other, only to lose interest when reality inevitably deflates the illusory fantasy on which the fetish is based. Additionally, there are those who make babies without a secure, tested relationship able to deliver the responsible teamwork of parenting. They bypass love in order to procreate.

Sadomasochism, with its psychology of power and control, is another way of ensuring the other's presence but also defends against recognizing the reality of loss, separateness, and the limitations of human intimacy. This is manifested as a failure of collaboration that dooms couples who need to work as a team in caring for children. These cases seem to demonstrate an ongoing tension between need for the other and an aggression that feels destructive. It reminds us how important the early experience of love is in one's childhood and how these developmental origins find their way into the dramas that unfold in family law.

Severe child alienation is a loveless business. It arises in families where other motivators dominate—collusion, defenses against trauma, blame, splitting, and hatred. Alienated children certainly struggle to love as they reach adulthood. There is a long-term impact on psychological adjustment. It should be expected. They were child soldiers employing the negative powers of hate and blame to expel one parent in order to bolster or even save another. They have been sacrificed to one's parent needs and have forfeited the right to innocence and to a loving, protective family. As much as they seem to be the instrument of destruction, they are victims.

In Pursuit of an Ethical Divorce
What This Means for High Conflict

Divorce is lifelong in its undoing of a vow. It seems counterintuitive, then, to designate the ex, the one left or taking the initiative to leave, as the object of ethical concern and responsibility. However, this is not an outlandish claim for many people. They harbor no ill will toward their ex-spouse and would prefer to treat them fairly, even warmly and responsibly, due to shared history and shared children. Moreover, they do not want to suffer more guilt than they already have by treating their ex-spouse with partisan zeal, trying to beat the other financially or limit their role or time with children. The divorce proceeds fairly and equitably, which then preserves the emotional capacity of the family system to help children process and adjust to the new circumstance. In this regard, ethics is not an issue.

The problem of ethics only arises when the divorce is contentious, and the conflicts numerous and sharp. It is much harder to speak about ethics when the other is now the opponent, the adversary in a court case, Doe versus Doe, and serious accusations are legion. At this moment, then, ethics is a much harder sell, although the fate of the divorce often proceeds from the willingness and capacity of the former couple to resolve their union ethically.

To do so can be challenging because of the psychological demand on divorcing partners to cope with a sense of failure and the profound guilt that often accompanies it. Making a place for guilt and failure is important but challenging. There is much embarrassment, shame, and helplessness in acknowledging failure, even though it is a painful and necessary step in working through a breakup. Failure is a blow to the sense of adequacy, and self-esteem suffers at least in the short term. We must forgive ourselves as much and sometimes more than forgiving the other. This takes time and perspective. It makes it very hard to parent children in the immediate shadow of the breakup when feelings are most raw; shame and guilt, highest; and hurt, most acute.

There is a paradox inherent to successful, healthy divorce. One must accept failure in order to move beyond it. Facing failure is instructive and allows for mourning, forgiveness, and inner change. What characterizes higher-conflict divorce is often the inability to tolerate guilt and failure. There is a sense of being wronged. The motivation to get rid of guilt in the form of aggressive blame is high. This is used to maintain a sense of innocence and victimhood. Hatred guards against despair, but it exacts a huge toll individually and on the family. One sees divorcing couples, even five or more years post-separation, who cannot look at each other or be civil but expect their children to overlook this limitation. In these circumstances, there is no anchor for ethics, no sense of continuing debt or responsibility to this person on whom so much was based. Without an ethical framework to guide behavior, however, everything can be decided on the basis of self-interest, and runaway conflict can easily become the currency of exchange.

It is understandable and even expected that people feel a debt to those whom they loved and who loved them. This goes well beyond marriage. There is always a deficit, a sense that we could have done more, a feeling of having failed to give all that one could have given. Indeed, children feel this about parents, and parents feel it about children. The idea that our obligation at a moral level has no real limit is puzzling because children need to become independent, and parents have their own lives as well. There is a limit to what we can do, but this does not stop parents, for example, from feeling responsible for their children for as long as the parent lives.

Of course, this sense of debt can be problematic in divorce because separation should imply a freedom from this other person, at least beyond the contractual necessities of finances and a parenting agreement. No one wants to feel like a hostage to their former partner, chained together by children, in what can only be described as a persecutory nightmare. Yet this is precisely the ambience of high conflict.

I suppose that the distinction rests on the difference between a link and a chain. A link can preserve an important connection, whereas a chain entraps. The link is residual of a marriage that bore children and that must survive the divorce in order to raise the offspring. A chain is the stuff of nightmares: trapped with your worst enemy and unable to escape. It is a path to destructiveness.

The legal system has its own way of speaking about and framing obligations. There is the obligation to pay child and sometimes spousal support or the obligation to coparent in a meaningful, collaborative way. The legal is contained in the ethical, which describes a continuing duty to care. This care is about maintaining a working, facilitating connection with the other parent without threat of invasion, violation, appropriation, or destruction. It is the ethical in the legal that aspires to justice.

In divorce, the bridge or link between parents serves the children of the union, who need a preserved family system to continue to evolve as people despite their parents' divorce. The duty to care includes the relationship of one ex-partner to another to respect the continuity of family relationships, the role and functions of the other parent, the children's right to parental relationships, and the need for peaceful coexistence while not draining the ex-partner of valuable energy in managing divorce firestorms.

Often, divorced parents are infinitely sensitive to their children while treating the other parent abysmally, as if ethical requirements stop at the border with the ex-spouse. This denies the essential responsibility to the other postseparation that is indispensable to a good outcome. Loving children includes the ethical treatment of the ex-spouse. One cannot be completely divorced from the other when there are children involved. *Divorce* as such is a misnomer, and this can have negative consequences when it is interpreted as the right never to deal with that person again, never to look, talk, or consider their views on child raising.

"I Could Have Done More"

There is always a lingering guilt in divorce. One could have done more to save the marriage, transcend a limitation, and make fewer missteps. Guilt and failure hang heavy for a time. It extends from the common impression that one has not done enough. Indeed, everyone has "egg on their face" in the case of marital failure. It is embarrassing to fail so publicly, no matter how this is rationalized. Even when providing therapy for a divorcing couple trying to be optimally fair to their children, there is a sense of failure that cannot be ignored. We can all relate painfully and mournfully to failure. Separation counseling, then, can be seen as an attempt to soften the blow, protect the family from the initial rupture, and promote a successful divorce. Nonetheless, it occurs in the context of the failure, which reverberates through the process, whether consciously or unconsciously.

Something has been irreparably lost and must be mourned. There is a necessary detachment of self from other and from the dream of what could or should have been shared. It is a guilt that, although painful, contains some degree of hope, maturity, and healthy self-regard. Blame is a temporary salve for guilt and the sense of failure. Attributing responsibility to the other, at least temporarily, lessens guilt. However, if the only way to assuage guilt is to blame, and this mechanism is favored by one or both divorcing parties, then conflict levels will ramp up quickly.

The addition of shame to the roiling mix of negative emotions will further intensify the pessimism of the postseparation climate. Shame might be experienced as depression more than conflict, but it can also be defended against and externalized. There are many examples of ex-spouses, raw with pain, shame, and guilt following a marriage breakdown, who take every opportunity to humiliate their ex-spouse, trying to make them feel small, inconsequential, incompetent, or inadequate.

The high-conflict-prone individual relies on externalization defenses. Self-reflection is simply too painful and humiliating, but without it there can be no real thinking or emotional processing. The focus on the failings and misconduct of the other ensures a battle-field discourse. There are often two disparate narratives, each telling a story that is highly polarized, discordant with the other, and reflecting an entirely different perspective. Each inhabits blame in a way that creates a bastion of defense, not only against external attack, but also against internal pressure arising from the verdict of reality.

As much as the legal system is aimed at conflict resolution, the conflict can be too defensively important to forfeit for the ready goal of resolution. The drama is enacted on two levels. On the first level, there is a legal conflict that mobilizes the family law system to action with the goal of resolution. On the second level, there is a tyranny of blame that has no natural resolution and will actually oppose it. It is conflict without the capacity to end, which is another way to define *high conflict*. Ironically, high-conflict individuals and couples are unsuited to successfully use the litigation process but are most likely to rely on it. Their children can be recruited as advocates to the point of alienation. These high-conflict couples are most riddled with disillusionments and least able to bear painful verdicts of reality. Their children might have views, but in high-conflict cases, the wrong views create emotional risk and retaliation, is a real possibility.

Diana and Matthew

It had been a tumultuous relationship from the outset, but Diana and Matthew had stayed together for 15 years before the union disintegrated into vindictiveness and accusation. It was a peculiar amalgam of dependency and struggle long before they had their daughter, Morgan, who was 9 years of age when they finally broke up.

In the aftermath, Morgan was whipsawed between a mother who was determined to protect her daughter from her father's abuse and lies and a father who could not stop himself from arguing incessantly with his daughter and thus making matters worse. Morgan was beginning to resist seeing her father, which Diana celebrated as an act of courage and good judgment, while Matthew openly blamed Diana and protested regularly to Morgan. Tensions were very high as Morgan's refusal to visit took hold.

Diana's background spoke to the black-and-white thinking that permeated her narrative. She had felt cheated and picked on her whole life. The impression that others failed her was a constant theme that framed her sense of herself in the world and how she perceived her ex-husband. She noted that she had raised Morgan to expose falsehood and stand up for what is right. In terms of family of origin, Diana described a selfish, controlling mother who allowed Diana's older brother to treat her terribly. She had been a much better student than her brother and was sure that his venom came from envy. She had not spoken to her brother in a long time and had no intention of ever talking to him for the rest of her life. Diana had left home as soon as she could, and she had stayed with relatives until she completed high school. She knew her parents loved her but felt betrayed by them as well.

According to Diana, Matthew appeared kind when they first met as college students. He was able to hide his real nature, especially his detached and punitive side. She felt very victimized by Matthew, who, she noted, would never want to socialize with others. It had been particularly awful when she discovered that he had been paying online prostitutes. She wanted to leave him then but became pregnant with Morgan. Diana related that she tried hard to make the union work but that Matthew was passive-aggressive and sabotaging. He was not what he pretended to be.

Matthew acknowledged the internet sex behavior and the financial debt he had incurred, which was now a burden for the family. He stopped when Diana confronted him and never went back to this conduct. He spoke of long-standing problems with social awkwardness and shyness. He had been bullied at school and acknowledged a tendency to retreat behind the wall of the internet, which he realized was not good for him or his family. His self-esteem had always been an issue. He admitted that he had become depressed during the marriage.

According to Matthew, he felt immediately comfortable with Diana when they first met because she was so exuberant and extroverted. However, when he displeased her, the negative reactions were huge. Diana would blame him for hours and bring up every injury and misstep that came to her mind, some of which he could not even recall. He felt like he had been thrown into a hole. Diana insisted that his parents did not like her, and this justified her refusal to see them. It fit a pattern where Matthew felt that he was being isolated from everyone except Diana, and this started to feel suffocating, even somewhat frightening. The hole kept getting deeper.

Matthew had hoped that having their baby would change the focus and give them a new start. It did not happen. Even in the hospital after Morgan was born, Diana accused him of demanding the limelight and pretending that he was the hero of the moment. She had been critical of his caretaking and seemed jealous if he enjoyed being with Morgan too much. He felt that there was no space to be himself and for them to be a family of three. It was either Morgan and her mother or Morgan and him. He went to therapy on his own, and this helped him make better sense of what was happening. He had not wanted the marriage to break up and had feared that this could lead to the end of his relationship with Morgan. Now it was happening. Matthew realized that he should not argue with his daughter. He wanted to be patient but found that Morgan picked fights with him, and her resemblance to Diana was uncanny.

Morgan was clear that her mother was a victim of her father and many other people in her life. She admitted feeling very sorry for her mother and harboring resentment of her father for being one more person who let her mother down. She accused her dad of wanting to destroy her mother with his e-mail messages to her. She lectured me that abuse is not only physical but also emotional and that she was determined not to let her dad get away with it. She had not decided when to start seeing him again or whether she even wanted to resume access.

Morgan noted that she was often late for school when staying with her dad because of their arguments. She wanted to do well in school, and this alone would justify not spending overnights with him in the future. Her mother had told her that her views were important and that she should speak truthfully and from the heart. Morgan underlined that her father lies a lot about her mother but that she, Morgan, knows the truth. When her mother was scared, Morgan was happy to comfort her. Her mother had told her that her cuddles were the best and all she needed.

Transgenerational Trauma and Marital Conflict

We leave embedded lives in the families who raise us but also in the historical context that is part of world history. The residue of these experiences is imported into marriages and is initially eclipsed by everyday challenges, perhaps even forgotten. There can be comfort in knowing that something experienced in one's youth, such as a political trauma, has been shared by the partner. As much as this represents an opportunity for deeper sharing and rapport, it can also disrupt the union and become a new source of shared trauma. In this case, what was seemingly forgotten is in fact disavowed and returns with a vengeance within the marital relationship.

Maria Teresa and Julio

Maria Teresa and Julio met at university and found commonality in their Latin American heritage and language. Julio was from Central America and had escaped a violent gang culture in his country. He had been a refugee but showed great adaptive capacity in his new life. After arriving, he worked in an abattoir for minimum wage but saved and invested, eventually opening his own business. Maria Teresa had also left her country precipitously in the wake of a civil war. She had immigrated, though, with her family, who had some financial means. Nonetheless, their exit had been precipitous and frightening. The family fled with the clothes on their backs. They got out just in time.

After 12 years of marriage, the couple had three children and their own home. Nonetheless, the union was in tatters, ripped apart by interspousal violence and conflict. Child protection services and police were a regular presence in the latter phase of the marriage. Julio accused Maria Teresa of being evil. She had attacked his humble origins, put him down mercilessly, and contradicted him in front of the children. In turn, Maria Teresa complained that Julio was violent with the children and her. She saw him as trying to be a gang leader in their family, forcing everyone to follow his whims and rules. She suggested that he was crazy and needed intensive therapy and medication.

There was mayhem in the family home before the breakup. Each filmed the other, and the children were recruited as allies. The family became a war zone. There were accusations that reached extreme threats of murder and sex abuse. If a child put the parent in a bad light to authorities, reprisals followed: "You will burn in hell if you lie," or, "Maybe you would prefer to live in a foster home." Each parent took a different child to the police to file reports against the other.

There was overwhelming tension spilling out regressively in all directions. Each parent was committed to the struggle. Obviously, something between them had gone terribly wrong. They were frightened, angry, deeply threatened, and acting out. The problem could never be solved at the level with which they were engaged with each other. It was deeply destructive. The children did not have the maturity to have their own perspectives. Instead, they accepted the parents' terms of reference, which included threats of murder and perversion.

As such, the parties were never functioning outside the struggle. There was no psychological distance from it that might have provided another point of view. It was high-conflict mayhem, an enactment of traumatic origins that they unconsciously repeated and forced their children to experience as well. In this respect, the attack on the children was evident: No one in the family could escape the trauma of war and violence. We will never know whether this catastrophe was solely due to unresolved trauma or whether there would have been too much envy if they allowed their children to grow up in peace and security.

There was no ethical line that this couple would not cross. When the marriage broke up, the children chose a parent to live with and had minimal contact with the other parent or siblings. There were alignments and battle lines. The siblings enacted their parents' split relationship. The family itself did not survive the breakup. Although there were attempts at family therapy, neither would meet in the same room as the other. Each continued to blame, and the children were emotionally scarred and burdened.

Not much changed after five years. The youngest child, a daughter, seemed the most resilient of the three and was the only one in a stable relationship. However, when seeking therapy for underlying sadness, she spoke a great deal of the pain she had endured, the sense of catastrophe, the broken links, and the failure of the system to help her or her siblings. Her parents, she noted, were less violent with each other, but each remained unforgiving and locked in blame. Neither had repartnered or showed any interest in other relationships.

Capacity for Concern

A robust almost-four-year-old boy holding his precious yellow front-end loader approached a child of similar age in the playground. They were both playing around a sandbox. "Want to play with this?" the boy asked the other. It was an act of caring arising from concern for how the toyless little boy might be feeling. It is not unusual for three-year-old children to demonstrate concern for others. This arises early in life. The concept that morality must be taught and essentially imposed through socialization does not stand up to evidence.

Of course, the toddler is given to episodes of aggressiveness as well as to caring and concern. Each modifies the other as they become integrated in the development of self-assertion and the sense of responsibility. Feelings of aggression are modulated by concern for the welfare of the loved and needed parent. Eventually, a special type of anxiety emerges called guilt, which signals that the child has considered or done something that could threaten the emotional availability of the parent on whom the child depends.

If the parent cannot tolerate the child's innate aggression and withdraws emotionally or retaliates, then guilt may become severe and destabilizing. Optimally, the parent's love and tolerance are internalized and help create basic trust and overall confidence in being lovable and desired. When the child internalizes this confidence, the parent is available to be psychologically used in development.

Although the capacity for guilt helps guide behavior, it might be better to speak about a capacity for concern, which brings us nearer to an ethical position rather than one based on moral judgment. Ethics is about doing the right thing out of inherent concern for the other rather than identifying when we are wrong and deserving of punishment or right and deserving of praise. This capacity for concern is at the forefront of ethics. It implies a double awareness: consciousness of the impact on others and acceptance of an unconditional duty of care.

Accordingly, conscious guilt is of limited value on its own because it tends to be short lived unless it extends to an attitude of concern. As such, concern brings one face-to-face with the other and the responsibility for the other's welfare. This capacity arises developmentally on its own. It is certainly part of the imperative need for survival and relates to the development of security, linked as it is to good care. Even young children can be wonderful therapists to their parents, showing kindness and compassion at precisely the right moment. I suspect that there could be examples of this empathic behavior even when children are not well parented. To be sure, it might happen more, which illustrates the link to survival.

Of course, mothers of toddlers will affirm the strange contradiction between caring, loving behavior one moment and aggressive disregard the next. Both currents are present and only gradually become integrated. Excessive guilt derives in this context, not from aggression only, but also from an experience of threatened attachment, which creates an internal alarm of guilty anxiety to avoid the feared loss of the needed parent or the parent's love.

There are a host of factors that strengthen the capacity for concern that is eventually tested in adulthood during both marriage and divorce. Parents who can accept what their children offer them, the gift of a scribbled drawing, for example, build bridges of recognition and reciprocity that reinforce the capacity for concern. Parents who "survive" their children's innate aggressiveness and pressing demands build confidence in the child that they can rely on their parents' emotional availability. No child wants to feel that they are too much for their parents to handle and are inherently destructive beings. This leads to pernicious guilt that can distort development.

Aggression, Emotional Control, and High Conflict

Often individuals and couples seen clinically through the family law system are not those who would usually seek psychotherapy. Their suffering is lived on the social plane of the family rather than in the mind. They are not incapable of introspection necessarily, but this may not be natural for them either. These cases take a different clinical approach. The therapist must work harder to build a working alliance and use an emerging sense of trust to work through paranoid anxieties and the politics of blame and threat. There is often a layering of disillusionments that may well go back to childhood. The working alliance can be fragile and mistrust, high, and there can also be fear that what the therapist learns and records in a file could be used against the patient in litigation. This must be addressed to establish a confidential space in which the treatment can unfold.[1]

Gerald and Susan

Gerald, a 50-year-old economist and father of two adolescent children, had spent the last 2 years in a court battle with his ex-wife, Susan. Ostensibly, he fought to protect his children from their unscrupulous mother, who had used and then discarded him. He devalued Susan's intellect, her contribution to the family beyond domestics, and her sincerity in marrying him in the first place. He felt duped and exploited, while he was sure that the children were brainwashed against him.

Susan had left him dramatically, taking the children with her and seeking refuge with her parents. She accused Gerald of being violent, uncontrolled emotionally, launching into endless diatribes that were merciless and distorted. Gerald denied everything. He doubled down and particularly emphasized Susan's coldness, unavailability, and willingness to influence the children against him. A family assessment, however, identified that Gerald was struggling with emotional control and a paranoid tendency.

Although Gerald downplayed his personality problems, there was evidence that behavioral control issues began in childhood. He could be violent in his childhood home, although again, he downplayed the significance. He had friends from school and extracurricular interests that he pursued, but he could be very reactive, although primarily within the family environment.

Everyone agreed that Gerald was an excellent student. His grades were superlative. He was the sole child and son of an illustrious inventor who owned his own company and held numerous technological patents. This father towered over the family and was idealized by Gerald's mother and the extended family on both sides. His father was beyond reach in all respects, as if he lived on a different plane.

This family structure that placed his father at the pinnacle of excellence and everyone else below proved to be extremely injuring to

---

[1] In my experience, the courts are very protective of patient confidentiality, even in jurisdictions where this privacy is not guaranteed in law. Children, in particular, may also need this confidentiality, lest their parents retaliate for what the child has reportedly told the clinician.

Gerald's pride and identity. He wanted to be close to his mother, but she in many ways subverted her own identity in favor of her husband. It was as if she, too, only existed for him. Gerald felt unseen, while his mother provided no counterpoint to his father's omniscience and omnipresence. By all accounts, Gerald's father was self-absorbed and self-aggrandizing. Work goals trumped parenting obligations and any other family focus or pursuit. Gerald felt that he had no real place in the family and could not understand why he had been born. Gerald's main contact with himself was through his rage.

He was 11 years old when the first eruptions occurred. These were so alarming that Gerald was sent to a pediatric neurologist because there was concern for an underlying seizure disorder. Gerald had smashed holes in walls and once pulverized his bedroom door. He also attacked his father's car and put his feet through the windshield. This certainly got him noticed, but he viewed these violent eruptions as an attack on family and home.

It took many years to get control of this rage, which he managed to accomplish with professional help and the influence of friends. This had not been an issue until it arose in his troubled marriage. As much as he sought to deny their severity, Gerald's anger management problems undermined any merits in his family law case. Both children found greater peace and security with their mother and were unnerved by their father's intermittent but frightening eruptive episodes. Gerald could not see his contribution or that his tantrums were cause for divorce. This fed his underlying theory that Susan had planned this all along and cleverly influenced the children to share her viewpoint. Nonetheless, pushed by his lawyer, he came for help, which required some expectation that he would own part of the problem. This was a huge challenge for Gerald. He came because his access to his kids depended on it. Susan could not take it anymore, and the children were unnerved by their volatile dad.

In Gerald's world, everyone was suspect, including me. He accused me of valuing the fee over his welfare and going through the motions of helping. He wondered out loud why everyone focused on him and not his wife. It seemed unjust. He seemed to be grieving the repercussions of a world where he did not seem to matter. In his view, he was a pawn, and any interest shown must be for some ulterior motive. He could not imagine that I would want to help him. It took approximately 6 months for Gerald to begin to speak more freely and to trust somewhat that I would not use what he revealed against him.

There were several turning points, but one in particular involved a dream that woke Gerald and left him feeling frightened and helpless. In his dream, he had gone to the backyard of the family home and used a shovel to unearth a bomb. It reminded Gerald of the bombs that are occasionally still excavated in London from World War II. In other words, it was a huge bomb. Gerald began unscrewing the top of the bomb. He realized that this was madness but did not stop. There was a disembodied voice that came out of nowhere: "Stop! You will kill us all!" He awoke in a panic. Gerald was not the type of patient who would normally report a dream spontaneously, given the family law context of the referral. Thus, it was surprising that he reported any dream, and this astonished him as much as me. We both appreciated its importance.

Like the dream itself, Gerald's rage and destructivity were not far beneath the surface. He noted that the "family home" to which he was referring in the dream was ambiguous. It was not clear whether this was his matrimonial or childhood home. Destruction was certainly on Gerald's mind, but he found it difficult to take responsibility for his feelings. He was sure that the bomb was planted and outside his control, but this was not specified in the dream.

I commented that he was perhaps saying that he did not start out in life as an angry person and that this fury was put into him. Gerald responded that his wife, Susan, had been very unfair and influenced the children to be afraid of any unhappy mood he might have. He always underestimated his explosiveness. I commented that his mother's submission to his father had effaced both herself and him and that something of this same experience was repeated in his marriage. Gerald thought that Susan was different when they met, although with the arrival of children, he felt that he had disappeared in her eyes. This upset him deeply and left him feeling resentful and on edge.

I related that as much as he felt the negation on the inside, perhaps he could be frightening on the outside when he got so angry. Maybe his wife felt that she had no choice but to protect the children from him. This was a hard message for Gerald to swallow. He resisted when I said anything that could lead to him feeling that I was on Susan's side.

Gerald had little sense or impression of his own anger. Reflective functioning was diminished when rage erupted. In his mind, Susan was the aggressor, blocking him out and revealing her disdain. He had no image of himself as a furious man who could cause damage and was a source of fear. When he had attended a course on anger management, which had been required for access to his children, he found it difficult to identify himself as abusive. Gerald could see that sometimes his mood soured, but he still looked for a plot to use his past against him. He struggled to take responsibility.

In Gerald's narrow world, where one is either doing or done to, there was no opportunity for a deeper perspective. There were moments when he seemed stuck on unfairness in a circular and defensive way, but there were also other times when he could clearly begin to think about himself. This was progress. It was again a dream that helped push the process forward:

> GERALD: I was at our family cottage, which I loved as a child. I left a sponge on the deck, and there must have been something in the sponge, a chemical, because it burned the deck. Discolored. I left to do something, but when I came back, large chunks of the deck were gone.

The dream was itself the fruit of reflection. He was again representing the fury of his suffering, in which he was destroying a family symbol. Gerald spoke about how invisible he had felt when the children came along. It was like a trick had been played on him, in which he contributed to creating what would eclipse him in Susan's eyes. He knew that this must be irrational, but he acknowledged that it felt like a catastrophe. He had not meant to destroy his marriage, but he could not live with how bad he felt either.

> GERALD: It was on my mind last night. There was only one person in my family growing up, and that was my father. My mother worked, but she came home earlier than my dad. I used to enjoy talking to her, but when he came home, all conversation had to be directed at him. No one else had a voice. I realize now that my mother must have been afraid of him. I wasn't afraid, but he never looked at me when he talked, even when he was talking to me. When I blew up in anger, it was because my dad was around. I wanted my mother to feel alarmed so maybe she would notice me, or maybe I wanted to attack him.

Gradually, Gerald was able to work out an accommodation with his ex-wife that allowed him to remain more regularly and safely in the children's lives. Mediation led to an accommodation in which the children would let him know if they felt scared, and he would allow either or both to speak with their mother and return to her care if this was what they wanted. Giving the children a safety valve because of their realistic anxiety proved ameliorative for Gerald and the children. His gradual capacity for self-reflection helped him be more aware of his sensitivities and trigger points. His self-containment improved dramatically, and with this achievement, he did better at cooperating and communicating with Susan. He shifted from projected guilt, experienced as blame and persecution, to a responsible and ethical position of concern. This brought their period of legal struggle to a close.

Conclusion

The endless loop of high conflict, conflict without end, captures its timelessness and capacity to dislodge individuals and whole families from the continuity of their lives. It can be contrasted with normal, linear conflict. It occurs within time; has a beginning and end; and is issue oriented, even when the discord is noisy and sharp.

In the circularity of high conflict, emotions remain strong, feelings stay raw, healing is nonexistent, and paranoid anxieties are dominant. The sense of failure is so disqualifying that it must be disavowed to protect self-esteem. Blame becomes a way of being. As much as there is always remorse in breakups, the feeling that one could have done more, this is absent in high-conflict cases. Remorse, guilt, regret, or any affect that would require acknowledging destructiveness is disavowed, and this perpetuates the harmfulness in a self-justifying cycle of blame. There is no anchor for ethics to take hold. The case thus unfolds as two soliloquies with little to connect them. In its imperviousness to reflection and severe tunnel vision, high conflict reveals its close ties to emotional trauma. It is destruction without any real reference point, torn as it is from the marriage and family context and appearing to the onlooker like a struggle to the death. It occurs outside time and is felt to be interminable.

The road to ethics must be grounded in the concern for the other, and this has its roots in love and attachment. This is the good object that must survive the divorce and provide a living anchor for children and ethics. This underlines the challenge in working with high-conflict couples. Creating an ethical space where the good can survive is essential, but then destructiveness must be faced and ways found to meaningfully address it.

8

Confronting the Nihilism of High Conflict

There is no path to ethics in the realm of high-conflict divorce that does not include confronting its inherent destructivity and how it was unleashed on the family. Focusing mainly on management, diagnosis, or dispute resolution amounts to sidestepping its destructive core. Recognizing this underlying psychodynamic can improve effectiveness in dealing with this most challenging population.

There is a tendency to use the term *high conflict* liberally and without the specificity that would help attorneys, judges, and mental health professionals distinguish between variants.[1] If there is not a serious undercurrent of destructivity, then it is not high conflict, no matter what form it takes. Something must either be attacked, destroyed, or at serious risk of being destroyed to meet the test. This could involve one or more of the following targets:

1. a link between a parent and a child
2. a child's mental health
3. a parent's health, socioeconomic well-being, or mental health to a significant degree
4. the capacity to function as a family capable of raising a child
5. a professional's identity or reputation

There are instances, for example, when ex-couples experience sharp and prolonged conflict and those when communication is a real challenge. There may be episodes that get out of hand, and resolution skills might be inadequate to the task. Nonetheless, there is nothing inherently destructive in the intent or, for that matter, the long-term

---

[1] Birnbaum, R., & Bala, N., (2010), Toward the differentiation of high-conflict families: An analysis of social science research and Canadian case law, *Family Court Review*, 48(3), 403–416.

consequence. Sharp and prolonged conflict can be troubling, but it does not usually destroy something.

The high conflict commanding the full attention of the legal and mental health communities has a very different feel because its destructiveness is apparent to anyone venturing close to it. At the bottom is something impenetrably nihilistic. The family is much worse off because of it, and recovery can take a lifetime. Children are frequently, if not inevitably, harmed.

The high-conflict-prone subject has a very different attitude toward the divorce and its resolution from other separated and divorcing individuals. They often want the other to bear full responsibility as well as to damage their reputation or hinder their capacity to live their life. They might revel when a child is critical of the other parent, subtly or not so subtly reinforce the attack, and credit the child with good judgment. They often hate rather than are simply upset. The verbal terms they employ to describe the ex-partner tend to be extreme—such as "evil" or "sick." Lawyers are hired and fired when they do not ally themselves with the destructive aim. There can be a deep urge to ruin the other. Mediators, lawyers, and mental health professionals may also become targets if they are deemed biased or identify with the ex-spouse. Neutral ground can be hard to come by or maintain. This is why professionals involved rely heavily on contracts and court orders to guide their interactions with this subgroup.

Destructiveness oozes from the wound of the divorce, and it is resistant to treatment through normal means. High-conflict individuals routinely create scenes in front of children; send shudders through ex-partners; never cooperate; and find any justification to refuse, obstruct, and otherwise stymie decision making and parenting. Spite can be particularly motivating. Such people will pay a hefty price, financial or otherwise, if they think that the ex-partner will pay more or can afford it less. Ruination may well be the goal, even if it is not acknowledged. Rather, the destructive aim is couched in a rationale of unfairness and victimization that gives cover and justification.

Intimidation is often also an important tactic—following the other's car; parking down the street in a stalking fashion but making sure to be seen; entering the other's house without consent; driving by the other's house to threaten; secretly damaging the other's property; stealing or redirecting mail; making false and incendiary reports to child protection, police, and taxation authorities; and endlessly sending e-mails, each more demanding and threatening than the last.

The desire to destabilize and destroy takes precedence over all other motives.

The ex-spouse who is subject to destructive attacks reels under unrelenting pressure. They often experience the divorce process as a nightmare and become worn down from the continual barrage. This is an expression of the nihilism. Whatever the specific mode of destructiveness, it usually has the desired impact. There are often exasperated legal counsel, burdened judges, strained mediators or parent coordinators, and stymied counselors and therapists. Assessors are required to write voluminous reports pleading for insight and self-reflection, which rarely make a dent.

There is what Henry Stack Sullivan labels a "malignant transformation": minimizing anxiety by tearing the other down in a dominant attitude of resentment and hatred that leads to isolation.[2] It is a defensive position, but the notion of transformation captures the deformation of the personality due to serious disillusionments and other stresses.

The severe-high-conflict individual bends the family law system to serve the destructive end. It is a hijacking of a rational and benevolent system that is crafted to serve important societal goals intended principally to protect children and families. This is justice. As much as legal and mental health professionals assume a constructive purpose and view their work through the lens of professional values and ethics, they are unprepared for the subversive and attacking motivation of the destructive, high-conflict individual or ex-couple. Routinely in my experience, the family law system underestimates the intent of the destructiveness or justifies ongoing destructive attacks on the ex-partner and children as simply misguided.

Serena and Robert

Serena had an exotic life prior to meeting Robert. She worked internationally for a global telecommunications company while raising a son. Her origins were Eastern European. There was an additional child, a daughter, whom Serena conceived while living in her home country. This child was raised by her parents in a rural community. She had not told Robert, however, that her parents intervened when Serena gave birth because of their serious misgivings about her capacity to parent.

---

[2] Sullivan, H. Stack., (1953), *The interpersonal theory of psychiatry*, Norton.

She had been a restless, rule-disparaging adolescent; recalcitrant to discipline; and very selfish.

Serena met and married a man when she had seemingly turned herself around and showed the charm and winning style that became the basis of her work success Their son, whom she did raise, arrived a decade after her daughter. The union ended, however, and the father had no contact. Serena's explanation was that she had only belatedly discovered that he lived a hidden criminal life, and she fled to protect this child. Robert never questioned this story nor knew that this man had been seeking contact with his boy for years.

Robert's marriage to Serena went well at the beginning. He was eager to serve as a caring stepfather, which she welcomed. When Serena became pregnant with another son, he was thrilled. It was then, however, that everything turned. Serena handled the pregnancy very poorly and treated it like an affliction. She blamed Robert and hated the bulge in her abdomen. She reinterpreted history to imply that she had been violated to satisfy his need for his own child. She accused him of being repelled by her son and eager to replace him. She started interfering with them having any relationship together.

Robert was stunned and disheartened. He felt panicky. After the baby was born and Serena recovered physically, she stormed out regularly in the wake of volatile episodes, in which she railed against Robert and terrified the household. She refused to breastfeed and alleged that Robert was using her as a "giant tit" to service him and his child. When Robert defended himself, she increased the volume, making sure that neighbors could hear and come to their own conclusion. The police were summoned on several occasions after neighbors called.

When the marriage finally broke apart, Serena fought to be able to take both children back to her home country, where she said she had family support. Her principal rationale that filled court papers was that Robert was physically and emotionally controlling and abusive. She alleged that it was akin to living under communist tyranny. Her affidavit evidence contained scurrilous accusations that depicted Robert as perverse, sadistic, and unfit to parent.

The gravity of the accusations against Robert attracted attention from child protection authorities. Eventually, an assessment was ordered and completed. The results, however, were equivocal. Certainly, the assessor perceived that Serena's bizarre and baseless allegations were problematic and antisocial and that her history indicated character problems, but the assessor concluded that it could be situational and would likely calm down. In effect, the assessment seemed to excuse her destructive behavior, citing cultural differences and poor communication between the parties. The stepson was not interested in further contact with Robert. The situation worsened, with the children caught in the middle.

Thankfully, Serena did not win the court's support to relocate, but the relationship between Robert and the stepson was poisoned. The younger son was torn between two solitudes: one in which his father was the enemy and the other in which he was a loved and nurturing figure. There was no resolving this split, which led to confusion. It was understandable, then, that this younger boy developed an anxiety disorder.

Serena had a poisonous side and a destructive intent. The psychoanalytic concept that comes closest to capturing this quality is "malignant narcissism." It describes a person who is self-centered, greedy, and exploitative of others. There is a poor capacity to take responsibility for one's actions or the hurt or damage caused. Antisocial and aggressive tendencies are common.[3] The term *malignant* is really a synonym for *destructive*.

Pathological narcissism can be an important ingredient in understanding some high-conflict-prone personalities. As this term is bandied about often and ascribed liberally to ex-spouses by aggrieved ex-partners, it might be useful to use this example to clarify its characteristics.

Serena is a good example of the incapacity to recognize the other's rights apart from the subject's own needs. Self-idealization is the glue keeping the narcissistic self together. Anything remotely bad that might arise from feeling inadequate or responsible is externalized and projected onto the other. They dread emotional dependence, as this implies weakness and neediness. Disruption often occurs at moments of vulnerability. Serena, for example, changed dramatically after she became pregnant.

When the destructive enters the discourse, it is aimed at dependent relationships, including children. This type of person hates the people who are needed but also those who need them.

---

[3] Kernberg, O. F., (2007), The almost untreatable narcissistic patient, *Journal of American Psychoanalytic Association*, 55, 503–539; Rosenfeld, H., (1971), A clinical approach to the psychoanalytic theory of life and death instincts: An investigation into the aggressive aspects of narcissism, *International Journal of Psychoanalysis*, 52, 169–178.

The hatred of the child is complicated. There would be too much envy if the child's emotional needs were met. In this regard, the malignant narcissist is consumed with resentment toward anyone who needs them, especially a child whom they are supposed to nurture and love. Thus, the destructive emerges as a need to destroy, and the case history will document this destructive path. Degrading attacks are inevitable. There can be sadistic pleasure in robbing the ex-partner of anything sacred or wholesome. The idea is to pull everyone into the gutter, even if there is a major personal price to pay. In this regard, entitlement is huge in the malignant narcissist, along with a righteousness that conceals the force of destructiveness.

Of course, there is no conscious acknowledgment of destructiveness, and a cover story appears that reverses reality and accuses the other of the precise crimes committed by the subject. Serena was consumed by her diatribes against Robert. She felt completely justified and shouted that she had been violated and mistreated, as had her older son. Her lies were legion and so prolific that there was no check or balance. Curiously, she welcomed the assessment and had no problem using it as a grand opportunity to spoil everything for Robert and the children. She was surprisingly effective in the short term.

Thus any attempt by Robert to stand up to Serena's repetitive belittlement was met with further and even more outlandish allegations against him. She asserted her superiority. Serena wanted to get her way entirely, which meant finishing Robert off in the children's lives as the ultimate triumph of her destructive power.

At some level, perhaps, the family assessor feared a retaliatory attack if this woman was fully confronted with her destructiveness. It takes courage to deal with such individuals because, apart from the normal legal route, they have recourse to attack the professional's career through regulatory complaints. This is a clear abuse of process, but it is very tempting for this high-conflict group due to its ease and destructiveness.

Serena fits the criteria presented. She attacked Robert's reputation and character and would have gladly seen him jailed if she might have achieved this level of triumph. She attacked the relationship between her older son and Robert, forcing the child to side with his mother. She had already eliminated other fatherly men in his short life, so he would have known her power. She attacked the innocence and inherent worth of her baby with Robert, seeing this child as an interloper on her freedom and envying any love that the child might receive from his father and paternal family.

One drawback of using this example is that it could give the erroneous impression that *destructive* is equated with *antisocial, sociopathy, malignant narcissism*, and even *evil*, but this is not the intent. Sociopaths are certainly prone to high conflict; indeed, some revel in it, but what is destructive is not necessarily sociopathic. However, there are instances in which severe personality disorder is relevant. When it goes unchecked, the results can be profoundly damaging.

More often than not, high-conflict cases feature layers of disillusionment, unresolved mourning, deep and enduring bitterness, and strong desires for vengeance. Whatever the specific character makeup, destructiveness runs through the saga. The following example illustrates this recurrent theme in high conflict.

Troy and Sharon

Troy grew up as the youngest child and only son of an airline pilot, who was often absent. His sisters were slightly older and functioned as a unit. They were closer to each other than to him. He was very close, however, to his mother when he was young and recalled often spending time with her while his dad was away working. Nonetheless, as his father's schedule was irregular and included considerable "off time," he also enjoyed activities with him. His dad was an avid outdoorsman, and as Troy got more physically capable, his father took him fishing and camping. It was a blossoming relationship.

Troy was dimly aware when, in the third grade, his mother became withdrawn. One day, while his father was away flying, his mother packed the children's suitcases, put everyone into her car, and soon joined a man with whom she was having an affair. It was 2 months before he saw his father again. Troy recalled feeling that he might never see his dad. He is sure that his father had no idea of his wife's extramarital activity or plans. He could not specifically recall their relationship at the time, but he did not recall any yelling or fighting between his parents.

It had been a profound betrayal of his father and the children for that matter. Eventually, his father was able to arrange to see his children regularly. Troy never felt close to the man who became his stepfather.

He papered over his darker feelings about his mother, which he had never expressed to her. In fact, he had not mentioned his feelings to anyone, including his sisters, who had endured the same experience. It was as if the event and its repercussions were forgotten.

Troy met Sharon through a mutual friend. They had common interests and were both employed in the same field. Sharon's childhood had been severely disrupted by a sexual encounter with a pubescent boy who lived nearby. She was 11 at the time. It was a sexual awakening for Sharon, despite her youth, and this troubled her greatly. She suffered bouts of guilt and anxiety. In Sharon's mind, she was more a coconspirator than a victim. Sharon's lingering anxiety led to problems gauging and managing relationships.

The liaison between Troy and Sharon was relatively brief. They lived together long enough for her to get pregnant, but it was unstable from the beginning. She found Troy very insecure, brittle, and reactive. He seemed suspicious of her and very mistrusting of her fidelity and demanded repeatedly to know her whereabouts. He was an appealing man in her eyes when she first met him, but the attraction wore off quickly. Within 4 months of living together and prior to their child's birth, the liaison ended badly.

This was just the beginning though. Troy did not even wait until their son was born before demanding equal time and shared parenting. He hounded Sharon and accused her of absconding with his son, much as his mother had done with his sisters and him. If he could send one e-mail, he sent 10, insisting on rapid replies and paying no attention to the fact that she was postpartum and caring for an infant.

Sharon felt that she was living a nightmare. It did not matter what she might say or do to appease Troy; nothing worked. He threatened legal action from the beginning and often threatened to involve the police if his demands were not immediately met. When he did see their child on his own, he refused to provide any feedback or inform her about the child's sleeping and eating. Eventually all issues had to be handled by lawyers, which proved very expensive and cumbersome.

Troy's sense of disillusionment, helplessness, and unfairness with its origins in his childhood easily transferred to his situation with Sharon. He raged, and she cowered. She feared Troy's communications and felt tyrannized by him. Of course, Troy saw none of this. He feared and thought the worst of her or anyone he identified with her. He could not tolerate anyone disagreeing with him without feeling attacked.

When their child had returned to Sharon with the beginnings of a fever, she inquired whether any symptoms were noticeable during the visit. Troy immediately became defensive: three e-mails, two phone messages, and 10 texts followed in quick succession, each recording his outrage at being blamed for not caring well enough for their child.

Troy ramped up legal fees, fired lawyers, complained about allegedly biased mediators, and harassed Sharon but was sure that he represented the best interests of their shared child. He attacked Sharon's character and reputation; the family law and mental health professionals attempting to help them; and day care providers, whom he believed were not neutral enough. Transitions between them were either a tense, uncomfortable standoff or a war zone. They were forced to use a public setting.

Troy was obviously too emotionally scarred to handle this situation. He sought allies who accepted his distorted view rather than examining his obvious difficulties. This is a hallmark feature of the high-conflict-prone personality. His attacks were destructive and intended to cause damage to Sharon and anyone associated with her. He was oblivious to his child's needs or the obvious requirement to work together with his ex-partner. The thin line that unconsciously separated Sharon from his own mother rendered her a suitable proxy for his rage and vengeance. This was bottomless, which is what Sharon sensed and left her feeling that she was trapped in a high-conflict madness that was destroying her. It had negative repercussions for the child, who was denied any semblance of parents who once came together in love to create him.

One can only imagine how extreme it would have become if Sharon was also of this high-conflict disposition. Those are clearly the worst, but this one was bad enough. It leaves the impression that nothing can be done to protect children from high conflict or the ex-partner trying to fend off repeated destructive attacks.

Was Sharon a proxy for Troy's mother? Indeed, this was the basis of destructiveness in this instance. Perhaps, though, I sided with Sharon, took her word for it, and underestimated the depth and breadth of her contribution. Sharon had a psychological vulnerability, the remnant of a confusing seduction that left her feeling more identified with the perpetrator than as a victim. Her confidence was low, and she lived with a residual shame that undermined her personality. As much as Troy found his hurtful, absconding mother in Sharon, she found her childhood abuser in Troy. Each replayed a terrible part of their lives that sadly had marked them.

If treatment were an option, then it would amount to a three-step process after the working alliance was established. First, it would be important to name the experiences of disillusionment, both historical and contemporary. Second, there would be a need for the therapist to contain and bear the pain and distress this caused the person, and then, third, the therapist would help to reframe the issue in better perspective, linking past to present and working to recover an ethical relation to the other.

Conclusion

These case reviews reach the apotheosis of destructivity rained down on the family and family law system. In severe-high-conflict divorce, all the noted problems come to the fore: the incapacity for concern and unrestrained attack without ethical consideration.

The clinician and legal specialist will certainly meet these "malignant" personalities whose pathological narcissism cannot be challenged by having to share and communicate with another adult, even if this individual is a former partner. They insist on unlimited control in the service of grandeur and will use every means available, from lies to distortion, to achieve their legal ends. Their destructiveness is fueled by a hatred of any limiting factor and, certainly, anyone who stands in their way. Every relationship is sacrificed to meet their egocentric needs without hint of remorse or equivocation.

These cases of malignant narcissism, though, are a minority. Mostly, high conflict is triggered by a culmination of disillusionments that prove traumatic and unleash a toxic brew of destructiveness aimed at the family ideal, which then reverberates through the mental health care and legal systems aiming to contain, repair, and resolve. It accounts for the chronic battle that can endure for years, which is so familiar to family law. The therapeutic goal is to turn dangerous destructiveness, with its surfeit of damaging conflict, into normal-range hatred that still registers the pain of a broken dream but is not in itself a nightmare.

Traumatic Conflict Disorder

Although I have met lawyers and mental health professionals who eschew ever working with high-conflict families due to depleting and even threatening professional experience, there are many more who brave the challenges. This is a testament to the dedication of the legal and mental health professional communities who serve this demanding population.

Of course, mention words like *court*, *custody*, or *high conflict* to many mental health professionals, and they will never go near the case. Professional risk keeps many worthy clinicians away from this important and valuable work. As a result, in most communities, one finds a small cadre of practitioners who specialize in this subgroup of the divorcing population. Their caseloads tend to be high, and the community relies on their expertise and experience to shoulder the burden inside and outside the courtroom, as there is as yet no widely accepted treatment strategy to mitigate the considerable damage done by such high-conflict individuals and couples. Severe-high-conflict divorce remains a serious public health concern with transgenerational consequences.

This is not dissimilar to the clinicians who work with such highly challenging cases as psychosis, which are viewed as largely organic problems barely manageable by medication and hospital services. Nonetheless, there is something very satisfying about working with complex and seemingly intractable cases, as if one can get a glimpse of humanity in the raw, bared, and transparent. There is no greater service than making every effort to protect children caught in such family mayhem, doing everything possible to mitigate the damage to their lives and growing personalities.

One should be skeptical of the lawyer allied with the worst aspects of a client's destructiveness and giving free rein to it and the health professional who writes glowing reference letters about the parenting capacity of someone they have never seen parent. Equally, it is plainly sad and terribly unfortunate when the regulatory systems designed to protect the public against unprepared or unethical practitioners are hijacked by high-conflict litigants abusing the process to attack the message through the messenger.

In the available literature, there is not much analysis of the source of high conflict other than references to personality disorders that favor excessive blame and other projective defenses. High conflict is multifactorial, however, and there is a growing appreciation for the role of previous trauma in the lives of these individuals and the saliency of trauma-based interventions.[1]

This points to examining the prior psychological and relational history of the high-conflict-prone subject and, particularly, the risk factors for high conflict. We need deeper insights into the specific characteristics of this demanding population rather than simply merging them conceptually with trauma theory and its remediation.

Despite some advances, the current legal and social science position has been mainly that these extreme family situations are often untreatable and must be managed. Hence, courts offer high-conflict judicial case management, both pre- and posttrial, while the clinical community provides parent coordination, assessment, and sometimes family therapy, including reunification therapy in cases of refusal to visit. The family law system has gotten much better at managing high conflict but no more successful at lessening it.

So far, I have identified two crucial underlying factors:

1. a layering of corrosive and often traumatic disillusionment in the life of the high-conflict-prone person who depletes hope and creates emotional vulnerability
2. a triggering of destructiveness, in which the goal is ruination of something related to the family that would otherwise be deemed precious

---

[1] Deutsch, R., Drozd, L., & Ajoku, C., (2020), Trauma-informed interventions in parent-child contact cases, *Family Court Review*, 58(2), 470–487; Drozd, L., Saini, M. S., & Velluci-Coo, K., (2019), Trauma and child custody disputes: Screening, assessment, and interventions, in L. Greenberg, B. J. Fidler, & M. A. Saini (Eds.), *Evidence-informed interventions for court-involved families: Promoting coping and healthy child development* (pp. 260–281), Oxford University Press; Fidler, B. J., Deutsch, R., & Polak, S., (2019), "How am I supposed to treat these cases?" Working with families struggling with entrenched parent-child contact problems: A hybrid case, in L. Greenberg, B. J. Fidler, & M. A. Saini (Eds.), *Evidence-informed interventions for court-involved families: Promoting coping and healthy child development* (pp. 227–259), Oxford University Press.

Thus, using the construct of "conflict" to describe these individuals or couples might obscure the specific nature of the problem. Not surprisingly, there is no clear definition of or accepted criteria for *high conflict*, even though 90% of court time is comprised of only 10% of cases handled by lawyers.[2] In this regard, the term itself has not especially clarified either the phenomenon or how it might be addressed.

Destructiveness is the key quality that determines the difference between high conflict and sharp conflict, acute conflict, reactive conflict, litigious conflict, or any other context or qualifier. Of course, there is general agreement that high conflict is destructive to families, but this is viewed as a consequence and not a cause. This needs to be reversed: a cause and not simply a consequence. When one casts a long view of human society, whatever sphere we might examine, there is a destructive variant of that realm. Here are a few examples, in no specific order:

1. alcohol → alcoholism
2. emotional dependence → parasitism or pathological dependence
3. Failure to accept individual differences → prejudice, antihuman rights, ethnic cleansing
4. male-female relations → misogyny, rape, gender-based murder
5. love of driving → reckless, stunt driving
6. tax avoidance → tax evasion

Postseparation interparental relations also have a pathological dimension, which is severe high conflict.

The common element in all these manifestations of the destructive in human behavior is that each represents a pathological expression of a normal dimension. At the same time, there is often a distorted idealization that lurks in the background. If we look at each of these examples, there is an underlying fantasy ideal that is somewhere in the psychic field. It is not a workable ideal, however, promoting adjustment and expressing healthy values and aspirations. Rather, it is a grossly distorted ideal, divorced from reality and inherently destructive:

1. Alcoholism and drug and food addictions, in general, feed on a fantasy of nirvana, the blissful state of nonanxiety, like an infant totally satiated

---

[2] Neff, R., & Cooper, K., (2004), Parental conflict resolution: Six-, twelve-, and fifteen-month follow-ups of a high-conflict program, *Family Court Review*, 42, 99–114.

and calmed at the mother's breast but with the human world replaced by a substance.

2. Parasitism or pathological dependence, in which the person clings to another, also hearkens to an early blissful state of total infantile dependence, when one's every need was met by an omnipresent, loving parent.

3. A country's wish and willingness to start a war, whatever its rationalization, often implicates its perceived manifest destiny, as either divinely given or achieved through some form of innate or cultural superiority. This is the basis of runaway nationalism, a collective delusion, which is paranoid and ultimately, in most instances, hateful and destructive.

4. Racism and pathological "othering" rest on the distorted ideal that one's own human subtype or culture or some combination of the two represents the ideal of human life. Again, this relies on a pseudo-distinction that is deeply exclusionary and paranoid and often leads to a vicious legacy.

5. As we are all born from mothers, there is a natural idealization of the woman, but at the same time, this can lead to a deep fear of her power over life and death. It is deeply distorted, essentially dehumanizing, but sadly too common. Misogyny can be seen as an expression of a pathological fear of female power. Women, on whom we are helplessly dependent at the beginning of life, need to be kept down so that maternal power is defused. The rape and murder of women can represent a symbolic destruction of the mother and her vital, life-giving, and sustaining role in human destiny.

6. The stereotyped male relationship with the car as an ideal of power and potency lurks behind the irresponsibly aggressive male who drives city streets and highways as if on a speedway, without regard for human life. It suggests a distorted ideal of masculinity that is inherently destructive and leads to needless injury or death of others.

7. Greed is fed by a bottomless, omnipotent wish to possess all the money and all the riches that the world can offer. It is an insatiable grandiosity that hates and seeks to destroy any limit or curb on that power. This includes taxes. Tax evaders will go to any length to avoid the shared civic duty to support the society that provides for us all. At its foundation lies a perverse sense of entitlement—an insatiable, ruthless infant who destroys the mother in order to possess the breast and all its goodness.

In all these examples, there is a close relationship between distorted idealization and destructiveness. It is the inevitable experience of disillusionment that acts as the trigger. Consider, for example, a bulimic young woman who idealizes the food before her as a magical breast that will fill her up and transform her. It will make her whole. Chips and ice cream in huge quantities offer the promise of a deep fulfillment that will end her quest. It is an idealized fantasy. Sadly, the moment she finishes gorging, she realizes that it is not magical or transformative at all but fatty food that will toxify and harm her. It is a moment of acute, traumatic disillusionment. Hence, she cannot wait to disgorge it through vomiting. She purges that which moments before had promised to be the solution to her ailing mood and weak identity. The cycle repeats endlessly without new learning.

Substitute the high-conflict-prone person for the bulimic patient, and we have a plausible progression toward a similar phenomenon. This individual marries full of hope and promise. The other, the new partner, is idealized as an answer to all the problems of the person's life. It is a new beginning. Unfortunately, at whatever stage or phase the bloom comes off the rose, usually sooner rather than later, the result is disastrous. The disillusionment is catastrophic and fatal to the relationship. Not only is there loss of a sense of love, but also the other is viewed as poisonous, a blight, and possibly a threat to the welfare of the children. Hatred can be palpable. It fuels a wish to destroy the other, to get rid of the toxin. But the other cannot be easily eliminated. Whatever blow is delivered, this noxious other remains. It is unvomitable. Thus, high-conflict hatred is never satisfied, disgorged, or abated. It is an endless cycle of destructive interactions in which no death blow can be delivered, which is why it becomes such a paranoid nightmare for the participants.

Identifying the traumatic disillusionment can be the key to recovering hope on a firmer and more rational basis. Let me provide another vignette to illustrate this relationship between distorted idealization and destructivity as it succumbs to disillusionment.

Neil and Belinda

Neil was a capable student who aimed to be the gold medal scholar that his dashing father had been. He was, in fact, more middling in his accomplishments, and there was an aching sense of inadequacy with which he struggled. When he married Belinda, it was a match made in heaven, as he saw it. He had never felt good enough to attract such a beauty. All his self-doubts were magically healed by her attention and love. He even thought his career would be better with her at his side. It was not long after they married, however, that Neil did not feel that much had changed. Belinda was not the magical amulet who would transform him into the handsome prince and scholar. Neil became increasingly negative, accusing Belinda of, among other things, being frigid, which she took badly and saw as degradation and abuse. Matters only got worse after they had their child. Neil felt deceived and envious of his child, who was getting much more love than he was receiving, at least as he saw it.

Perhaps, Belinda hoped that Neil's career would take off, but it stalled. He did not receive the promotions he thought were his due. He became angry, resentful, depressed, and very negative. Everyone was getting ahead but him. He found increasing fault with Belinda, and they fought over which of them was the biggest disappointment. His adoration for her plummeted, and in its place, he felt a growing vitriol. When their marriage broke under the onslaught, severe disillusionment transformed into endless conflict and encompassed all their interactions.

It was as if hope itself had perished with the death of the fantasy of the idealized Belinda. High-conflict individuals and couples often live without hope. One might say that all Neil's hope was contained in the image of Belinda as a magical ideal who would make him the person he wanted to be. This was the unconscious fantasy that propelled the union from his side. She would be transformative for Neil, and he would be forever grateful and loving to her. It was an overestimation of what any marriage could deliver. In his eyes, Belinda had failed him, and she fought this indictment at every turn in their long, fruitless legal battle. Disillusionment led to hopelessness, and this fueled the destructive high conflict.

In Neil's case, the magical image of Belinda was a defense against painful realities tied to his own feelings of inadequacy. His case against his now ex-wife, prosecuted through endless court battles, never emptied or satisfied his blame of her. As much as his behavior was ruinous to his family and himself, destructive to the core, Neil could never see any of it. He was filled with a self-righteousness that was blind to his own conduct. Even witnessing his child lose sleep and suffer meltdowns at school did not alter Neil's behavior. It was a pox on his own house and family because this included Belinda.

Reconceptualizing High Conflict

High conflict would be better understood if reconceptualized as traumatic conflict disorder (TCD) to capture its links to psychopathology and psychic trauma. The role of disillusionment, then, would be central to understanding and responding to its clinical and judicial challenges. TCD is based on defensive illusions that cover up painful vulnerabilities. Disillusionment, then, opens the door to destructiveness, which becomes a bottomless appetite for struggle that is never quenched. The important question is whether there is a treatment for TCD.

First, there is no viable solution based mainly on the reduction of conflict. For example, mediators and assessors will put special effort into making the parenting plan so specific that there will be nothing to fight about. Of course, this is impossible and itself an unrealistic ideal. Conflict is analogous to lava that flows across the surface but gives no hint of what is occurring below ground, where the problem originates.

Second, TCD conflict can rarely be managed because it is fueled by destructiveness that works against resolution. Mainly, it can be accommodated through court and extrajudicial dispute resolution and mental health services. It has a circular, self-combusting rhythm that has no end because it is unmournable.

Third, destructiveness is an essential ingredient to the disorder. It cannot be TCD if it is not destructive. Sufferers never acknowledge destructiveness, especially as a primary aim. Rather, they experience themselves as victims, sometimes martyrs to justice, fairness, and truth. The destructive aspect is mentally unsymbolized and thus unavailable to reason. If the subject engages legal counsel that fans the flames of victimhood, however, the result can be appalling.

Finally, the destructiveness of TCD needs to be approached indirectly through tackling and working through traumatic disillusionments. Each disillusionment should be named for the illusion on which it was based, described in its path to downfall, experienced with the therapist, and mourned to the extent possible. This is mainly work that needs to be done individually unless, there is sufficient working through to have the capacity to meet the ex-partner outside the zone of conflict. As noted previously, there is a triphasic process of naming, containing, and reformulating in a way that facilitates a return to ethics.

There are two separate strands to disillusionment. First, there is the realization that the reality is not the equal of what was expected. Second, there is an inability to find value or sustain interest in the way things are.[3] Traumatic disillusionment intensifies that experience. The destructiveness that follows speaks to its core significance for the subject.

---

[3] Rycraft, C., (1968), *Imagination and reality*, International Universities Press.

These illusions create a fragile strand of hope. They are often idealized appraisals of the other and what the other can do. This idealization and the resulting illusion cover old wounds and vulnerabilities. In TCD, illusions are defensively held to avoid painful realities, which is why when they disintegrate, everything about the relationship disintegrates with it. The catastrophe is experienced as a personal assault, and a destructive hatred fills the space.

High conflict is a description of observed behavior that is ambiguous and hard to define. It is a label that suggests quantity versus quality. Where does high conflict begin, however, and how should the clinician or the court differentiate high conflict from general divorce conflict? The problem has less to do with identifying such cases, for they are often flagrant and hard to miss, than with providing effective intervention to undo the toxic dynamic that fuels its interminability.

One area where there has been an effective shift from description to underlying clinical dynamics is child alienation. Understanding of this concept shifted in 1985, when psychiatrist Richard Gardener reconceptualized the problem as "parental alienation syndrome."[4] His emphasis on parental conduct and motivation oversimplified the problem and put the onus squarely on the shoulders of the preferred parent. It would be like calling depression "harsh parent syndrome" by ascribing the cause to the sufferer's parents.

Nonetheless, there was no turning back. The mental health and legal communities saw merit in pathologizing a behavior that was clearly alien to the standards of the best interests of the child. Parental alienation syndrome has never made it into the psychiatric lexicon, but alienation is today understood as an abnormal family pattern that deserves treatment. I prefer the term *child alienation*, which is more accurately descriptive of what occurs while omitting apparent causation. As discussed previously, these cases are usually complicated, involving a child and specific adult factors. Others refer to "refusal to visit" or "entrenched parent-child contact problems," which are accurate terms in that the phenomenon encompasses a range of estrangement behavior and situations with no single causation.[5]

---

[4] Gardner, R., (1992), *The parental alienation syndrome*, Creative Therapeutics.

[5] Fidler, B. J., & Bala, N., (2010), Children resisting post-separation contact with a parent: Concepts, controversies, and conundrums, *Family Court Review*, 48, 10–47; Fidler, B., Deutsch, R., & Polak, S., (2019), "How am I supposed to treat these cases?": Working with families struggling with entrenched parent-child contact problems: A hybrid case, in L. Greenberg., B. Fidler, & M. Saini (Eds.), *Evidence-informed interventions for court-involved families: Promoting healthy coping and development* (pp. 227–259), Oxford University Press.

The advantage of the term *traumatic conflict disorder* is that it retains the signifier, conflict, but buffers it within the bookends of trauma and psychopathology. In this regard, it is more akin to other traumatic conditions, such as PTSD, than to disorders of personality. Of course, if an individual has an emotional vulnerability, they could well be more prone to PTSD, but one does not have to be disordered to develop PTSD. In the same way, personality problems would increase the risk of TCD, but personality disorder is not a necessary ingredient. A history of prior traumatic experiences, beginning in childhood, is very much a predictor of PTSD.[6] The same can be said of TCD, which stems from radical disillusionment.

The term *TCD* is preferable to *high conflict*, which obscures its destructive impact on families. It implies that conflict itself is the issue rather than the layering of traumatic disillusionments and destructivity underlying the problem. Conflict is the manifestation, but it is necessary to address the underlying cause to have an any appreciable impact. In these couple dynamics, conflict seeps from a deep wound of one or both parties, but it is not reducible to the wound itself.

Viewing high conflict as a disorder also captures its pathological dimension. Sufferers vociferously condemn their ex-spouse and find no cause too small to ignore or any issue unworthy of grievance. The lack of perspective can be jarring to the outsider, the self-righteousness beyond proportion or reason and a capacity to rationalize spending every dollar available and then some, presumably to defend themselves and their children. Destructiveness is in the air, whether acknowledged or not. TCD, in this respect, is a traumatic disorder that can overwhelm a family's adaptive resources, make children sick, and fully occupy the courts and mental health professionals trying to assist them.

I recall a savvy family law lawyer reflecting on a case that seized his attention. It was the tail end of a prolonged saga in which every effort, judicial and mental health, had failed to contain the destructive current that had crippled the family. The children grew old enough during the protracted struggle to devise their own solution. The lawyer related how sad it was to see a parent offering the same distorted, unserviceable theory of the ex-spouse's villainy to the judge, despite countless court appearances and mental health input. There was no insight, no new perspective, and no appreciation of the role this

---

[6] Verhaeghe, P., & Vanheule, S., (2008), Posttraumatic stress disorder (PTSD), actual pathology, and the question of representability, *Psychoanalytic Psychology*, 25(2), 386–391.

parent had played in the family affliction. This was clear to everyone in the courtroom that day except this unfortunate individual.

It would have been a clear case of TCD. The sufferer was likely in the grip of a destructivity that was circular and never-ending. Parents are usually spent, emotionally, physically, and often financially. In the lawyer's recollection, there had been numerous awful incidents, explosive moments of both physical and emotional violence. These occurred in many different venues where the parents and children interacted. The man in this case, pleading that the court needed to protect the children from their mother, would have had limited capacity to see any side but his own.

In this regard, TCD is also a problem of representability. The individual tends to gloss over moments of startling regression and does not seem to have any awareness of their own functioning within the conflict. There is clearly no retrospective reflection, what French analysts call après coup, that would allow for new learning. Thoughts and perceptions occur within an entirely closed system, in which there is no other thinkable view.

This narrowing of reality of the ex-spouse can impair judgment, perspective, emotional control, and reflection within the circumscribed realm of the conflict. This paralyzes the capacity for empathy and the ability to see the merits or perspective of the ex-partner. It is not psychosis in the diagnostic sense but a form of psychotic thinking regressively provoked by traumatic ruptures and disillusionments that create an unbearable state of mind.

The goal in TCD tends to be solely confirmation of one's interpretation of reality. This has little to do with actual conflict resolution or the best interests of the children. Instead, confirmation often functions like a fixed idea, and the whole case is aimed at proving this usually deeply distorted and starkly polarized reality. It is reminiscent of the worst cases of conspiracy theorists.[7]

Although health professionals and courts attempt to intervene between the warring parties, there is often no space for a third

[7] The link between disillusionment and destructiveness was on full display on January 6, 2021, when an unhinged, riotous mob of disillusioned American citizens, ablaze with the conviction of betrayal, destructively turned on the very symbol of the nation's family ideal, the Capitol, or "People's House," in Washington. Chanting, "Whose house is this?" they ransacked the building, assaulting and destroying while claiming to be the nation's only real protectors. The fragile thread of hope, linked to a Trump reelection, shattered. It was a loss too great to acknowledge or mourn and triggered a destructive attack on the very symbol of the family.

perspective that might help create new forms of thinking and problem solving. There is, instead, a refusal to acknowledge disturbing but essential realities, such as the impact of the conflict on the children. Assessing reality becomes very difficult in the zone of the conflict as well as for staying positively focused on family obligations and tasks. Unfavorable court judgments are either ignored or dismissed as judicial misunderstanding. Detailed family assessments by mental health professionals are read only for what they might say negatively about the ex-partner. They fail to influence.

It is the idea of destructiveness that can be hard to grasp because it runs counter to family values. As noted previously, the goal is to bring the family house down, like the priest who turns on the parishioner, the doctor who turns on the patient, or the disillusioned rioter who attacks the house of government. TCD is not about conflict any more than sexual abuse is about sex. It is about destructiveness, which shifts the paradigm from life and love to destroying a reality that has been so painful and disillusioning that it must be destroyed. Once the individual crosses this threshold, there is often no turning back. Nonetheless, there are better and worse ways of responding to and dealing with it.

Sara and Sam

Sam could not keep his voice down. He was immediately yelling, exasperated by how unfairly he was being treated and how despicably unjust his ex-wife was. He ignored his ascending rage until it burst. He always felt fully justified but never stopped trying to explain himself. His children were nervous of him.

His now ex-wife, Sara, had her own struggles. She came from a large family warped by internal conflict. Siblings and parents fought regularly, and periods of estrangement were common. Sara had left home very young and dropped out of high school. She lacked formal education but was an intelligent and well-read person. Nonetheless, she had a sharp temper and a cutting manner, honed by the combative family who had raised her. She hated this quality about herself and had felt that Sam and she would never repeat the problem, which made her disillusionment especially bitter when the atmosphere in their marriage turned sour. It happened slowly, but with two young children to raise and busy work lives, they both felt strained. Instead of supporting each other, sparks started to fly. They each felt a sense of inadequacy and held the other to account for what felt like failure.

Sam was denied a promotion at work, on which he had counted. This made matters decidedly worse between them. Stung by the career setback, he defensively showed little respect for Sara's intelligence, and she lashed out about his "hippy loser family" or whatever criticism came to mind. His condescension, underlying shame, and Sara's dripping derision created a toxic atmosphere for the two children, a boy and a girl. On Sara's initiative, they agreed to a temporary marital separation with the hope of lowering the temperature, but it only added to their mutual disillusionment. It was not long before Sara gave up trying and declared the marriage over. Sam felt set up and betrayed. There was a huge shift, and conflict consumed them like a wildfire.

Sam's upbringing had also been deeply disillusioning. His parents were return-to-the-land types who lived off the grid and viewed poverty as a form of self-sufficiency and moral purity. They chastised their offspring for wanting anything material and not making do. They demanded chores of their children to a degree that Sam experienced as a cruel tyranny, more slavery than childhood. His mother made ill-fitting clothes, and this was a cause for ridicule at school. His parents apparently took pride in this response, as if it signaled that they were doing something right. Sam grew up ashamed of his origins and very angry and disillusioned by parents whose morality was self-serving rather than caring.

It seemed no accident that these two people found each other. Both Sam and Sara had grown up feeling disgruntled and disillusioned. Neither had been able to give comfort to the other, and each used blame and aggression to keep the other at bay. Each understood too well the other's vulnerabilities and self-doubts and rubbed it in with venom. Neither had known sufficient love or reassuring attachment. They were soon in the grip of a very destructive dynamic that bore no resemblance to how they had begun as a couple.

But what is this destructivity? Very painful, traumatic experiences that are deeply disillusioning allow destructive impulses to foment and take over the psyche and family field. Outward aggression is a mere fraction of what is actually destructive. It is mainly the crushing effect on all family members, whether there is overt aggression or not. It emanates from radical despair, a deeply damaged psychic image of the family as a source of hope.

Sara's inclination was to protect the children from Sam, not as much as to alienate them as to expose his guilt and failure and make him assume the blame. She minimized her own family history of endless feuds and estrangements. What she visited on Sam was exactly what she had learned as a child. His loud vocal retort and lack of a clear strategy seemed to seal his fate as the loser in their struggle. He appeared to lack a capacity for self-preservation and dug a hole with his children and Sara.

Sam meant well when trying to help their son in particular, who has having difficulties achieving at school, but failed to ensure Sara's support and became too outwardly frustrated for the child to handle. Inevitably, he said too much, did too much, and managed to make himself the focus, even when he was trying his best to be helpful.

Yet the major share of destructiveness did not derive from Sam necessarily but from Sara. She could not stop delivering a beating and encouraged her children to do so as well. She looked like the rational one on the surface but was deeply undermining Sam and found solace, if not pleasure, in putting him down in retribution. She was not completely wrong with respect to Sam, but this hardly justified the depth of damage she inflicted on the family. Both children were hurt by what occurred; their link with their father was compromised to their detriment.

The son continued to struggle academically, while his parents argued incessantly whether he even had a scholastic problem. Sam lost his capacity for self-care. He developed worrisome health risks. He felt like a worm under Sara's heel. This was not dissimilar to how he had felt with his own father.

There is no single emotion or life factor that triggers this current of destructiveness. It is an independent factor. Yet we see it play out in human society in so many ways: self-inflicted damage on the body; attacks on important relationships; endless, pointless wars that chart human history; and uprisings by disenchanted citizens who violently attack symbols of the government that they believe has betrayed them. In Sara and Sam's case, one could identify the dynamics of underlying shame and humiliation releasing a torrent of destructiveness on one another. Sara was deeply aware of her dysfunctional family background, people seeming to live for their hatreds, rivalries, and grievances. Sam was ashamed of his family and his own situation. The loss of the promotion was especially humiliating and seemed to him to confirm Sara's doubts. If Sara was relishing in delivering beatings, he was doing little to curb the blows.

As a parenting couple, and despite their dysfunction, Sara and Sam were still helpable. The bridge between them was the deep shame each had felt in their lives: the fear of being exposed as having come from inferior families, those worthy of contempt and ridicule.

Sam began the conversation. He had taken the children to gym class and was aware that Sara was in the viewing stands while he was sitting on the gym floor, where some parents were permitted to observe.

> SAM: All I could think of was that Sara could see me—gross and pathetic. Why are you there looking down at me? I could not stand it and wanted to run out. I know you hate me and wish you had never met me.

Sara defended being in the building, as this was allowed according to their parenting agreement. She insisted that she was simply looking for a quiet, unobtrusive corner. She then berated Sam for focusing on her and not on the pleasure of seeing their children doing so well in the gym. Of course, this only made Sam wince more.

The conversation eventually turned to Sara and her feelings of utter humiliation when Sam would make her feel stupid about what she did not know about world affairs.

> SARA: You make me feel awful about myself sometimes just because I am not as smart as you and educated. I know that you think I'm stupid, and I am afraid that the children will think the same as you. I never felt that I could be good enough for you.

Sara and Sam needed to make the link between their deep shame regarding themselves, their family backgrounds, the depth of disillusionment each suffered as a child, and how the whole tragic history repeated with their own marriage and now their divorce. It was a layering of disillusionments. What each had gone though as a child was painfully and harmfully repeated.

There were three steps to amelioration. First, they needed to acknowledge that what they were calling divorce conflict had little to do with conflict or divorce. It was traumatic, tragic, and destructive. If they could not accept that their relationship pattern reflected a problem that implicated both their psyches, then I could not have helped them.

Second, they needed to find a way to think about and bear the real underlying feelings rather than to blame or engage destructively with one another. In this case, Sam and Sara were able to get outside the conflict with help and reflect on themselves in the struggle. Often, this is not achievable without preliminary work on self-reflection— becoming aware of self-states, feelings, background thoughts, flashes of memories, or associations—and to be able to convey them without fear of having it used against them. This is what is meant by the term *mentalizing*.[8] In some situations, it is this prework of identifying thoughts and emotional states of mind that paves the way to work through the painful layers of disillusionment.

Third, TCD sufferers, such as Sam and Sara, need to identify and trace the history of traumatic disillusionments and accompanying shame and regret that fed the vicious cycle of their interaction. It is in in many ways an individual journey and not something that can be solved at the level of the couple. This would not preclude each exploring this aspect with the therapist in the context of the couple if this capacity was present.

Sara admitted that she had always wanted to have a "perfect" life to counter the shame and disillusionment she had experienced in her formative years. She held Sam responsible for ruining her dream, but she also felt bad that she could not be more successful in everything she did. Sara noted that what drew her to him was his strong ability and endless fund of knowledge and worldliness. She admired this greatly and even envied him. She felt discouraged by Sam and his way of treating her, but she also found her own self-esteem fragile and easily rocked when she did not live up to her own expectations. Her cutting sarcasm made her feel good for the moment but was also a source of guilt. She was aware when she did not support Sam with the children, and she could never explain why she would go so far in damaging him in the children's eyes. It came from a depth of rage that she could hardly justify.

Sam was aware that he dug a hole for himself and often did the opposite of what he needed to do. It took a while for him to understand that he was as much interested in shaming and punishing himself as in rehabilitating and affirming his image as someone worthy of respect and love. He was deeply resentful toward his parents for sacrificing the family to their twisted hippy ideal that was a poor justification for poverty. In a curious way, when he felt cruelly treated by Sara, he somehow felt that his parents were being punished as well. He needed to

---

[8] Fonagy, P., (2015), Peter Fonagy, Anna Freud Centre chief executive: What is mentalization? Interview, *Anna Freud Centre*, 1(1), 2.

stop the vicious cycle of eruptions and excesses followed by remorse, shameful self-torment, and suffering exclusion by his children.

Over the next 6 months, Sara and Sam made progress. Though they continued to have some conflicts, mainly due to communication problems, there was diminishing venom and anguish. Yet, there was no going back on the separation: too much water under the bridge and a sense that they were too similar to transcend their issues. They discovered, however, that dealing with conflict was not their issue. They became better able to pull together as parents. Sam no longer felt scorned by Sara, and she understood better that using Sam as an outlet for her own issues was unfair to him and their children. She was able to express gratitude to Sam for their family, and he was able to thank her for her openness and self-responsibility.

TCD and Destructivity: The Role of Hatred

TCD features two people, at least one of whom is struggling to discredit the other to demonstrate the other's utter unworthiness and fault. The entrenched TCD sufferer seeks to be pure victim, unblemished by fault and on the side of righteousness and virtue. There is no longer a private relationship. If there is to be a shaming, then it is a public shaming. Of course, everyone has something to hide. Failure sticks to both participants, while ascribing it solely to the other is a way out. Hence, the struggle is interminable because we are all discreditable over something and no one wants to be stigmatized.

Let us return to the man standing before the judge, pleading his case despite a painful, protracted legacy of damaged children and damaged adults, claiming the righteousness of his position after years of abhorrent high conflict. What is remarkable, I expect, is that he presumably continued to represent the ideal in his own mind: the one who really loved his children and sought justice for them. Moral narcissism in TCD clashes with reality, and the reality is far less clear and absolving of responsibility.

This is the precise cocktail of destructiveness: a claim of excessive moral virtue, deep disillusionment, shame, and unacknowledged guilt as well as disavowed hatred and aggression. We might imagine that this man probably could not even begin to see his hatred, not only of his ex-wife, but also of his children. This disavowed aggression would apparently burst into the family field, with moments of mayhem affecting everyone. After the explosions, the attack would be completely denied, as if it never happened. It would be disavowed.

But why the hatred? We can suppose that he felt that his wife and children ruined his life, drained him emotionally, and discredited him in front of community and family. As to his children, they are not just offspring but also witnesses to his failed record; victims of his disavowed aggression; and betrayers who continue to love, choose, and benefit from the comforts of his ex-wife. Of course, he would know that this is their mother and someone they needed to love, but he would expect them to see the truth, especially their mother's nastiness; to acknowledge that they have been deluded or brainwashed; and to see their father's ideal protective love and righteousness. However, the children's continued loyalty to their mother might have clashed with his ideal view of himself as the only moral parent. This would have intensified the hatred and fed his destructiveness. Attacks on the children for loving the other parent are not uncommon in TCD cases, although they are rationalized as loving parenting gone awry.

Often, the conflict is expressed through one child in particular. This child is both the target and the prize. It could be a child who lends him- or herself to the parents' struggle, or it could be the parents who triangulate this child as a battleground. It is never good news for the child. They might be empowered by the parents as the one who gets to judge and choose but also disempowered in that they are not free to engage their energies and focus on growing up. Peer relationships, academic progress, and mental health may suffer.

Mentalization and TCD

A major part of the difficulty of dealing with TCD and resulting high conflict is that individuals are impervious to outside influence. They function within the closed system of the TCD. Because there is no aperture to the external world, there is no opening to a new perspective or to thinking itself. The TCD sufferer never seems to acquire new knowledge as the legal process unfolds, which is not the case with normal divorce, even among those where there is heightened and sharp conflict. There is usually learning and better perspective acquired through the long resolution process, which is missing in TCD. In-depth custody reports by mental health professionals that can take months to complete tend to fall on deaf ears. What does not fit with the TCD parent's dogmatic view is rejected out of hand and often attacked. It is spit out and cannot be taken in and digested.

There must be a theory of mind that applies to others and not just oneself. Determining reality is often a group effort. The capacity to have a successful relationship, including a marriage, then, requires each partner to attend to what the other is experiencing or feeling to coconstruct truth. This is missing in entrenched TCD.

One should not ignore as well the defensive aspect of refusing to think—a form of rejecting thought and repudiating what is complex, interpersonal, and self-implicating. When parts of the self and reality are disavowed, individuals are more likely to feel invaded or controlled. In this case, the high-conflict sufferer narrows their vision and sees everything objectionable in themselves in the ex-spouse, who is then perceived as a persecutor, betrayer, or bully. For example, an assaultive ex-husband who could never respect a boundary asserts in testimony that his former wife is a "control freak."

Sheila and Geoffrey

Sheila's parents had separated when she was 14, and it was shortly after that her mother was diagnosed with a rare form of epilepsy that resulted in unpredictable, difficult-to-control seizures. Her mother had to give up driving, and she had to maintain a low-stress life that limited her capacity to participate in Sheila's life. Her father's leaving and subsequent disowning of responsibility for his ex-wife meant that much of the burden fell on Sheila to help her mother cope. It was a double blow to her mother, who never really recovered from either catastrophe. Sheila left home when she turned 23, which coincided with her mother moving to an assisted living residence. It had been a long and difficult road already for this only child.

After marrying Geoffrey, the couple had a son and daughter. It was never a happy, relaxed union, and there was often an underlying mistrust. This extended to child-rearing, especially from Sheila's side. She felt used by her husband. It ended painfully after 12 years of being together. Geoffrey had experienced Sheila as coveting the children and excluding him. It was as if there was no place for him in the family. Their son, then 8 years of age, could be difficult. He had a temper and struggled with behavioral control. An episode occurred, and Geoffrey grabbed the boy by the arm more roughly than he should have. Sheila erupted and, running into the room, yelled, "I won't let your father hurt you anymore!" The son was bewildered. His mother had reported the incident, and when interviewed by the child protection worker and subsequently, the police, the son insisted that nothing terrible had happened.

The marriage was over at this moment, but Sheila was just beginning to find her focus, which was Geoffrey. After physically separating, she made it very difficult for the children and their father to have an independent relationship. The son reported that his mother spoke negatively about his father and expressed exasperation that she was being "forced" to send them. She could only see Geoffrey as an aggressive threat.

All roads for Sheila led to Geoffrey, who became the focus of her fury and intense mistrust. Geoffrey was fearful that any misstep on his part could lead to an assault charge. He felt hampered with the children for the same reason. Sheila had a vendetta against him and would have gleefully seen him excluded from the children's lives. Moreover, the children were not beyond using their mother's fury against their father, threatening, for example, to tell their mother about some limit-setting parenting action he took. At the same time, they did not corroborate their mother's view of their father. Of course, she saw this support of their dad as based on fear of him, but it was evident that the children feared their mother's upsets much more than feared their father.

Shelia seemed unable to think about Geoffrey, about herself in relation to Geoffrey, or about how her children might feel about their father independently of her. She only knew that he was a threat, and this perspective took over. Thus, her capacity to mentalize within the circle of the family was poor. Her pent-up aggression was disowned and projected fully onto Geoffrey.

Seeing them individually at the outset seemed to be the optimal approach. It was necessary to focus on identifying feelings as feelings and thoughts as reflections and to use these building blocks to help make sense of mental states. This was necessary before considering that the other had a separate mind, which meant that the ex-partner would have independent thoughts and feelings that must be understood in their own terms.

When it was time to meet together, it was clear that progress would be slow. Sheila wanted to leap at Geoffrey, almost literally, and he would withdraw and become steely and stoic. Her sense of him as violent and abusive made it hard for her to see how she also compromised his sense of safety. They needed ground rules within the session. Sheila had a difficult time recognizing Geoffrey and simply assumed that whatever she thought about him must therefore be true. Repeatedly, I had to assert boundaries between Sheila and Geoffrey as well as boundaries between what was believed and what could be considered truth.

It would have been tempting to explore the roots of Sheila's rage in her own childhood: the father who abandoned her mother and the mother who went from a vital person to a semi-invalid who could not be stressed without fearing for her health. It would not have worked. Sheila needed to do the prework of learning to reflect on her own feelings and beginning to think and mentalize within the couple relationship. She had to see that her children were separate from her and had their own minds and perceptions. Whatever she felt about Geoffrey, he, too, had thoughts and feelings that guided his behavior and approach to her and the family. Recognizing how and why she acted the way she did would not mean that this was the only way to see it. Sheila's narrative was a manifestation of mind, not objective truth. She needed to develop a place for mind and make a space between thought, belief, and action that left room for other perspectives.

In working with them, I paid careful attention to their feelings and thoughts. They were cautioned not to make categorical conclusions or label the other. Sometimes after sessions, I wrote e-mails to them, capturing the essence of what they were saying about how they saw themselves and each other. I did this to encourage thinking.

It was only after Sheila was able to make a place for her thoughts and feelings as a reflection of mind and an equivalent place for Geoffrey's mind that she was able to focus on the layered disillusionments that powered the TCD and severe high conflict that had gripped the family. Sheila's fury at her husband for not being a trustworthy ally and stalwart and her disillusionment with her children for supporting their father had unleashed a destructiveness aimed at the family. Current disillusionments occurred on top of earlier traumatic ones surrounding the loss of a vital mother and the abandonment by her father.

Mentalization in divorcing high-conflict couples is impaired by the disruptive, disorganized interaction between the two. There is limited or no capacity to repair any rupture or resolve any issue. This leads to a layering of broken interactions, each associated with unresolved, painful distress. The challenge when treating the TCD couple is to bear the unbearable rather than trying to find middle ground or mutually palatable solutions. In my experience, solution-based approaches do not work when a destructive dynamic is in play. There is no such thing as middle ground.

Any professional dealing with these entrenched, destructive dynamics can attest to the imperviousness to new input or perspective. Shelia, for example, was adamant that Geoffrey was a horrible, abusive man with no regard for the feelings of others, including their children. When asked simply to describe her experience of Geoffrey in an effort to create space for her to acknowledge that her feelings were not the only reality, Sheila would note repeatedly, "I know what he is." "You are like everyone else," she would add. "You haven't seen him rip into the children and treat me like dirt." I knew that Sheila felt completely undermined, powerless, and helpless because of the formative events she had experienced. Her sense of certainty seemed to be a way of avoiding ever feeling helpless again. This predisposed her to seeing difference of opinion or perception as attacks on her reality.

Whatever capacity for reflective thinking or mentalization that Sheila could muster was greatly diminished by the high conflict. Geoffrey's disillusionment history was perhaps less clear. He had a very pragmatic mother, awkward with affection, and critical but very committed. He reported several important episodes when he did something that his mother found socially embarrassing and she emotionally withdrew. It was very much about appearances. His father, however, was the opposite: warm and engaging although often away from home due to his work.

Geoffrey's style was to appease and conciliate. Nonetheless, there was never any appeasing Sheila, and he found himself increasingly frustrated, both in the marriage and after the breakup. He was not the cruel, abandoning man whom Sheila portrayed, but in the end, he could not stay the course in the union and effectively left, as her father had done. In the final phase of the marriage, he had been too frustrated, and this made it a particular challenge for the children, who nevertheless felt close to their father and enjoyed his natural warmth. Clearly, Sheila was another woman whom Geoffrey could not emotionally satisfy. It was the repetition of a painful pattern and not its remedy.

In each instance, though, the formula would remain the same: the sum of traumatic disillusionments in interaction with how the disillusionment pattern is distributed between the parties. This would then predict whether the TCD is in the individual or the couple. It was possible to work with Sheila and Geoffrey then because, as much as Sheila was a TCD sufferer, Geoffrey was not in that category. He could mentalize and represent his feelings in words and metaphors despite the challenges growing up. This capacity for metaphor work is diminished in complex trauma as well as TCD.[9]

It is the life-altering disillusionments that seem to be the biggest contributor to TCD. These are the kind that shake the identity. One can imagine what it would mean to a child to have one's mother get sick and their father leave almost at the same time. This condemned Sheila to a caretaking role when she should have been learning to be in the world and enjoying the freedom of her youth.

It is these gut-wrenching disillusionments that deliver the blows energizing the high-conflict climate of TCD. In my experience, these disillusionments often are not really acknowledged. They tend to be presented as bland history, as if there was no ill effect. It is why they must be identified and worked through in order to drain the emotional toxin that fuels the destructiveness and prevents mourning.

Disillusionment Therapy

Disillusionment therapy would, in such cases, need to represent and reflect the ethics of the court, lawyers, and mental health professionals. It should label TCD as a clinical rather than management problem. The approach would reconceptualize high-conflict divorce as a failure to mourn linked with multiple layers of traumatic disillusionment and reaching a crescendo in the marriage itself. Optimally, case management would rely on a multidisciplinary team approach under the auspices of the court.

The focus on traumatic disillusionment would be central, as this is the common gateway to destructiveness in postseparation families. Destructivity would be identified and not accorded the usual justifications that high-conflict individuals and couples routinely employ to rationalize their damaging behavior. The case management team would need to provide containment by insisting on accountability for the destructiveness itself and developing an organized approach to both, recognizing and working through the distorting disillusionments and the destructiveness that flows from it.

---

[9] Leonoff, A., (2013), Metaphor-work in the treatment of complex psychic trauma, *Canadian Journal of Psychoanalysis*, 21(2), 247–269.

The problem is that the parties are engaged in a high-stakes legal struggle while gripped by noticeably destructive conflict with ongoing attacks on important family links. This leads to a legal case that resembles an avalanche in its turbulence and tenacity. The incapacity of the parties to reflect on themselves or their children is evident. There is no adaptive perspective regarding the ex-partner that allows the two to work together. This explains why new learning is usually out of reach and why the destructive aspect of the divorce dominates despite all attempts to address it.

Recognizing the destructive current of TCD as a pathological reaction to severe disillusionment could lead to the conclusion that children should have independent legal counsel when possible. The children need to be protected from the worst aspects of the parents' behavior, and the court needs to demonstrate to the parents that TCD limits their capacity to provide meaningful protection of them. High conflict would then be seen for what it is: a parenting ex-couple caught in the maelstrom of a very destructive dynamic that puts the family at serious risk of harm—emotionally, socioeconomically, and sometimes physically.

Jasminka and Harry

Jasminka and Harry were an unusual, separated couple in that they came for help together two years after breaking up. It had been a second marriage for Harry, and he did not have any biological children of his own. However, he was very much identified with Jasminka's son and daughter from her first marriage, who were 15 and 13, respectively, at the time.

The marriage between Harry and Jasminka had been extremely volatile, including one episode when they were both flailing on the ground and Jasminka was injured by a kick to the ribs. Harry felt terrible and admitted being responsible. The actual incident as it was described, however, involved both parties in profound regression, each out of control. This did not excuse Harry's actions, but neither was he asking to be excused. They were as a couple subject to regular, explosive episodes of emotion, yelling, screaming, and blaming. Each had seen the folly of continuing to live together and the impact this was having on their children. At the same time, neither could explain why two people who still professed love aimed such vicious attacks at one another in periods of dissociated rage.

Each had the goods on the other. Jasminka had a deeply traumatic history stemming from her Serbian childhood. She had lived through the terrors of war. Indeed, her father was killed in the backyard of their home, and Jasminka and her mother took refuge with a neighbor.

Harry's home life had not been scarred by murder and war. He had come from a bleak, empty home. His mother was an alcoholic and took to her bed every afternoon. She was chronically unavailable and more or less an invalid. His father did not pick up the slack or ever speak to Harry about the situation. Rather, he had a long-standing girlfriend, whom Harry knew, with whom he spent most of his time. No one ever spoke to Harry about his feelings. He just silently lived it. Harry retreated within himself, although he credited Jasminka with breaking the shell of his isolation and helping him better to engage the world. Nonetheless, the union was simply too volatile, and they were damaged physically and emotionally by these awful, explosive episodes that were profoundly destructive for the family.

War was very much home territory for Jasminka. She could be very cruel when enraged, but underneath she was deeply afraid. Her father's antifascism had cost him his life. Immigration was fraught with difficulty. Learning English and fitting into a foreign culture were complex and strenuous. Her first marriage to a Serbian man had failed. She had thought that they would find comfort together, but he liked alcohol too much, and Jasminka could not abide it. He was still involved with her two children, though, seeing them one weekend every second month, as he resided in another city. He was also able to take them during holiday periods, as long as he kept strictly to his agreement not to drink. The children understood this restriction and were to inform their mother if their father was not abiding by the injunction. She made sure that they had their own phones.

Harry was shocked that his marriage to Jasminka had descended into violence. He noted that he was a very inhibited person emotionally and never even knew that he had a temper. His relationship to Jasminka could not find solidity, even though he was very much drawn to her and the children. Jasminka saw Harry as a person who had no idea how to be involved with another human being. She had still not anticipated how frustrating it would be to live with him. Whatever her problems, Jasminka asserted, she knew how to love. Moreover, she understood that Harry wanted to have a relationship with her children but observed that he was equally awkward with them as with her and that they did not know what to think or want from him.

The word *disillusionment* landed with a thud for Jasminka. In her mind, it summarized the story of her life. She idealized her family's life before the Balkan war. Her father's death seemed meaningless in her eyes, an outcome of a twisted, spiteful, and retaliatory culture. Two husbands later, she was jaded with love. She saw her life as waiting for the next disaster, and it resonated with her when I spoke of a disillusionment so profound that hope itself might perish.

Harry's history of disillusionment was no less simple. Neither parent had made him a priority, although his greatest anger was directed at his father, who knew that his mother was essentially an invalid from alcoholism but still left him under her noncare. Harry had not been able to succeed in relationships as an adult. He would retreat deeply into himself, which made it extremely difficult for any partner. Harry had lashed out at Jasminka, blaming her for being too crazy to love, but he also realized that he could be very distant and that this was hard on anyone trying to be close to him.

Jasminka and Harry found some commonality in the mutual exploration of their crushing disillusionments. Each could acknowledge carrying a chronic sense of hopelessness that they had expected the other to heal. The fury was aimed at the partner's failure to make this feeling go away. It felt like a broken promise and became the focus of a rageful, spiteful fury that each directed at the other. At these regressive moments, there was no awareness of the children and what they might be feeling, being forced to endure a war zone as helpless witnesses to destruction.

Harry was able to appreciate Jasminka's offer to help him relate better to her children and have some relationship with them, despite the end of the marriage. They were able to apologize to each other in a way that was meaningful and healing. The relationship with the children became a mutual project in which both could take part, finding opportunities to be a successful divorced couple, able to mourn while retaining some remnant of the original dream.

Integrating TCD Concepts into Clinical Interventions

Family systems theory seems to be the most widely accepted framework for designing interventions in the case of high-conflict families, especially those where there is a refusal to visit and rejection of that parent. Family members are seen in various combinations to unlock dysfunctional patterns and reunify the children with the ostracized parent.[10]

Walters and Friedlander highlight the application of a multi-modal family intervention (MMFI) model that very much fits current practice when the professional resources are available and affordable.[11] The MMFI involves a team approach, including a family therapist, individual therapists, and either a parent coordinator with decision-making powers or direct access to a judge. The idea is to create a framework of accountability in which the complex and often destructive or disturbed resist/refuse dynamics can be treated. The destructive aspect can lurk behind even hybrid cases, where the rejected parent contributes to the alienation as much as it is promoted by the preferred parent in conjunction with willing children.

Fidler, Deutsch, and Polak offer an example for this type of comprehensive intervention in what they describe as a case of moderately severe resist/refuse dynamics.[12] A 42-year-old man, Michael, left his 40-year-old wife, Maria, who is the mother of the couple's three children. Maria had a history of depression but had been asymptomatic for the five years prior to the marriage ending. Michael left Maria for a coworker, Sonya, whom he offered as an alternative maternal figure once the divorce was finalized. Michael used Maria's mental health history against her to pursue sole custody. She became transiently depressed after the union ruptured but responded well to psychotherapy. She also showed initiative in seeking mental health resources to address the troubling situation that developed.

Michael made sure that he shared his misgivings about Maria with the children's school and gave Sonya as the emergency contact person in case he could not be reached. He told his children that he had to leave their mother to protect them from her. It was not long before the two older children referred to their mother as "the nut" and expressed

[10] Baker, A., & Sauber, S., (Eds.), (2013), *Working with alienated children and families: A clinical guidebook*, Routledge; Judge, A., & Deutsch, R., (Eds.), (2017), *Overcoming parent-child contact problems: Family based interventions for resistance, rejection and alienation*, Oxford University Press.

[11] Walters, M., & Friedlander, S., (2016), When a child rejects a parent: Working with the intractable resist/refuse dynamic, *Family Court Review*, 54(3), 424–445.

[12] Fidler, B., Deutsch, R., & Polak, S., (2020), "How am I supposed to treat these cases?" Working with families struggling with entrenched parent-child contact problems: A hybrid case, in L. Greenberg, B. Fidler, & M. Saini, (Eds.), *Evidence-informed interventions for court involved families: Promoting healthy coping and development* (pp. 227–259), Oxford University Press.

fear that she would commit suicide if they were to spend time with her. Refusal to visit became pronounced in two of the three children. The youngest was spared but felt pressure and lack of support from her father for continuing to see her mother.

Michael's behavior, self-serving and self-protective on the surface, covered the profound destructiveness at the core of his actions. It was an attack on his wife, Maria, that could have had lethal consequences if depressive illness and suicidality was actually an issue. Indeed, Michael's plan could well be framed as an attempt to isolate her, break the link between the children and her, and drive her to despair and suicide. There is no mention in the case history of why he would want to do any of this other than that he fell in love with Sonya. However, Michael went much further in his conspiracy. He tried to have Maria replaced by Sonya in the children's lives. Again, we see the murderous intent, although none of this is acknowledged in the case description. What is missing is a rationale or motive for the alienating behavior and clear intent, not only to leave Maria, but also effectively to rub her out as a mother.

Matricide is a complex topic, but there is certainly an omnipotent form of masculinity that seeks to destroy the mother as a source of dependence and attachment. Michael's attempt to murder Maria, at least in the children's lives and potentially even in terms of her own life, seems matricidal. There is a natural separation and individuation that could be psychically matricidal—our childhood relation to our mothers is "murdered" to gain emotional autonomy. What Michael had in mind, though, is something much more malignant. We can only wonder what Michael had against his own mother, what was so disillusioning that it returned with a vengeance to strike Maria.

The good news is that Michael did not succeed in his unethical mission, according to the authors, although I would not believe that a happy ending was possible unless his destructiveness was named, confronted, and worked through therapeutically. Maria did become transiently hopeless, and an assessment indicated periodic yelling on her part during the marriage, but there was support overall for her case from the court as well as from therapists. She had a propensity to depression but no serious mental illness. A court-appointed reunification therapist assisted the family. Whether Michael's destructiveness would find other outlets in the future is hard to know. His new partner, Sonya, might have been helped by the reunification therapist to form an independent view, and this might have limited Michael's destructive options. If Sonya had been a coconspirator in matricide, however, the case could have taken a more malignant turn.

Conclusion

Severe high conflict seems much more than its name implies. There is something of an archaic struggle between two people, rife with trauma and destructiveness, in which each perceives the other as a threat. This chapter focuses on the destructive element and its roots in layering disillusionments underpinning a toxicity that attacks the family crucible in some aspect. If one could identify a specific loss that seems most germane to high conflict, then it is not the partner as much as hope itself. Children are not necessarily targeted by the destructiveness, but neither are they immune. Unless one has lived it as a child, it can be a challenge to appreciate what it means to have parents attacking the family ideal that they have cocreated. They might claim virtue and love for their children, but from the child's perspective they are bit players in a destructive drama that essentially overlooks them.

The concept of traumatic conflict disorder (TCD) isolates destructiveness as a core ingredient, whatever the decibels registered or the specific reasons offered for the discord. Sometimes one only sees the effects of the destructiveness, its imprint on the family: burdened children struggling to progress, worsening psychopathology in family members, broken parent-child relationships, incapacity to make any decisions or achieve consensus. The traumatic element reveals the roots of TCD in disillusionment but also the annihilation anxieties that are often near the surface of afflicted ex-couples. Survival is not certain, and yet this is not sufficient to persuade the parties to change paths. It takes a very particular type of intervention, a therapeutic approach that recognizes destructiveness and resists the usual circuitous self-justifications that fill endless pages of affidavits and testimony. Locked in the interminable struggle of TCD, change is impossible. Tragically, the worthy goal of self-preservation does not apply, which is another way to identify the true destructiveness of this divorce pathology that needs our urgent attention.

Implications for Legal, Judicial, and Mental Health Services

B efore concluding, there is some additional information to help pinpoint the decisive features of the high-conflict, TCD individual or couple. This is essential to avoid pigeonholing individuals and couples into a category that will shape how they are understood and treated. The false negative, those who actually prove to be TCD, is much less of a concern in this regard than the false positive, those who are labeled TCD when they are not. This, then, opens the way to examine how the family law and mental health systems can better address this serious public health problem in evidence daily in family courts.[1]

Classifying Features

Recognizing traumatic conflict disorder (TCD) is crucial for making sure these individuals and couples receive the right legal and mental health services. This is especially important because the term *high conflict* is potentially so encompassing that it captures cases that do not require any specific accommodation or approach. They might be acute conflict, relational conflict, separation conflict, or sharp conflict, but they are not TCD.

When cases are labeled "high conflict," the determination acts like an official diagnosis in shaping perceptions and expectations. Divorcing couples can be inadvertently influenced by their attorneys and others who convey an expectation, which can distort the case and serve as a self-fulfilling prophecy. The designation needs to be clinically meaningful, which requires achieving greater clarity and specificity. False positive diagnoses, in this regard, can lead to iatrogenic

---

[1] Brownstone, H., (2009), *Tug of war: A judge's verdict on separation, custody battles, and the bitter realities of family court*, ECW Press.

consequences. It corrals couples into a mind-set that shapes the outcome and defines them before they can really define themselves.

For example, a couple in their early 30s met and conceived in what was described as an accident. They were educated and accomplished but with little relationship experience. They shared ethnicity but little else. The relationship turned sour even before the birth, although they continued to share a house. She wanted time to bond and nurse her infant, while he demanded shared parenting. She put a lock on the nursery door, and he broke it. Their situation was a complete muddle of communication and expectation. They had attorneys who emphasized their respective positions, referred to them as "high conflict," and set in motion an expensive court process.

What was missing was a rational and ethical approach to this child and some sense of perspective, timing, and a rational plan that would begin with the child and not reinforce their growing battle lines with each other. It was an inflamed situation that needed boundaries and leadership. It was certainly not TCD. It was a clash between two strong-minded young adults who were both scared and overwhelmed by their unplanned situation. They realized that they were permanently linked through their mutual child, and this frightened them even more. They needed help to adjust, not litigation.

Classification is thus important. Look for a flagrant incapacity to see the other as a real person. The ex-partner tends to be seen in extreme negative terms or not considered at all in a refusal to acknowledge. In the TCD mind, the former partner bears little resemblance to an actual three-dimensional person. There is usually a high pitch of conflict that shows no appreciable variability. It is a scene of unchanging enmity. Whatever one can say to the TCD sufferer fails to make a difference. All they can hear is what reinforces their polarized view. There is no chance for insight because this would require reflection and some openness to new ideas. TCD is fundamentally antipsychological.

Previously, I captured these qualities by describing four elements directly pertinent to TCD:

1. a fundamental breach with the other, leaving a bunch of projections without any authentic acknowledgment or recognition of the other
2. the destruction of the intrapsychic representation of the couple that leaves the other existing only externally
3. a lack of a self-observing capacity
4. a huge self-justification while convinced of one's innocence and the other's guilt

Besides these four mainly internal characteristics, there are four other markers of TCD that could help properly identify these cases. The first two are attitudes linked to observable feelings. The third is evident in the personal history, and the fourth is a way of relating to the ex-partner and often others identified with that person.

Scorn

If shame and guilt are common emotions in a painful divorce, then scorn is the attitude du jour in TCD. Scorn holds the other in a tight grip that keeps at bay the disturbing feelings of humiliation, inferiority, inadequacy, and even longing for the other. The individual holds their nose in the face of the ex-partner. Contempt feeds scorn, which contaminates the family field. It has a poisonous feel and often knows no bounds. It can be noisy scorn, expressed as outright disdain, or silent scorn, in which the other is completely ignored, as if they do not exist.

Psychologist David Matsumodo reports that the presence of contempt even in married couples is associated with greater marital dissatisfaction, longer periods of separation, and increased health problems.[2] It makes it easier for violence to occur within social groups, and this could certainly apply to high-conflict ex-couples.[3] An important distinction needs to be made between anger and contempt.[4] Anger is a negative affect that does not necessarily require a judgment of the other's moral or social standing. Contempt, however, radiates a sense of superiority or condescension, and this makes divorce and violence more likely than does anger alone.[5] Scorn is the externalization of contempt.

Antagonism

The hostility experienced in TCD is an active, ongoing anger that is relatively constant rather than ebbing and flowing according to circumstance. In this sense, it is antagonistic and reflects the roots of this

---

[2] Matsumodo, D., (1992), More evidence for the universality of a contempt expression, *Motivation and Emotion*, 16(4), 363–368.

[3] Rosenberg, E., Ekman, P., & Blumenthal, J., (1998), Facial expression and the affective component of cynical hostility in male coronary heart disease patients, *Health Psychology*, 17(4), 376–380.

[4] Bilewicz, M., Kamińska, O. K., Winiewski, M., & Soral, W., (2017), From disgust to contempt-speech: The nature of contempt on the map of prejudicial emotions, *Behavior and Brain Sciences*, 40, e228.

[5] Gottman, J. M., (1994), *What predicts divorce?* Lawrence Erlbaum Associates.

word, implying opposition but also *agon*—contest. It is competition but not like two people playing a competitive game; instead, it is two gladiators in a battle that only one or perhaps neither will survive.

Disillusionment

Disillusionment is particularly painful and disruptive when linked to figures on whom the subject was deeply reliant. There is also the converse, where the parent idolized the child and projected onto the child unrealistic qualities and expectations. In this latter instance, the subject's parent or someone equally important became disillusioned with them, which represented a catastrophe that subsequently became painfully repeated in the marriage.

The ex-partner does not gradually fall from the grace of idealization, succumbing to a more realistic and mature appreciation with time. Rather, the union collapses. What was wonderful is transformed into something terrible; the good, into the bad; or the safe, into the dangerous. Once, the bubble of illusion bursts, there is no going back. As previously indicated, there is nothing left on which to support the relationship after the illusory bubble breaks. Psychically, this sudden rupture can be perceived as an attack, as if the partner did this deliberately.

Conflict

The relationship history reveals clearly that conflict is sustained as a state of mind, even when there is no specific contentious issue. Everything is conflictive, or nothing is nonconflictive. Whereas antagonism is the attitude in TCD, conflict is a way of relating. It has a very different function in TCD than it has normally. Conflict is a way of coping with the other's presence in TCD. It expresses the underlying gross disillusionment while preventing emotional collapse and sustaining self-esteem. It is a suit of armor that reinforces a shaken identity.

To make matters worse, conflict invariably spreads like a toxic spill. If one thinks of a puddle, then the extent of TCD can be measured by the degree of spread. Hence, it has the potential to extend from the couple relationship to the children, extended families, school, neighbors, extracurricular activities, lawyers, mental health professionals, child protection agencies, police, mediators, and the courts. Wherever the TCD extends, there is a distorting effect that warps intention and function. It is stymying and depleting to be in its proximity. Impasse is always the result, with no or limited capacity for resolution.

The need for conflict as a maladaptive coping mechanism can be so great that the individual will engage or discard friends, relatives, and professionals entirely on the basis of whether they agree to side with them. This opens the door to attorneys who "specialize" in high-conflict cases and willingly serve as unblinking alter egos for the destructive conflict on which the client insists. There is the mental health equivalent, a counselor or therapist who easily takes on the coloration of the client, writes letters, extols their virtue in areas of which they have no evidence or experience, devalues and diagnoses the ex-spouse, and remains totally identified with the aggrieved and troubled client. Professionals who are themselves deeply and traumatically disillusioned in their lives can unfortunately be attracted to this work.

Identifying TCD

The combination of scorn, antagonism, disillusionment, and conflict describes the specific character of the ongoing hostility in severe high-conflict divorce. It is a sure sign of TCD. Once traumatic disillusionment takes hold and the other is ejected from the register of the lovable into the contemptible, the destructive current can emerge full force. It often plays out in the legal arena as a battle of attrition. Even when the children are not specifically targeted, there is a blindness to the emotional effects on children or an appreciation of the battering each endures without any real resolution or legal victory possible.

Although I describe the syndrome as a single entity for purposes of clarity and definition, there is actually a continuum. In extreme cases, the capacity for self-reflection is so poor and the other so fundamentally demonized that the discourse is essentially psychotic. Other cases are less extreme, in that there is residual capacity to relate to the other beyond projection. Nonetheless, the core ingredients of scorn, antagonism, and conflict are present and fueled by profound disillusionment. What is crucial in all cases, however, is that the destructiveness is turned on the family. Whatever way it is rationalized, the damage to a child, an adult, or a relationship is an unmistakable manifestation of the wish to do harm.

Recommendations for the Legal System

Although there are certainly jurisdictional differences in how these cases are handled, recognizing intrinsic destructivity as primary to toxic high conflict offers a new and hopefully important shift in how these cases can be addressed. It is a change in paradigm. In no other family law context does protecting the best interests of the child have more urgent significance. Toxic high conflict and TCD are a specific risk for children, who are routinely triangulated by warring parents, for whom they are either pawns or targets, while being denied any measure of emotional security and safety. The court needs the legal capacity to order child protection investigations and, if absolutely necessary, place children in alternate care arrangements, including foster care, until their parents are capable of responding to their real interests. Judges need all the tools available to protect children in cases of severe TCD precisely because the parents are not able.

As an assessor, I wrote countless reports over many years, detailed family assessments intended as much to be teaching tools as custody and access prescriptions. The premise was that with this added knowledge and, in interaction with their lawyers, the parties would gain better insight that they could use to see the situation more adaptively. This conceptual and methodological approach did achieve benefits for the broad majority of disputed cases. In terms of TCD couples and individuals, success, if any, was minimal. TCD and toxic, high-conflict divorce occur in a closed and often paranoid system that only takes notice of the adversary. The tunnel vision can be extraordinary. The concept of an accountable client is unrealistic in these severe high-conflict cases. It is the system that must create a framework of accountability with everyone involved: judges, lawyers, and mental health professionals working toward the same end.

Once cases are triaged and the severe high-conflict subgroup identified, access to justice must be understood through the eyes of the child and not the adults. It is the child whose human and legal rights need protecting. Case management, then, would have a different goal than managing or facilitating the resolution of conflict. It would instead be focused on accountability, child protection, and establishing the therapeutic means to defuse the destructivity that is a direct threat to the children and their parents. Any future right to litigate would then be based on the adults first undergoing a therapeutic process to address the TCD.

As much as children are often the direct targets in toxic high-conflict divorce and TCD, they should be represented by a children's lawyer, an attorney ad litem, when required. This would underscore that the parents are unable to protect their children's welfare and have demonstrated this incapacity in the mayhem of high conflict that has already engulfed the family. In itself, this insistence on a legal child advocate imparts and adds to accountability, which is important in dealing with this most difficult clinical and legal problem.

As much as many legal jurisdictions recognize specialization in family law, such a specialization should include education in working with severe high-conflict families. Some lawyers may demonstrate a special aptitude and interest and could be listed in a subspecialization roster. They would have undergone some extra training. Unless the lawyer fully comprehends the powerful role of the destructive current in these cases and can find a way to both represent the TCD client while not sacrificing the children to blind advocacy, they should not be involved. Although the right to the legal counsel of one's choice cannot be abrogated, it is still the legal system itself that needs to be accountable to its fundamental purpose.

Judges must protect children and not the right of adults to monopolize court resources and use it as a battleground to enact a destructive purpose. This should include supervisory jurisdiction over lawyers who either passively take instructions from clearly harmful TCD clients or who identified so closely that they enacted the same twisted and undermining projections. If the children knew or understood, they would shudder, as the presence of these attorneys amplifies the destructiveness of the case. These are a minority, but it happens enough to deserve mention as a contributing problem to dealing with toxic high conflict and TCD.

Recommendations for Mental Health Professionals

It is difficult for any mental health professional acting as a family therapist to single-handedly assist a TCD family. There are simply too many levels of dysfunction fueled by a core of recalcitrant destructiveness. A small team of therapists who have the savvy and experience to work with this difficult population is the optimal approach. It is not enough, then, to have different mental health professionals involved; they must be able to work together for the good of the family.

There are then five steps or levels to the intervention. First, in cases where reflective functioning is poor, the individual must be helped to identify thoughts and feelings; distinguish these from facts; and begin to appreciate that the other has their own mind with their own respective thoughts, feelings, and perceptions. This prework is vital for anything else to succeed. The result does not have to be perfect by any means, but it must create some crucial distance, where the person can begin to distinguish mind from objective reality. A completely self-aware, mindful person is an unrealistic goal. Rather, there must be sufficient understanding within the context of the conflict-ridden union that assumed truths are in fact feelings, perceptions, and reflections of mind.

Second, the TCD component must be located within the couple, specifically an assessment of whether this toxic element is situated in one or both adult participants. This diagnostic step is important for guiding the treatment that follows.

In the third step, the TCD sufferer(s) meet with an adult therapist in the team to address the historical antecedents and source of risk for TCD. This would include, in particular, layered traumatic disillusionments beginning in childhood and its painful repetition in the marriage. If the TCD appears to be more in one partner than the other, then it is still necessary for both to be seen by individual therapists in order to maintain balance and work through the challenging hurdles ahead. Concurrently, the parties should take advantage of community-based resources offering programs for high-conflict divorce as well as anger management in cases where interpartner violence or child abuse have occurred.

Fourth, in parallel with adult therapy, the children should be seen separately from the parents to help them maintain parental relationships while receiving support and protection, if required, from the clear harm to which they are being exposed. Therapists would not assume when working with these children that their parents are misguided though loving individuals with distorted perceptions and personality problems. It is crucial that the destructive core of TCD be kept at the forefront of the therapists' minds so that children can be protected. It is the denial of destructiveness by legal and mental health professionals that allows for its devastating effects to continue unabated while the family moves chaotically through the family law system.

Finally, the parents must be brought together for the difficult post-separation work. If there are outstanding criminal charges for assault, then some variance in bail conditions might be required. Although there could be situations in which bringing the two ex-partners together would not be advisable or feasible, it is an important step in the return to ethics whenever possible. The two parties must come together in some way as a family who bore these children in hope and desire. Unless they can constitute or reconstitute this unity, the children will always be exposed to the dangers of splitting, fragmentation, and destructive ways. It is the notion of family that allows the children to go from one household to the next. It is a bridge that, in its absence, leaves them perilously exposed and unable to link what their parents constantly destroy.[6]

In the first chapter (page 21), I offer the example from the literature of a mother of two children who attacked the marriage, ended it, and then used authorities to have the father jailed and expunged from the children's lives for alleged perverse behavior. The therapist met with the children and their father, who was wrongly excoriated and alienated by the mother. In this case, the mother would be identified as the TCD sufferer. Nonetheless, she was left on the sidelines of treatment because it was deemed that the father and the children were the ones needing help to restore their relationship. This therapeutic work was successful, although the mother, in a final coup de grace, left her children and the area. In the model I propose, the children's mother would be seen by a different therapist, who understood precisely the destructivity that was at the base of this type of problem. The mother would have been helped to identify her destructiveness and, only then, aided in self-exploration to address the history of traumatic disillusionments that eventually led to her major role in ripping apart the family.

Clearly, the mother's inability to tolerate her children loving their father, leading to a multilevel attack on him, suggests that she perceived her children's paternal attachment as a serious betrayal. We can only wonder what type of traumatically abandoning experience in her own childhood would have led to this destructive rage within her. Of course, untreated, she exacted the same fate on her children and betrayed them. The therapy of the mother would be crucial to making her accountable and restoring her to ethics. Bringing the mother and father together, then, would have helped to build this capacity

---

[6] Consider, for example, those divorcing parents who want mediation to develop a parenting plan but who refuse to ever be in the same room. This has multiple consequences stemming from the attack on the link between them that is itself destructive.

for triangular stability—mother, father, children—which is essential to achieving a rudimentary capacity for a family, likely absent in her case. Thus, the children's love of their father proved traumatic to her. She struck out willfully in rage to destroy it.

Maybe, though, she would have resisted therapy. Here is where the court becomes crucial for insisting on ethics and providing a container where children can be truly protected. There might have needed to be an order for therapy or even an order for the children to be removed from her care until she received proper help. It would certainly not be ideal, but in these cases, nothing is ideal. One must do what one can do, which is why the therapists must be skilled and capable of building alliances, even with individuals who cannot see their part.

Optimally, court jurisdiction would include supervisory control over this process. This would encompass aligned lawyers who do not recognize ethical limits to accepting clients' instructions. It would also comprise therapists and counselors who act as unblinking advocates in unhealthy collusion and health profession regulators who allow high-conflict litigants to subvert the public complaint processes through vexatious attacks.

The court has an obligation above all else to protect children, and judges must be free to do what needs to be done. This includes temporary protection orders and ensuring the integrity and functionality of the process so that these families can be helped. It is surely not a matter of limiting access to justice but rather tailoring the legal process so that children's rights are not superseded by parents acting out with uncontrollable destructiveness.

Conclusion

Lancing the boil of destructivity in the individual or couple opens the door to resolution of high conflict and TCD. When it is allowed to fester, unnamed and unrecognized or rationalized in some way or another, then all that can be accomplished is management, which is usually an endlessly moving target. When the destructive is not faced directly, its negative impact deepens. The cases get worse over time, and the system becomes increasingly less able to manage the consequences. It is an ethical crisis as much as a legal one. This can continue for years and is only eased when the children become older and take fate into their own hands. Sometimes, they become ill from the chronic harmful dysfunction. This can be hard to witness.

There is more that needs to be done. Having an integrated judicial, legal, and therapeutic approach to dealing with TCD-affected families would offer an opportunity to provide containment, accountability, and therapeutic momentum. It is equally important that the destructiveness be identified, and its links to traumatic disillusionment, uncovered and worked through. There is no perfect solution because the population is so difficult. Yet a system that recognizes destructiveness at the core of high conflict has greater capacity to protect children and assist their engulfed parents.

11

Tabling High Conflict
On the Path to Ethics

There is broad agreement that broken marriages must be mourned. Indeed, all our losses must be grieved in order to be given up. This is the promise at the heart of the human spirit, the quid pro quo that rewards those who can mourn with the chance of living a more fruitful, contemporary life. If we are guided by ethics, then this clearly requires a commitment to truth and a willingness as well as capacity to face reality. Mourning requires relinquishing what was loved and valued while also acknowledging its importance. Paradoxically, then, successful grieving is an essential contributor to happiness.

In 1917, Freud identified melancholia as a pathological mourning and distinguished it from normal grieving. It is the failure to mourn and the nonrecognition of the loved one's value. He wrote, "In mourning it is the world which has become poor and empty; in melancholia it is the ego itself."[1] One way to understand this observation is that in mourning there is an emotional reformation and integration, while in melancholia there is only psychic discord—one part of the mind turning on another without end.

The couple in the throes of divorce is faced with an overdetermined choice: mourning or melancholia. Either they will be able to preserve and remember what was good even as they part ways and reintegrate their lives or, at the other extreme, they will engage in a chronic struggle, emotionally violent, and sometimes physical, in interminable cycles of unforgiving anger and hatred. Of course, these are the extremes, and there are many variations in between.

There is an inextricable link between melancholia and disillusionment, and this holds true for high-conflict divorce. These are fostered in

---

[1] Freud, S., (1957), Mourning and melancholia, in J. Strachey (Ed. & Trans.), *The standard edition of the complete psychological works of Sigmund Freud, Vol. 14* (pp. 243–258), Hogarth Press, (original work published 1917), p. 246.

unions built on illusion about the other instead of unions with mature knowledge, mutual recognition, and tested compatibility. Whether the unions are short lived or long, they are mainly held together by the children they produce and raise. Disillusionment is shattering, and the result is fragmentation that each experiences as a no-holds-barred attack stemming from the other. This unleashes destructiveness.

Nelson Mandela once observed in an interview with Oprah, "There is nobody more dangerous than one who has been humiliated."[2] This can play a powerful role in politics, for example, when groups or classes experience profound disillusionment in their governments, feel that they have been deceived and let down, and face deep humiliation and fury. Humiliation and disillusionment go together. When trust and belief in another is exposed as false, an illusion that was never going to deliver what was promised, disillusionment results, and humiliation often follows. The loss of dignity is huge and dangerous.

Thomas L. Friedman, a senior opinion columnist for the *New York Times*, clearly captures this dynamic in human society: "Humiliation, in my view, is the most underestimated force in politics and international relations. The poverty of dignity explains so much more behavior than the poverty of money."[3]

Disillusionment, the impoverishment of dignity, and consequent rage are characteristic of many of the most painful aspects of human society. This includes high-conflict divorce. It is a laboratory in the study of disillusionment. In this regard, these issues deserve to be studied as a focus for intervention with couples who will go to any lengths to attack and devalue the other, despite sharing offspring.

As I have emphasized, unless one uproots, exposes, and treats destructiveness, there will be no real answer to severe high conflict. Thankfully, we have psychologists and other researchers who have the expertise to operationalize these concepts and devise treatment strategies that can be tested against criteria for change.

Once the notion of destructiveness is elevated from consequence to cause, the perspective on existing therapeutic approaches to helping severe high-conflict families changes. For example, reunification therapy between an alienated parent and child must concomitantly address the destructive motivation of the alienating parent. A child who reconciles

---

[2] Winfrey, O., (2001, April), Oprah talks to Nelson Mandela, *O: The Oprah Magazine*, https://www.oprah.com/world/oprah-interviews-nelson-mandela/6

[3] Friedman, T., (2020, September 8), "Who can win America's politics of humiliation?" *The New York Times*.

with a targeted parent could become a target and might, therefore, be frightened of such a prospect. This would then function under the surface as a hidden resistance to making anything better. This might look like alignment with a preferred parent, but it is in fact something else.

Consider a young adult who, as a child, had attacked and devalued his father who was divorced from his mother. During joint sessions with his son, in which he was blamed, criticized, and treated with utmost scorn and disrespect, the father stoically, if not masochistically, suffered through it, to no avail. Now an adult, the son is dealing with the fallout of his parents' dysfunctional and destructive divorce. He suffered considerable shame from his underlying awareness that he never had any intention of improving his relationship with his father when he attended joint sessions with him. The sessions were opportunities to punish his dad. He spoke about his mother's hatred of his father and how he always felt her encouragement, approval, and even admiration. She credited him with good judgment and deplored that he ostensibly did not have the father he deserved.

Of course, publicly and in court filings, the mother spoke of her hope that father and son would find some resolution. She blamed the whole situation on her ex-husband and observed that he was failing with his son in the same way that he had failed with her. There was no acknowledgment of her destructive intent to attack her ex-husband through his relationship with his son. Even less accessible to consciousness was her intent to attack her son by appropriating him into her revenge strategy and destroying any chance of her son having a father to love and admire. As a young adult man, however, the son was able to reflect on the circumstance and could see how his mother coveted his love but created a world dominated by antipathy. He was finding his way back to his father, although it was painful for father and son to acknowledge what they had lost.

The issue in devising treatment strategies for severe high conflict is to name overtly the manifestations of destructiveness and find the source in the parent's history, with particular attention to painful and at times humiliating disillusionments.

Role of Trauma

A further area of study concerns the role of psychic trauma in severe high-conflict divorce. The problem that arises is one of definition. What exactly is trauma, and what trauma are we talking about? The term is so overused that it has lost its specific meaning and is equated with stressful events, as if the event itself determines the designation. Of course, there are many events in life that are overwhelming and overtaxing and that have no immediate solution. These can occur during childhood but also can happen at any phase of life. Neglect and mistreatment and other adverse experiences in childhood are associated with trauma but should not be equated with it.

Before writing "Beyond the Pleasure Principle" in 1920, Freud's view of "psychical trauma" was restricted to an excess of affect that could not be fully discharged—the impact of unconscious memories linked to powerful, compulsively repeated emotions. In 1920, he added a new dimension for understanding psychic trauma: the concept of a protective shield: "We describe as 'traumatic' any excitations from outside which are powerful enough to break through the protective shield (Reizschutz). It seems to me that the concept of trauma necessarily implies a connection of this kind with a breach in an otherwise efficacious barrier against stimuli."[4] Freud conceptualized the protective shield from a neurological standpoint as a barrier that stands between the external world and the receptive cortex, which he described as a protective envelope or membrane that keeps out dangerous stimuli. It is the breaking through of this barrier that defines the psychic trauma. Although incomplete and clearly missing the psychological component, which is fundamental, Freud's description is important in terms of definition because it implicitly contains the notion of vulnerability or its converse, resilience.

Any definition of what constitutes trauma must take into account that the event itself, even chronic exposure, is not a sufficient cause.[5] Normal associative channels by which memories are processed fail in these cases.[6] A trauma, then, is the confrontation with an identity-threatening event or experience that cannot be elaborated in a normal, associative, and meaningful way. The reason for this impossibility can be understood in the light of preexisting vulnerability, whether this is

[4] Freud, S., (1955), Beyond the pleasure principle, in J. Strachey (Ed. & Trans.), *The standard edition of the complete psychological works of Sigmund Freud, Vol. 18* (pp. 3–64), Hogarth Press (original work published 1920), p. 29.

[5] Paris, J., (2000), Predispositions, personality traits, and posttraumatic stress disorder, *Harvard Review of Psychiatry*, 8, 175–183.

[6] Van der Kolk, B. A., (1994), The body keeps the score: Memory and the evolving psychobiology of posttraumatic stress, *Harvard Review of Psychiatry*, 1, 253–265; Van der Kolk, B. A., & Fisler, R., (1995), Dissociation and the fragmentary nature of traumatic memories: Overview and explanatory study, *Journal of Traumatic Stress*, 8, 505–525.

earlier trauma, a genetic predisposition, or a more vulnerable personality structure.

At the beginning of my career, I saw some patients who had survived Nazi death camps and were immobilized by psychic trauma, but it was their children who were the main symptom group, developing life-inhibiting problems and post-traumatic disorders. In the latter situation, we can see that the external event itself was much less important than the capacity of the survivor parent to help their offspring process what they, the parent, had experienced in their life. It is no surprise, then, to verify clinically that children of survivors experience more post-traumatic symptoms than the survivors themselves.[7]

One can think of an internal mother, father, and parental couple who provide comfort and containment and to whom we turn in order to tolerate very stressful life events, even those that threaten survival. The child psychologist and psychoanalyst James Herzog describes a triadic scaffolding of parental representations in the mind that supports the child's development. Self with mother, self with mother and father, and self with father depict the holding environment in which the child's sense of identity is protected and fostered. This is the stimulus shield that Freud discussed but now in very human terms.

Herzog makes an important point toward understanding children of high-conflict divorce: "The child who is possessed by one parent as the needed or seduced other, or by each parent separately in that manner, is deprived of the protective and facilitating experience of being recognized and loved by the parental couple together."[8]

Trauma needs to be understood, then, in its human context as the radical unavailability of the other to foster mental processing of stressful life events. It is, at base, a breach with the other, a severing experience that is felt as a threat to survival. This includes the internalization of the parental couple as a coming together in love to create and protect the child. High-conflict divorce destroys this element, which leaves the child held by one or the other in a broken structure, in which the parents are never together in the child's mind.

Moments of severe disillusionment can stand out in some cases and represent traumatic ruptures that alter how the individual sees themselves and their life. I recall a woman suffering from complex

[7] Yehuda, R., Schmeidler, J., Giller, E., Jr., Siever, L., & Binder-Brynes, K., (1998), Relationship between posttraumatic stress disorder characteristics of Holocaust survivors and their adult offspring, *American Journal of Psychiatry*, 155, 841–843.
[8] Herzog, J., (2005), Triadic reality and the capacity to love, *Psychoanalytic Quarterly*, 74, 1048.

psychic trauma who related huddling in the basement of the family home at age 5, as a hurricane raged outside. There was a shattering moment for the patient that was only indirectly linked to the deafening sounds of the storm. It was her sudden awareness that her parents were totally unable to protect her that demolished in an acute moment her sense of being magically protected by them. This highlights an important aspect that links trauma closely to massive disillusionment: Trauma represents the failure of the human world to hold and protect.

Research on high-conflict divorce needs to be informed by an understanding of trauma very much linked to the failure of an internal parental structure to mediate between the self and the external world. It cannot be reduced to external events. In this regard, the focus is not solely on whether the parents were in conflict as much as whether, in the midst of their conflict, they were still able to recognize and respond to their children's needs. The trauma, then, would not be reduced to the cacophony of dispute in the family, the stormy sounds of divorce war, but rather to the incapacity of the parents and parental couple to maintain a holding presence and to help the child weather these events and process fears and emotions in a meaningful way.[9]

For those adults who succumb to serious high-conflict divorces, research could focus on preexisting psychological vulnerabilities, which I describe as a layered history of significant disillusionments. From the perspective of mind, this could be conceptualized as ruptures in the individual's own psychic world, with internalized parents failing to mediate, contain, or help process experience. In this regard, high conflict can be seen as a transgenerational transmission of trauma, in which the disorder is defined not by symptoms but by the incapacity to think and process psychically at crucial moments when identity is most threatened. High-conflict divorce, in the same way, suggests a disorder of nonthinking, in which repeated acts of destructiveness predominate. This conforms to the experience of clinicians who observe the entirely closed and impenetrable views of the high-conflict sufferer that are never examined or open to change.

---

[9] Drozd, L., Saini, M. S., & Velluci-Coo, K., (2019), Trauma and child custody disputes: Screening, assessment, and interventions, in L. Greenberg, B. J. Fidler, & M. A. Saini (Eds.), *Evidence-informed interventions for court-involved families: Promoting coping and healthy child development* (pp. 260–281), Oxford University Press; Landis, J., (1960), The trauma of children when parents divorce, *Marriage and Family Living*, 22, 7–13.

Although there is research linking unrealistic appraisal, amounting to an idealization of the partner, as a risk factor for disillusionment and marital failure, it is important to distinguish the severe high-conflict group from the wider population of divorced individuals and couples.[10] In the wider divorce group, disillusionments are met with disenchantment and marital unhappiness. In the severe high-conflict subgroup, disillusionments are experienced traumatically as a severe, unforgivable injury and betrayal.

It is perhaps not surprising that multiple disillusionments are also a risk factor for suicide, which can be perceived as a solution to unbearable emotional pain.[11] Here the violence is turned inward, but the destructiveness is clear. As clinicians treating suicidal patients can attest, the story is not of lack of fulfillment but rather the individual's perception that their entire basis for wishing and believing has been shown to be false. Psychoanalyst Lucy Lafarge describes this state as "going off a cliff."[12]

Disillusionment in the partner has also been related to the severity of symptoms of postpartum depression.[13] This represents another version of the "cliff" at a time when the woman would feel very vulnerable and reliant on her partner. As such, disillusionment is a risk factor for mental distress and shakes the foundation of the relationship or exposes what is then felt to have been a lie or illusion.

This quality of experience is important in distinguishing disillusionment from simple disappointment. In the high-conflict divorce scenario, the despair of disillusionment triggers splitting, in which the "bad" is deposited into the ex-partner, who is then hated and deemed capable of all kinds of odious conduct. This use of splitting explains the commonly observed correlation between high conflict and certain personality disorders, especially in the cluster B category of the DSM (antisocial, narcissistic, and borderline).[14] Idealization and states of illusion meet a harsh end in these individuals when reality proves

---

[10] Niehus, S., & Bartell, D., (2006), The marital disillusionment scale: Development and psychometric properties, *North American Journal of Psychology*, 8, 69–84.

[11] Tillman, J. G., (2018), Disillusionment and suicidality: When a developmental necessity becomes a clinical challenge, *Journal of the American Psychoanalytic Association*, 66(2), 225–242.

[12] Lafarge, L., (2015), The fog of disappointment, the cliffs of disillusionment, the abyss of despair, *Journal of the American Psychoanalytic Association*, 63(6), 1225–1239.

[13] Malus, A., Szyluk, J., Galińska-Skok, B., & Konarzewska, B., (2016), Incidence of postpartum depression and couple relationship quality, *Psychiatria Polska*, 50(6), 1135–1146.

[14] Kreger, R., & Eddy, B., (2011), *Splitting: Protecting yourself while divorcing someone with borderline or narcissistic personality disorder*, New Harbinger.

disillusioning. The sense of persecution is then extreme, defenses are exclusively externalizing and projecting, and the fighting back constitutes the high-conflict position that one is being victimized by a nefarious enemy.

Disillusionment-Oriented Divorce Therapy

There are many "acronym" therapies today, CBT and DBT being the two best known. These are treatments that are more defined and condition specific. Could there be a therapy for high-conflict divorce that would target its underlying structure? In this case, high-conflict divorce would be seen as a pathologically traumatic response to severe disillusionment, both in the marriage and at other significant moments of the individual's life.

The trauma, both historical and marital, needs to be reconstructed within its interpersonal and historical context because this will chart the pathway to understanding the source of the disillusionment crisis that sets in motion the destructiveness. High conflict is often precipitated by a sense of utter abandonment or betrayal by the partner. The other is transformed psychically into someone feared and hated, one who is seen as the worst enemy and responsible for ruining the subject's idyllic life.

Each pillar of disillusionment must be identified and worked through so that mourning could occur. This often requires the therapist to move the client away from arguing their case to exploring the specific impediments to mentally processing what occurred and to find a better, less conflictive path forward. It leans toward a focus on reflection and is aimed at promoting thinking versus acting. The more the interview is allowed to focus on conflict and reinforce the client's harsh, toxic views, the less effective the intervention. It is not a confrontation with the client but with the futility of engaging in a destructive, depleting conflict that would otherwise never end. Although the deepest fear inherent to this client group is utter despair, shifting the focus to disillusionment can be a relief.

Final Reflections

At its best, divorce is a resolution and not an ending. At its worst, divorce is a malady of love, a disillusionment so great that love as a hope seems to die. The dream of love crumbles into despair. We can think of a loss so fundamental that it can never be mourned. One would be nothing in the face of such a catastrophic loss—a subject without identity, a lover without the possibility of love. This describes the traumatic mind-set where high conflict can take hold. The process stalls and circles endlessly without anyone having the key to end the agony. The family as an ideal and source of promise is attacked. The interminability of traumatic conflict disorder (TCD) accounts for its persecutory nature. Retribution masked as justice leads to endless conflict, which can be managed but not easily resolved.

Return to Ethics

In this era of no-fault divorce and best interests of the child, is there even a place for ethics? Yet a system solely focused on conflict at whatever tenor and intensity is at risk of being appropriated for the aim of enactment rather than solution. The family law system is then forced into the role of witness, unable to stem the tide harming the family.

What ethics? Whose ethics? These are cogent questions. Consider a divorcing man who informed his 16-year-old daughter about his financial dealings. The child was told she could never share this with her mother, lest her mother use it against her father in court. He intended to brief his daughter fully, including providing her mother's affidavits in their ongoing conflict. This is misguided, but in a divorce beyond ethics, such conduct is commonplace. The father's wish for alliance outweighed any ethical obligation to protect his child's bond with her other parent.

It is clearly destructive in that it emanated from a deep well of disillusionment: a man who felt used, discarded, unfairly blamed, and devalued by his former partner and mother of his children. His enmity and sense of his spouse as evil was profound; his fury, palpable and diverted into exacting revenge that easily sacrifices the daughter to the conflict.

High conflict begins where ethics end. It is in this realm that the destructive can take hold. Children have no defense because their love for their parents is elemental. Hence, love in this destructive context becomes inherently traumatic and damaging to the child's identity. If ethics could survive, then the family would have a chance of a better future. Destructiveness ignores boundaries, violates them, and fails to protect or views protection through such a distorted lens that it justifies harmful behavior.

In the previous example, the fact that this man would seriously damage his daughter's maternal relationship is obscured by a current of destructivity that would want to see the wife exposed as unworthy of love and respect, especially to her child. It is twisted and disguised as protective love. Again, this is a world beyond ethics, in which destructiveness has taken hold and serves its own perverse logic.

How might the family law and mental health systems introduce ethics in a situation akin to an all-out brawl? One must return to the seat of ethics: its primal origin in the early care provided by a mother for her baby. It is an ethical relation that acknowledges the baby's absolute dependence on its mother for survival. This is where maternity and ethics come together—not to privilege the woman over any other gender identity but rather to give priority to a human encounter that makes one person absolutely responsible for the well-being of another.

In this brief example, how do ethics apply to the father determined to twist his daughter's mind and interfere in her relationship with her mother? Would he have denied his baby primary care: food, sleep, a clean body, holding, and affection? Are these more advanced needs any different? Certainly, she could be damaged by her father's avenging seduction, shaped by hatred presented as protective love. He has lost what it means to be a parent, which is fundamentally to be wholly and unequivocally responsible. Is this man prepared to know this? Perhaps he must.

> Mr. ___, you sit on the precipice of forfeiting what it means to be a parent and ex-spouse to the other parent. Your daughter's emotional fate is in your hands. Will you abandon her to your burgeoning hatred, force her to ally with you against her mother? It is a choice you must make with full knowledge that you and you alone are fully responsible for this child's well-being, no matter how much you protest that your conduct is justified.

In truth, this example is reeling from the effects of disillusionment and its link to destructiveness. This must be confronted as a disorder, with its most serious symptom being the disavowal of ethics. It is the recovering of ethics, the parent's abiding, unremitting, and overriding responsibility for the other that is the sole route out of this mind-set. Judges, lawyers, and mental health professionals must stand together in the resolve that there is no future without ethics and no ethics without a direct and meaningful confrontation when it has been destructively obliterated.

Conclusion

This book explains the complexity of high-conflict divorce, especially in its relation to ethics, disillusionment, and destructiveness. Indeed, writing and thinking are so intertwined, it is hard to know where one stops and the other begins. In the midst of dealing with such couples and individuals, it can also be hard to think. The forces created (mainly destructive) paralyze thinking and make problem solving even harder to achieve. Yet there is a great need for reflection on this important societal and public health issue. Although the rate of divorce ebbs and flows, there is no relief from the burden that these toxic divorce situations impose, not only on children, but also on the courts and mental health systems. Nonetheless, there is an eagerness to find solutions. My hope is that this book contributes in some measure to that end.

Index

ethics: attitude lack of, 12; for baby, 91, 96, 208; of Barbara/Jeff, 112–13; children and, 86, 93–95; concern/guilt comparison, 141–42; crisis of, 196–97; for debt, 94, 134; dilemma in, 5; for disillusionment therapy, 96–97, 180; divorce education for, 31, 33, 36; of Donald, 89, 90; enforcement of, 29–30; in family law, 134–35, 208; high conflict and, 199–201, 207–8; in high-conflict divorce, 2, 14, 24, 33, 149; in human nature, 11, 91–93; in legal system, 37, 135–36; for life, 91; in marriage, 11–12, 84–85; maturity of, 46; mental capacity for, 36; in no-fault divorce, 207; for parent, 91; problems arising for, 133; psychopathology compared to, 94; responsibility in, 12, 92; transformation of, 93; of William and Julie, 15–17
ethos, 11
evil behavior, 99

failure: acceptance of, 134; disavow of, 51–52; guilt and, 135
family: alienation and, 119–23; background, 28–29; disillusionment in, 19–20; love basis for, 96; matrix in, 13; mental concept of, 26–27; mother dominance in, 61–62; mourning by, 121
family assessor, 118, 151–54, 192, 194
family law: case management in, 20, 37–38, 79–80; children counsel in, 181, 193; clinical-work mandate by, 142–43, 143n1; conflict enactment during, 136; court time of, 161; destructiveness and, 151, 194; ethics in, 134–35, 208; high conflict and, 149, 159; in high-conflict divorce, 3, 5, 14–15, 82; judicial oversight in, 24; for LGBTQ, 73; specialization in, 193; TCD and, 167–68, 192–93
family systems theory, 183–84
fatherhood, 74–75; ideal, illusion of, 106–8; son relationship destroyed in, 201
Fidler, B., 184
5 Types of People Who Can Ruin Your Life (Eddy), 6
food: addiction for, 161–62; in bulimia, 162–63; emotions and, 105
Freud, Sigmund, 21, 38, 199, 202–3
Friedlander, S., 184
Friedman, Thomas L., 200

Gardener, Richard, 166
Geoffrey, Sheila and, 176–80
Gerald, Susan and, 143–47
government divorce provisions, 81
gratitude, 59, 63

greed, 162
guilt: blame and, 134, 136; concern compared to, 141–42; in ethical divorce, 133; failure and, 135

Harry, Jasminka and, 181–83
hate, 154, 175
Henry: Mary and, 120; Nicole and, 27–30
Herzog, James, 203
Hetherington, E. M., 9
high conflict: amelioration of, 172–73; attitude reflecting, 150; behavior, 166–67; blame in, 147; bulimia compared to, 162–63; case management of, 5, 160–61; classified, 187–88; conflict compared to, 2, 147, 149–50, 161; definition of, 136, 161; ethics and, 199–201, 207–8; factors hidden in, 160; family law and, 149, 159; judicial system administration of, 192–93; marriage, 139–41; pathology of, 166–67; personality disorder link to, 205; psychopathology link to, 164–65; reconceptualization of, 165–69; services for, 160; source of, 160; TCD compared to, 167; trauma-based interventions for, 160; trigger for, 158; of Troy/Sharon, 155–58
high-conflict divorce: atonement after, 92; of Carol/Daniel, 71–72; children of, 48–49, 203; clinical work for, 7, 10–11; community and, 5, 20; as complex, 209; concept of, 9–15; conflict compared to, 51; couple destructivity by, 20–21; CQ in, 64–67; of Denise/Pauline, 75–78; destructivity in, 2, 12, 19–21, 79–80, 149–50; disillusionment-oriented divorce therapy for, 206; duration never ending in, 31, 136; duty rejection in, 13; egocentricity in, 93–94; emotional states in, 59, 189; ethics in, 2, 14, 24, 33, 149; failed marriage compared to, 55; family law in, 3, 5, 14–15, 82; framework for, 24, 47; gratitude in, 59; illusion cause of, 96; of John/Melissa, 102–5; of Kenneth/Irene, 83–85; loss disavowed in, 51–52; love in, 206–7; of Marianne/Derek, 17–19; mental health and, 10, 23, 149; mental health professionals administration of, 159; mentalization in, 178–79; mourning in, 68–69; narcissism in, 88; nonrecognition in, 60; parent and, 53, 118, 135; psychological demand in, 133; psychopathology in, 6–10; research needs for, 204–5; sexual allegations in, 8, 28, 30; in society, 20; support services for, 51, 82; of Sylvia/Murray, 7–8; therapy in, 21–23; trauma and, 79, 201–6; violence in, 31–32; vulnerability in, 63–64; of William/Julie, 15–17. See also conflict
Hopkins, Anthony, 99

mentality: of coupleness, 64, 79–80; of
family, 26–27; of parenthood, 74–75; self-
recognition lack of, 53–54, 104
mentalization, 104, 173; in high-conflict divorce,
178–79; TCD and, 175–76, 194
Michael, Maria and, 184–86
misogyny, 161–62
MMFI. *See* multi-modal family intervention
Moloney, L. J., 6
Monique, Pierre and, 60–63
morality: definition of, 91; empathy with, 93,
102; obligation of, 86, 91; taught, 141
Morgan, 137–39
mother: baby nurtured by, 14; destructivity of,
23; family dominance by, 61–62; link repair
to, 108; with TCD, 195–96
motherhood, 74–75
mourning: with anger, 68; of Carol/Daniel,
71–72; emotional states of, 68; by family,
121; in high-conflict divorce, 68–69; of
loss, 19, 199; marriage allowance for, 199;
melancholia compared to, 199; of Serena/
David, 69–70
multi-modal family intervention (MMFI), 184
Murray, Sylvia and, 7–8
mutuality, 113, 115–16

narcissism: crisis of, 95; definition of, 87;
destructivity of, 88–89; disillusionment
caused by, 87; of Donald, 89; egocentricity of,
88; grandiose personality of, 87–88; in high-
conflict divorce, 88; of Kayla, 85–86; labeled
as, 88–89; love type, 109; malignant, 153–55,
158; psychopathology of, 11, 87–88, 96, 153,
158; of Serena, 151–55; vulnerability excess
of, 87
Nazi death camps, 203
Neil, Belinda and, 163–64
neurobiology, 105, 202
Nicole, Henry and, 27–30
nihilism, 149–51
no-fault divorce, 207
Norman, Kayla and, 85–86

orphanage, 103
Outsiders to Love (Howell), 100

parasitism, 162
parent: attitude mirrored, 129–30; behavior
codes, 35; child alienation of, 117–20,
122, 166; child and role reversal of, 128;
coparent attitude for, 35; death of, 56; ethics
for, 91; high-conflict divorce and, 53, 118,
135; identity bolstered for, 122; of LGBTQ
marriage, 73; management of, 53; mental

concept of, 74–75; new, 111; parental
alienation syndrome in, 166; preferred, 121–
23, 129; psychotic, 128; targeted, 122–24,
129
Pat, Danny and, 55–57
pathology: behavior, normal compared to,
161; of high conflict behavior, 166–67;
melancholia as, 199; of parasitism, 162; of
racism, 162
patrimony, 45–46
Pauline, Denise and, 75–78
personality: destructivity by, 99–100; disorder,
110, 205; grandiose type, 87–88; malignant,
158; psychopathic, 102; violent, 143–46
Phillip, 123
Pierre, Monique and, 60–63
Polak, S., 184
pornography, 21, 28, 61, 103, 120
postmarital conflict, 6–7
postpartum depression, 205
postseparation relationship: discordant, 15–16,
134; pathological dimension of, 161; shame
after, 136; TCD therapeutic work by, 195–96
post-traumatic stress disorder (PTSD), 167, 203
prostitute, 137–38
protective shield, 202
psychic trauma, 79, 201–4
psychology: divorce demand of, 133;
neurobiology with, 105; of sadomasochism,
130
psychopath, 100
psychopathology: of antisocial personality
disorder, 99–100; of children, 9–10, 48–49;
of disillusionment, 33; as ethical problem, 94;
in films, 99; of high-conflict divorce, 6–10;
high conflict link to, 164–65; of love, 130–
31; of narcissism, 11, 87–88, 96, 153, 158;
normal compared to, 161; personality types
of, 99–100; of Sylvia, 100–102; of Sylvia and
Murray, 7–8; of TCD, 167
psychosis, 128, 159
PTSD. *See* post-traumatic stress disorder

racism, 162
recognition: domination guaranteeing, 116–17;
for mutuality, 115–16; sadomasochism and,
116–17; of self, 116
relationship: apology in, 59; capacity for, 64,
79; chauvinism in, 45–46; coupleness in, 64,
79–80; end of, 40; love motivation for, 96;
narcissistic, 88; postseparation, 15–16, 134;
sadomasochism destroying, 113; in society,
81
religion, 27–28, 42–43, 77, 81
remediation route, 52

responsibility: by children, 92–93; in CQ, 66; denial of, 12; in ethics, 12, 92; struggle with, 94

retaliation, 1

Robert, Serena and, 151–55

Romeo and Juliet (Shakespeare), 82

sadism, 99, 102

sadomasochism: definition of, 113; psychology of, 130; self-recognition lack in, 116–17

Sam, Sara and, 169–74

same-sex marriage, 73–75

Sara, Sam and, 169–74

scorn, 50, 189

self-recognition: capacity for, 116; denial of, 57; mental concept lacking in, 53–54, 104

Serena: David and, 69–70; Robert and, 151–55

sex: abuse, 8, 21–22, 28, 30, *41*; adult complexity of, 50; allegations, 30; birth control for, 82; destructivity of, 156; pornography and, 61, 120; sadomasochism and, 113

shame, 136

Sharon, Troy and, 155–58

Sheila, Geoffrey and, 176–80

The Silence of the Lambs, 99

Smyth, B. M., 6

social services, 31

society: high-conflict divorce in, 20; relationship in, 81; women emancipation by, 82

sociopathy, 99–100, 111, 155

Sophie, Terry and, 49–50

Stanley, Melanie and, 109–11

stress, 105

subjugation, 116

suicide, 205

Sullivan, Henry Stack, 151

Susan, Gerald and, 143–47

Susanne, 106–9

Sylvia: Jerome and, 100–102; Murray and, 7–8

TCD. *See* traumatic conflict disorder

Terry, Sophie and, 49–50

therapy: apology in, 58–60; case management in, 22n24; couples mandate for, 142–43; of Danny/Pat, 55–57; for disillusionment, 53–55, 57–60, 80, 96–97, 180, 194, 206; dream deconstruction in, 107–8, 145–46; in high-conflict divorce, 21–23; of Irene, 84; judicial system mandate for, 196; TCD concepts for, 183–86, 194–95

tie the knot, 81

till death do us part, 95

trauma: definition of, 201–2; destructivity compared to, 18–19; of Diana/Matthew, 137–39; disillusionment and, 40–41, *41*, 180, 194, 204, 206; of high-conflict divorce, 79, 201–6; of Marianne/Derek, 17–19; of Maria Teresa/Julio, 139–41; marriage and, 139; protective shield for, 202; psychic, 79, 201–4; transgenerational, 139, 204; unconscious, 38–39, 103; vulnerability link to, 202–3

trauma-based interventions, 160

traumatic conflict disorder (TCD), 159; adult therapy for, 192; antagonism in, 189–91; case management of, 165, 180, 192–96; children and, 175, 194; classification of, 188; clinical work for, 183–86; conflict relation to, 167, 190–91; conflict types compared to, 187; conspiracy theory compared to, 168, 168n7; couple diagnosis of, 187–88; destructivity and, 165, 169, 174–75, 186, 196–97; disillusionment contributor for, 180, 190; elements of, 188; ethical divorce and, 169–74; family assessor for, 194; family law and, 167–68, 192–93; hate and, 175; high conflict compared to, 167; historical trauma intervention for, 173, 194; identification of, 191; illusions and, 166; legal system and, 192–93; mental health professional administration of, 193–96; mentalization and, 175–76, 194; mother with, 195–96; psychopathology of, 167; PTSD compared to, 167; of Sara/Sam, 169–74; scorn in, 189; of Sheila/Geoffrey, 176–80; stereotype avoidance of, 187; therapeutic interventions for, 183–86, 194–95; treatment for, 165

Troy, Sharon and, 155–58

Trudeau, Pierre, 36

Trump, Donald, 168n7

violence: of Dennis/Lila, 113–15; in high-conflict divorce, 31–32; of Jasminka/Harry, 181–83; personality disorder from, 143–46

vulnerability: in high-conflict divorce, 63–64; narcissistic, 87; trauma link to, 202–3

Wallerstein, Judith, 9–10, 31

Walters, M, 184

William, Julie and, 15–17

Winnicott, Donald, 14

About the Author

Arthur Leonoff is a psychologist and psychoanalyst whose clinical practice extends more than 40 years. This is his third book on family law and divorce. He cowrote *Guide to Custody and Access Assessments* (1996) and authored *The Good Divorce* (2015), which was republished as *The Ethical Divorce* (2021).

Dr. Leonoff is a supervising and training analyst with the Canadian Psychoanalytic Society. His scholarly contributions include numerous clinical papers on psychoanalysis. He is a regular teacher, supervisor, lecturer, and former board member of the International Psychoanalytic Association and current chair of International New Groups. Dr. Leonoff is a frequent speaker and contributor to international legal and mental health communities.

www.ingramcontent.com/pod-product-compliance
Lightning Source LLC
Chambersburg PA
CBHW022311280326
41932CB00010B/1065